Issues and Methods in Comparative Politics

Why do we compare countries? How do we compare countries? What are the 'big issues' in comparative politics? *Issues and Methods in Comparative Politics* provides students with the answers to these fundamental questions. It is an accessible and user-friendly text which explores the strategies of comparative research in political science. It begins by examining different methods and then highlights some of the big issues of comparative politics, using topical examples which emphasize the act of comparing as a means to explain observed political phenomena.

- Part I shows how and why comparative politics is important, the strengths and weaknesses of different comparative methods, and the problems encountered in conducting political research.
- Part II addresses dominant issues in comparative politics, including economic development and democracy, violent political dissent and revolution, non-violent political dissent and social movements, transitions to democracy, and institutional design and democratic performance.
- Part III draws important lessons for comparative politics and discusses the key challenges for the field in the next century.

This book has been designed to make a complex subject easy and accessible to students. Features of this textbook include:

- briefing boxes located throughout which explain key concepts and ideas;
- suggestions for further reading at the end of each chapter;
- a glossary of terms.

Todd Landman is Lecturer in Politics at the University of Essex.

Issues and Methods in Comparative Politics

■ An introduction

Todd Landman

London and New York

First published 2000
by Routledge
11 New Fetter Lane, London EC4P 4EE

Simultaneously published in the USA and Canada
by Routledge
29 West 35th Street, New York, NY 10001

Reprinted 2002

Routledge is an imprint of the Taylor & Francis Group

Typeset in Century Old Style by Keystroke, Jacaranda Lodge, Wolverhampton
Printed and bound in Great Britain by
St Edmundsbury Press Limited,
Bury St Edmunds, Suffolk

British Library Cataloguing in Publication Data
A catalogue record for this book is available from the British Library

Library of Congress Cataloguing in Publication Data
Landman, Todd.
Issues & methods in comparative politics: an introduction / Todd Landman.
p. cm.
Includes bibliographical references and index.
1. Comparative government.
I. Title: Issues and methods in comparative politics.
II. Title.
JF51.L346 2000
320.3′07′2–dc21 99–048348

ISBN 0-415-18727-3 (hbk)
ISBN 0-415-18728-1 (pbk)

Contents

Figures

Tables

TABLES

Briefing boxes

Acknowledgements

It has been both a challenge and a pleasure writing this book. I am grateful to Patrick Proctor, who approached me while at a book launch in London and asked me whether I would like to write a book on methods in comparative politics. From my experiences teaching Latin American politics and other comparative courses in the United States, the United Kingdom, and Italy, it became apparent that few students understand the logic and purpose of systematic comparative analysis. I am grateful to Routledge for supporting my ideas for this book, and I am particularly indebted to Tom Mackie at Strathclyde University who patiently and diligently read drafts of the chapters as they were produced.

After studying political science at the University of Pennsylvania and Latin American Studies at Georgetown University, my formal study of comparative methods began at the University of Colorado, where I had the pleasure of working with Claudio Cioffi-Revilla, J. Samuel Fitch, Sven Steinmo, Jeffrey Kopstein, TJ Pempel, and Mark Lichbach. At the University of Essex I have been fortunate to benefit from a stimulating intellectual community and an outstanding research environment. While the facilities and surroundings provided the necessary support and infrastructure to complete the book, it has been the people in the Department of Government that have mattered the most. I wish to thank Joe Foweraker, Hugh Ward, David Sanders, David Howarth, and Roman Krznaric for their comments, discussion, suggestions, and assistance. Paul Carter, my research assistant in the summer of 1998, read many drafts to provide an undergraduate perspective. I would also like to thank my many students on whom I have inflicted the logic of inference and to whom I have evangelized the virtues of systematic comparative analysis.

A number of personal friends and family have made my time thus far in the United Kingdom an absolute pleasure, and the social network that has built up over the years makes my daily life a joy. Dave Smith and Leigh Amos have been dear friends throughout the process of writing. Thanks to my British family members

Pat and Tony Warren, Catherine and Keith Law, Jeremy and Sarah Warren, Lawrence and Louise Warren, and Frank and Isobel Warren. Across the 'pond', thanks to Drew and Kate Landman, Hank Landman, and my mother Laura Landman. Since the first days in Wivenhoe, my relationship with my wife Miriam has flourished and she has been a pillar of unflagging support in my life. Finally, it is to our new daughter, Sophia Laura Landman, that I dedicate this book.

Todd Landman
Colchester, Essex

Introduction

This book is intended to be an accessible and 'user-friendly' text on the strategies of comparative research in political science. It is aimed at upper-level undergraduate and first-year postgraduate students taking courses or doing degrees in political science, comparative politics, area studies (European politics, Russian and post-communist politics, Latin American politics, Third World politics, African politics, or Asian politics), public policy, human rights, and political explanation. The book self-consciously puts method first, and then interrogates some 'big issues' of comparative politics through the lenses of the methodologist in an effort to teach students to think about the logic behind comparison as well as the need for systematic research in political science. In this way, the book sees comparison as an important means to an end; namely, explanation of observed political phenomena.

The book is necessarily grounded in a certain way of 'doing' political science. Without becoming mired in the ongoing debate about different approaches to political science and social science in general, suffice it to say that this book assumes there are observable political events, actors, interests, structures, and outcomes about which political scientists can make reasoned, informed, and intelligent analytical statements.[1] Variously called 'positivism', 'behaviouralism', or 'post-behaviouralism' (Fay 1975; Von Wright 1971; Sanders 1995; Lane 1996), this style of political science concentrates on *observable* political behaviour and events at the individual, group, or national level, and assumes that explanations of that behaviour are 'susceptible to empirical testing' (Sanders 1995: 58). It is thus grounded in the position that the ultimate objects of comparative politics exist for the most part independent of and prior to their investigation (see Lane 1996; Lawson 1997). This book is meant to aid those with a similar outlook on studying the political and social world in making statements about politics based on the best empirical evidence available, given the natural constraints on resources. In this way, it accepts that these statements are imperfect and uncertain, but by advocating systematic and well-grounded 'procedures of inquiry' (King *et al.* 1994: 6) it aims to help students of politics make such statements the best that they can be.

To achieve this objective, the book is organized into three parts, which can be read separately or in the order in which they are presented here. Part I establishes the scientific justification for doing comparative politics, including why political scientists compare countries (Chapter 1), how they compare countries (Chapter 2), and strategies for choosing countries and problems of comparison (Chapter 3). Part I shows how comparative methods can help students explain and understand observed political phenomena in the world. It shows what analytical leverage can be added to a research problem by comparing one country to another, a few countries together, or many countries at once. It shows how comparative methods help generate, clarify, and support important theories and propositions of political science. It shows the key problems to avoid in order to maximize the impact of comparative research. Finally, it seeks to unify these comparative methods into one *logic of inference* (King *et al.* 1994), where *no one method is favoured over another.* Rather, the strengths and weaknesses of the methods are outlined given their ability to achieve valid inferences.

Part II uses the comparative 'architecture' established in Part I to address some dominant issues in comparative politics. These issues were chosen using the following criteria: (a) they receive wide attention in the extant comparative literature, (b) they have a certain resonance with and attraction to students of comparative politics, and (c) they are particularly suited to examining the different ways in which comparative methods can be applied. The comparative issues include economic development and democracy (Chapter 4), violent political dissent and social revolution (Chapter 5), non-violent political dissent and social movements (Chapter 6), transitions to democracy (Chapter 7), and institutional design and democratic performance (Chapter 8).

Each chapter in Part II identifies the main research problem or question, specifies the ideal ways in which to investigate the problem with different comparative methods, and reviews the main findings of comparative research on the topic. In this way, the chapters in Part II seek to 'compare comparisons' in an effort to demonstrate how scholars choose research questions, formulate theories, specify hypotheses, and use comparative methods to test their hypotheses. Students who are new to comparative politics can begin by reading the chapters in Part II to get a flavour for the types of issues that have received significant attention in the comparative literature. They can then return to the chapters in Part I to see how the different methods of comparison have developed and how each offers different strengths and weaknesses for the study of politics. For students that have been studying comparative politics, or other related disciplines, it is suggested that the book be read in the order in which it has been presented. For all readers, it is suggested to read Part III last.

Part III summarizes the main conclusions from Part II and looks forward to the challenges that the field will face in the foreseeable future. Chapter 9 highlights the common themes, methodological trade-offs, and sources of difference that arise from the comparison of comparisons in Part II. Chapter 10 concludes with an examination of the substantive and methodological challenges that the field will confront in the future. The chapter reviews briefly the evolution of the field since its early 'public law phase' (Valenzuela 1988), examines new methods that are being developed for cross-national comparison, argues for ways in which to transcend traditional dichotomies in the field, and discusses new issues that will capture the attention of comparativists.

The text also includes tables and figures drawn from the findings of comparative research; 'briefing' boxes in each chapter clarifying concepts, terms, and relationships; suggestions for further reading at the end of each chapter; a glossary of terms; and a bibliography. Taken together, the book progresses from a discussion of different comparative methods, through a treatment of issues popular in comparative politics, to reflections on the field in the past and the future. As primarily a text on method, it should be read as a companion volume to more theoretically oriented comparative textbooks, such as Dogan and Pelassy (1990) *How to Compare Nations*; Chilcote (1994) *Theories of Comparative Politics*; Lichbach and Zuckerman (1997) *Comparative Politics: Rationality, Culture, and Structure*; and Peters (1998) *Comparative Politics: Theory and Methods.*

Note

1 The divisions in political science are discussed in Almond (1990) and Goodin and Klingemann (1996b); the post-modern criticisms of social science are well outlined in Rosenau (1992); general criticisms about science can be found in Kuhn (1970) and Feyerabend (1993); and responses to these criticisms can be found in Gross and Levitt (1994), and Couvalis (1997).

Part I

WHY, HOW, AND PROBLEMS OF COMPARISON

The chapters in this part of the book establish the rationale for the systematic comparison of countries, demonstrate the different ways in which countries can be compared, and examine the various problems that scholars have confronted or will confront when comparing countries. Too often, both the choice of countries and the way in which they are compared are decided for reasons not related to the research question. In contrast, these chapters argue that the comparative research strategy matters. From the initial specification of the research problem, through the choice of countries and method of analysis, to the final conclusions, scholars must be attentive to the research question that is being addressed and the ways in which the comparison of countries will help provide answers.

To this end, Chapter 1 shows that the comparison of countries is useful for pure description, making classifications, hypothesis-testing, and prediction. It then shows how methods of comparison can add scientific rigour to the study of politics in helping students and scholars alike make stronger inferences about the political world they observe. This is followed by a discussion of key terms needed for a science of politics including theory and method; ontology, epistemology, and methodology; cases, units of analysis, variables, and observations; levels of analysis; and quantitative and qualitative methods. Chapter 2 delves deeper into the different ways in which countries can be compared and why these different methods matter for making inferences. It argues that scholars face a key trade-off between the level of conceptual abstraction and the scope of countries under study. It shows how comparing many countries, few countries, or single-country studies all fit under the broad umbrella of 'comparative politics', and that all have different strengths and weaknesses for the ways in which political scientists study the world.

Finally, Chapter 3 outlines the main problems that confront comparativists and suggests ways in which to overcome them. These problems include 'too many variables and too few countries', establishing equivalence between and among comparative concepts, selection bias, spuriousness, ecological and individualist fallacies, and value bias. Together, these chapters offer a synthesis of comparative methods and provide a 'toolchest' for students and scholars that can be used to approach both existing and new research questions in political science.

Chapter 1

Why compare countries?

Making comparisons is a natural human activity. From antiquity to the present, generations of humans have sought to understand and explain the similarities and differences they perceive between themselves and others. Though historically, the discovery of new peoples was often the product of a desire to conquer them, the need to understand the similarities and differences between the conquerors and the conquered was none the less strong. Growing up in the late twentieth century, citizens in all countries compare their position in society to those of others in terms of their regional, ethnic, linguistic, religious, familial, and cultural allegiances and identities; material possessions; economic, social and political positions; and relative location in systems of power and authority. Students grow up worried about their types of fashion, circle of friends, collections of music, appearance and behaviour of their partners, money earned by their parents, universities they attend, and careers they may achieve.

In short, to compare is to be human. But beyond these everyday comparisons, how is the process of comparison scientific? And how does the comparison of countries help us understand the larger political world? In order to answer these important questions, this chapter is divided into four sections. The first section establishes the four main reasons for comparison, including contextual description, classification and 'typologizing', hypothesis-testing and theory-building, and prediction (Hague *et al.* 1992: 24–27; Mackie and Marsh 1995: 173–176). The second section specifies how political science and the sub-field of comparative politics can be scientific, outlining briefly the similarities and differences between political science and natural science. The third section clarifies the terms and concepts used in the preceding discussion and specifies further those terms and concepts needed for a science of politics. The fourth section summarizes these reasons, justifications, and terms for a science of comparative politics.

Reasons for comparison

Today, the activity of comparing countries centres on four main objectives, all of which co-exist and are mutually reinforcing in any systematic comparative study, but some of which receive more emphasis, depending on the aspirations of the scholar. *Contextual description* allows political scientists to know what other countries are like. *Classification* makes the world of politics less complex, effectively providing the researcher with 'data containers' into which empirical evidence is organized (Sartori 1970: 1039). The *hypothesis-testing* function of comparison allows the elimination of rival explanations about particular events, actors, structures, etc. in an effort to help build more general theories. Finally, comparison of countries and the generalizations that result from comparison allow *prediction* about the likely outcomes in other countries not included in the original comparison, or outcomes in the future given the presence of certain antecedent factors.

Contextual description

This first objective of comparative politics is the process of describing the political phenomena and events of a particular country, or group of countries. Traditionally in political science, this objective of comparative politics was realized in countries that were different to those of the researcher. Through often highly detailed description, scholars sought to escape their own ethnocentrism by studying those countries and cultures foreign to them (Dogan and Pelassy 1990: 5–13). The comparison to the researcher's own country is either implicit or explicit, and the goal of contextual description is either more knowledge about the nation studied, more knowledge about one's own political system, or both. The comparative literature is replete with examples of this kind of research, and it is often cited to represent 'old' comparative politics as opposed to the 'new' comparative politics, which has aspirations beyond mere description (Mayer 1989; Apter 1996). But the debate about what constitutes old and new comparison often misses the important point that all systematic research begins with good description. Thus description serves as an important component to the research process and ought to precede the other three objectives of comparison. Purely descriptive studies serve as the raw data for those comparative studies that aspire to higher levels of explanation.

From the field of Latin American politics, Macauley's (1967) *Sandino Affair* is a fine example of contextual description. The book is an exhaustive account of Agusto Sandino's guerrilla campaign to oust US marines from Nicaragua after a presidential succession crisis. It details the specific events surrounding the succession crisis, the role of US intervention, the way in which Sandino upheld his principles of non-intervention through guerrilla attacks on US marines, and the eventual death of Sandino at the hands of Anastasio Somoza. The study serves as an example of what Almond (1996: 52) calls 'evidence without inference', where the author tells the story of this remarkable political leader, but the story is not meant to make any larger statements about the struggle against imperialism. Rather, the focus is on the specific events that unfolded in Nicaragua, and the important roles played by the various characters in the historical events.

Classification

In the search for cognitive simplification, comparativists often establish different conceptual classifications in order to group vast numbers of countries, political systems, events, etc. into distinct categories with identifiable and shared characteristics. Classification can be a simple dichotomy such as between authoritarianism and democracy, or it can be a more complex 'typology' of regimes and governmental systems. Like contextual description, classification is a necessary component of systematic comparison, but in many ways it represents a higher level of comparison since it seeks to group many separate descriptive entities into simpler categories. It reduces the complexity of the world by seeking out those qualities that countries share and those that they do not share.

The process of classification is not new. The most famous effort at classification is found in Aristotle's *Politics* (Book 3, Chapters 6–7), in which he establishes six types of rule. Based on the combination of their form of rule (good or corrupt) and the number of those who rule (one, few, or many), Aristotle derived the following six forms: monarchy, aristocracy, polity, tyranny, oligarchy, and democracy (see Hague *et al.* 1992: 26). A more recent attempt at classification is found in Finer's (1997) *The History of Government*, which claims that since antiquity (*ca.* 3200 BC), all forms of government have belonged to one of the following four basic types: the palace polity, the church polity, the nobility polity, and the forum polity. Each type is 'differentiated by the nature of the ruling personnel' (ibid.: 37). In the palace polity, 'decision-making rests with one individual' (Finer 1997: 38). In the church polity, the church has a significant if not exclusive say in decision-making (ibid.: 50). In the nobility polity, a certain pre-eminent sector of society has substantial influence on decision-making (ibid.: 47). In the forum polity, the authority is 'conferred on the rulers from below' by a 'plural headed' forum (ibid.: 51). Aristotle's classification was derived deductively and then 'matched' to actual city states, while Finer's classification scheme is based on empirical observation and inductive reasoning (see below for the distinction between these two types of reasoning). Both scholars, however, seek to describe and simplify a more complex reality by identifying key features common to each type (see Briefing Box 1.1).

Hypothesis-testing

Despite the differences between contextual description and classification, both forms of activity contribute to the next objective of comparison, hypothesis-testing. In other words, once things have been described and classified, the comparativist can then move on to search for those factors that may help *explain* what has been described and classified. Since the 1950s, political scientists have increasingly sought to use comparative methods to help build more complete theories of politics. Comparison of countries allows rival explanations to be ruled out and hypotheses derived from certain theoretical perspectives to be tested. Often seen as the *raison d'être* of the 'new' comparative politics (Mayer 1989), scholars using this mode of analysis identify important variables, posit relationships to exist between them, and illustrate these relationships comparatively in an effort to generate and build comprehensive theories.

Arend Lijphart (1975) claims that comparison allows 'testing hypothesized empirical relationships among variables'. Similarly, Peter Katzenstein argues that 'comparative research is a focus on analytical relationships among variables validated by social science, a focus that is modified by differences in the context in which we observe and measure those variables' (in Kohli *et al.* 1995: 11). Finally, Mayer (1989: 46) argues somewhat more forcefully that 'the unique potential of comparative analysis lies in the cumulative and incremental addition of system-level attributes to existing explanatory theory, thereby making such theory progressively more complete'. The symposia on comparative politics in *World Politics* (Kohli *et al.* 1995) and the *American Political Science Review* (vol. 89, no. 2, pp. 454–481), suggest that questions of theory, explanation, and the role of comparison are at the forefront of scholars' minds.

Briefing box 1.1 Making classifications: Aristotle and Finer

Description and classification are the building blocks of comparative politics. Classification simplifies descriptions of the important objects of comparative inquiry. Good classification should have well-defined categories into which empirical evidence can be organized. Categories that make up a classification scheme can be derived inductively from careful consideration of available evidence or through a process of deduction in which 'ideal' types are generated. This briefing box contains the oldest example of regime classification and one of the most recent. Both Aristotle and Samuel Finer seek to establish simple classificatory schemes into which real societies can be placed. While Aristotle's scheme is founded on normative grounds, Finer's scheme is derived empirically.

Constitutions and their classifications

In Book 3 of *Politics,* Aristotle derives regime types which are divided on the one hand between those that are 'good' and those that are 'corrupt', and on the other, between the different number of rulers that make up the decision-making authority, namely, the one, the few, and the many. Good government rules in the common interest while corrupt government rules in the interests of those who comprise the dominant authority. The intersection between these two divisions yields six regime types; all of which appear in Figure 1.1. The figure shows that the good types include monarchy, aristocracy, and polity. The corrupt types include tyranny, oligarchy, and democracy. Each type is based on a different idea of justice (McClelland 1997: 57). Thus, monarchy is rule by the one for the common interest, while tyranny is rule by the one for the one. Aristocracy is rule by the few for the common interest, while oligarchy is rule by the few for the few. Polity is rule by the many for the common good, while democracy is rule by the many for the many, or what Aristotle called 'mob rule'.

		Those Who Rule		
		One	Few	Many
Form of Rule	Good	Monarchy (kingship)	Aristocracy	Polity
	Corrupt	Tyranny	Oligarchy	Democracy (mob rule)

Figure 1.1 Aristotle's classification scheme
Sources: Adapted from Aristotle (1958: 110–115); Hague *et al.* (1992: 26); McClelland (1997: 57)

Types of regime

Finer (1997: 37) adopts an Aristotelian approach to regime classification by identifying four 'pure' types of regime and their logical 'hybrids'. Each regime type is based on the nature of its ruling personnel. The pure types include the palace, the forum, the nobility, and the church. The hybrid types are the six possible combinations of the pure types, palace-forum, palace-nobility, palace-church, forum-nobility, forum-church, and nobility-church. These pure and hybrid types are meant to describe all the regime types that have existed in world history from 3200 BC to the modern nation state. Finer concedes that there are few instances of pure forms in history and that most polities fit one of his hybrid types. These pure forms, their hybrids, and examples from world history appear in Figure 1.2. The diagonal that results from the intersection of the first row and column in the figure represents the pure forms, while the remaining cells contain the hybrid forms. Many regime types that were originally pure became hybrid at different points in history. Of all the types, the pure palace and its variants have remained the most common through history, and despite it popularity today, the forum polity that represents modern secular democracies is a relatively rare and recent regime type (Finer 1997: 46).

	Palace	Forum	Nobility	Church
Palace	*Pure Palace* Persian, Roman, Byzantine, Chinese, and Islamic Empires; 18th-century absolutisms	*Palace–Forum* Greek tyrants, Roman dictators, Napoleanic France, modern dictatorships and totalitarian regimes	*Palace–Nobility* Court of Louis XIV, Britain 1740–60, Poland, Mamluk Regime in Egypt, and pre-1600 Japan	*Palace–Church* Traditional Thailand: the *sangha*; European Middle Ages
Forum		*Pure Forum* Greek *poleis*, Roman republics, and medieval European city-states; modern secular democracies	*Forum–Nobility* Roman republic, Republic of Venice	*Forum–Church* Ephrata Mennonites 1725, Amish 1700–present,[†] both near Lancaster, Pennsylvania
Nobility			*Pure Nobility* 17th- and 18th-century Poland	*Nobility–Church* Teutonic Order 1198–1225
Church				*Pure Church* Vatican; Tibet 1642–1949

Figure 1.2 Pure and hybrid regime types with examples from history
Source: Adapted from Finer (1997: 34–58)
Note: [†] Author's addition

Furthermore, the publication of truly comparative books in the field continues to demonstrate the fruitfulness of this mode of analysis. For example, Luebbert (1991) compares Britain, France, Switzerland, Belgium, The Netherlands, Denmark, Norway, Sweden, Czechoslovakia, Germany, Italy, and Spain to uncover the class origins of regime type in inter-war Europe. Rueschemeyer *et al.* (1992) compare the historical experiences of the advanced industrial countries with those of the developing world to uncover the relationship between capitalist development and democracy. Wickham-Crowley (1993) compares instances of revolutionary activity in Latin America to discover the causal configuration of successful and unsuccessful social revolution in the region. Foweraker and Landman (1997) compare the authoritarian cases of Brazil, Chile, Mexico, and Spain to illustrate the relationship between citizenship rights and social movements. Finally, Inglehart (1997) compares survey data from forty-three societies to assess the mutual relationship between the process of modernization (or post-modernization) and changing value systems. In all these works, key explanatory and outcome variables are carefully defined and the relationships between them are demonstrated through comparison of empirical evidence (see Briefing Box 1.2).

Briefing box 1.2 Hypothesis-testing

Voting participation

In *Contemporary Democracies*, Powell (1982) examines a number of key hypotheses concerning voter participation in twenty-nine democratic countries. Participation is measured using voter turnout, or the percentage of the eligible voters who actually voted in national elections. He argues that voting participation ought to be higher in countries with higher levels of economic development (per capita GNP), a representational constitution, electoral laws that facilitate voting, and a party system with strong alignments to groups in society (Powell 1982: 120–121). His statistical analysis of the data from these countries reveals positive effects for all these variables on voter participation, which are depicted graphically in Figure 1.3.

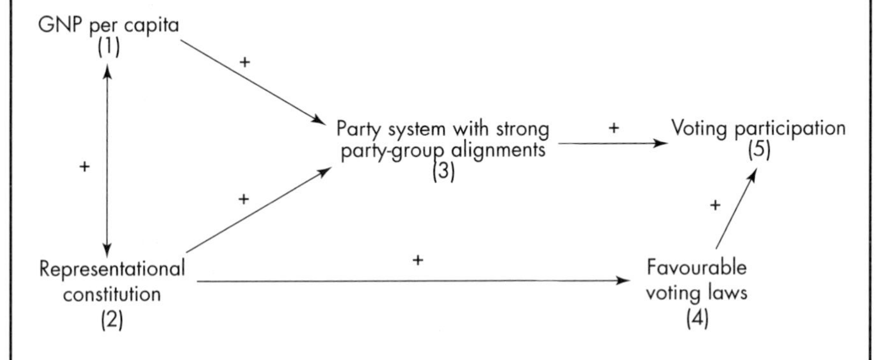

Figure 1.3 Four hypotheses on voting participation
Source: Adapted from Powell (1982: 121)

Moreover, his analysis shows that the level of economic development and constitutional structure are not directly related to voter participation, but that they 'lead to or help sustain the development of party systems and the choice of voting laws, which do get the voters to the polls' (ibid.: 120). This causal ordering is depicted in the figure with the arrows and the numbering of each variable.

Prediction

The final and most difficult objective of comparative politics is a logical extension of hypothesis-testing, namely, to make predictions about outcomes in other countries based on the generalizations from the initial comparison, or to make claims about future political outcomes. Prediction in comparative politics tends to be made in probabilistic terms, such as 'countries with systems of proportional representation are more likely to have multiple political parties'. In this example, a political scientist would know the likely effect of a nation switching its electoral system from a plurality or 'first-past-the-post' rule to a proportional one (Hague *et al.* 1992). Another predictive example involves the benefits accrued to political incumbents in contesting future elections. Based on the empirical observations of past electoral contests, political scientists could be reasonably secure in predicting that the incumbent in any given election has a higher probability of winning the election than the non-incumbent (see King *et al.* 1994).

Although prediction is less an aspiration of comparativists today than in the past, there are those who continue to couch their arguments in predictive language. For example, weak predictive arguments are found in Huntington's (1996) *The Clash of Civilizations and the Remaking of the New World Order*, and strong predictive arguments are found in Vanhanen's (1997) *The Prospect of Democracy*. Huntington (1996) identifies nine key cultural groupings which he believes currently characterize the world's population, and predicts that future conflicts will be more likely to appear in the areas where two or more of these cultures meet or 'clash'. Not only does Huntington seek to predict future conflicts in the world, but claims that his 'civilization' approach accounts for more post-Cold War events than rival approaches. Similarly, based on observations of the presence of economic resources and the occurrence of democracy in the world from the middle of the nineteenth century until today, Vanhanen (1997: 99–154) predicts the degree to which individual countries and regions in the world are likely to become democratic (see Briefing Box 1.3).

The science in political science

The preceding section specified the four main objectives of comparison in political science and hinted, through reference to questions of explanation, theory-building, and prediction, how comparison might be considered a science. The key term used throughout the discussion was *inference*. Simply put, making an inference is 'using facts we know to learn something about facts we do not know' (King *et al.* 1994: 119

Briefing box 1.3 Making predictions

Democracy in East and Southeast Asia

Using similar methods as Burkhart and Lewis-Beck, Vanhanen (1997) seeks to predict the expected level of democracy in specific countries and regions of the world based on their distribution of 'power resources'. Democracy is measured by a combination of the smallest parties' share of the vote and the percentage turnout (ibid.: 35). The distribution of power resources is measured by an index that combines the urban population, the non-agricultural population, proportion of students, the size of literate population, the number of family farms, and the degree of decentralization of non-agricultural economic resources (Vanhanen 1997: 59–60). By examining the relationship between the level of democracy and the distribution of power resources from 1850–1993, Vanhanen compares the actual 1993 values of democracy to those that were predicted using regression analysis. Figure 1.4 shows the actual and predicted values of democracy for sixteen countries

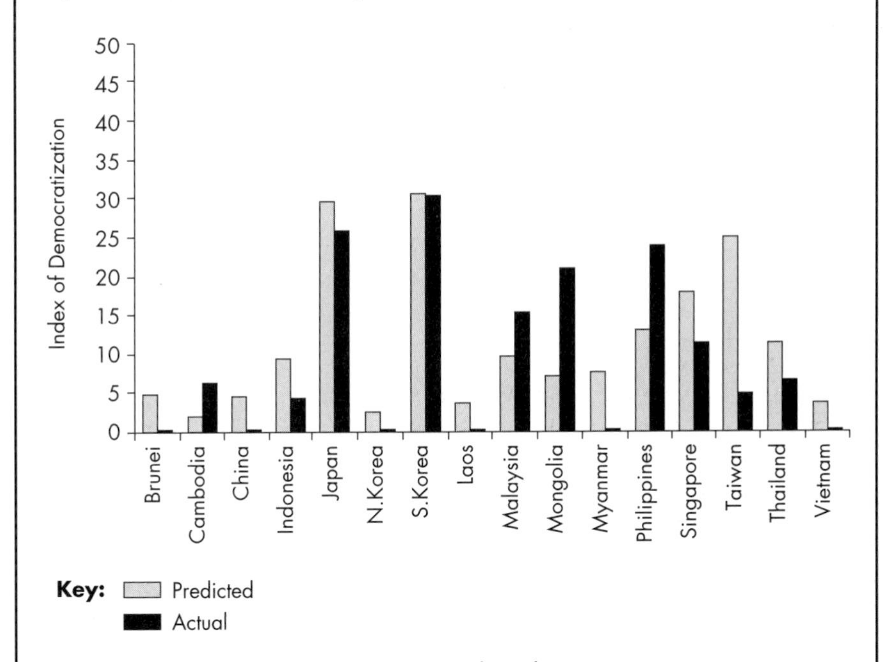

Figure 1.4 Predicting democracy in East and Southeast Asia
Source: Adapted from Vanhanen (1997: 88–89)

from East and Southeast Asia. The sixteen countries are listed along the horizontal axis and the values of the index of democratization are listed on the vertical axis. The predicted scores of democracy represent the level of democracy that each country ought to have obtained by 1993, given its corresponding distribution of power resources. The actual level is the score for 1993. The difference between the two values is known as the residual. Japan and South Korea appear to have obtained the levels of democracy that were predicted, while Malaysia, Mongolia, and the Philippines have higher levels of democracy than expected and Brunei, China, and Taiwan have lower scores than were expected. These varied results have several implications. First, the discrepancy between the actual and the predicted values may mean that something other than the distribution of power resources accounts for the level of democracy (see Chapter 3). Second, the deviant cases whose level of democracy is unexpected for 1993 may be temporary exceptions to the overall pattern. Third, the indicators that were used may not accurately reflect the concepts Vanhanen seeks to measure (see Chapter 3). Overall, however, the process of making predictions can raise new research questions and identify the need to focus on those cases that do not 'fit' the pattern (see Chapter 2).

après Mill; see also Couvalis 1997). Gabriel Almond observes that 'the object of political science . . . is the creation of knowledge, defined as inferences or generalizations about politics drawn from evidence'; and Mayer (1989:56) claims that 'comparative analysis . . . [is] a method that plays a central role in the explanatory mission of political science itself.' Thus, comparative politics seeks to achieve the goal of inference about politics through comparing countries. This section of the chapter clarifies how the process of making inferences is the underlying principle of comparative politics, and how the methodological assumptions of natural science are important to a science of politics.

For the purposes of this volume, science is defined as the gradual accumulation of knowledge about the empirical world through systematic practices of inquiry, including the collection of evidence, the generation and testing of hypotheses, and the drawing of substantive inferences.[1] But beyond this basic definition, what are the parallels between political science and natural science? What are the main differences between the two? And how does comparison help resolve these differences? The strong case for a science of politics suggests that both (comparative) political science and natural science share the same basic goals, namely, description, classification, hypothesis-testing, and prediction. Both activities require the systematic collection of evidence; an ordering of the evidence and the search for discernible patterns; the formulation and testing of contending explanations for the occurrence of the patterns; and the building of more general theories. Thus, a science of politics always contains this 'evidence–inference methodological core' (Almond 1996: 52), or the 'customary pair' of theory and observation (Feyerabend 1993: 23).

Two examples from the natural sciences may help make these points clearer. Both the theory of evolution and the theory of gravity are based on the systematic collection of evidence. Charles Darwin sought to document the entirety of the Earth's flora and fauna. Originally in an effort to demonstrate the glory of God's creation, Darwin soon discovered a pattern in what he was observing for which an alternative explanation was possible. The theory of evolution, buttressed later by the theory of natural selection, emerged as the new explanation for the variety of species found in the natural world. Similarly, Isaac Newton formulated the theory of gravity based on the collection of evidence (the falling apple!). Neither scientist had actually seen evolution or gravity but merely *observed its effects*. In this way, evolution and gravity are mental constructs, whose repeated empirical verification has given them a law-like status.

Political scientists also collect evidence systematically (e.g. archival records, interviews, official statistics, histories, or surveys), search for discernible patterns in the evidence, and formulate theories to account for those patterns. In comparative politics, the political scientist compares countries in an effort to verify the theories that have been formulated. Thus, both the natural and political sciences seek to make inferences based on the empirical world they observe, and both seek to maximize the certainty of these inferences. Despite these general similarities between natural science and political science, there remain two important differences: experimentation and the generation of scientific 'laws'. These differences are discussed in turn.

The first difference between natural science and political science is the role of experimentation. The advances in natural science are supported by evidence gathered through experimentation, which involves the controlled manipulation of the subject under study in an effort to isolate causal factors. Evidence in political science tends not to be gathered through experimentation, although some political scientists use experiments in their research (e.g. those who work on game theory, focus groups, and 'citizen-juries'). Comparative politics, in particular, cannot use experimentation for both practical and ethical reasons. For example, it is practically impossible to re-run the same election in the same country with a different electoral system to observe the differences in the outcome of the two systems. Ethically, it is impossible to redistribute income intentionally in a developing country to see if civil strife erupts. These examples demonstrate the use of *counterfactuals*, or situations in which the researcher imagines a state of affairs where the antecedent factors to a given event are absent and where an alternative course of events or outcomes is considered (Ferguson 1997b).

Whether it is different electoral systems, different distributions of income, different levels of economic development, or the absence of particular revolutionary groups, political scientists implicitly suggest a counterfactual situation when making claims about important explanatory factors. The claim that 'single-member district electoral systems tend to produce two-party systems' is in effect also claiming that countries *without* such electoral systems will necessarily have different political party systems. While some historians may construct alternative historical scenarios based on 'calculations about the relative probability of plausible outcomes' (Ferguson 1997b: 85), political scientists compare countries that differ in ways that supply the counterfactual situation. For example, by comparing the political party systems across countries with different electoral systems, the comparativist seeks to demonstrate that the type of electoral system has some bearing on the type of party system. In this way, comparative research 'simulates' experimentation (Lieberson 1987: 45; Ferguson 1997b).

The second difference between natural science and political science involves the law-like status that is given to certain scientific theories. Experimentation and repeated empirical verification give theories in the natural sciences the status of laws (e.g. the law of conservation of energy, or Boyle's Law of Gases); however, the nature of evidence marshalled in support of theories of political science is such that law-like generalizations are rare. Two famous 'laws' of political science are well known. Michels' 'Iron Law of Oligarchy' suggests that the natural processes observable in the dynamics of organizations and small groups are such that over time, all groups and organizations develop a hierarchical structure of authority with a small elite at their head. In an example from the comparative literature, this law has been tested in the examination of social movement organizations, where evidence suggests that the most successful and longstanding social movement organizations tend to have formal bureaucratic structures and authoritative bodies composed of elites from the movement (see Tarrow 1994). The second law, called 'Duverger's Law', argues that electoral systems based on single-member districts tend to produce two parties while systems with proportional representation tend to produce multiple parties. This law has been repeatedly tested in comparative studies on electoral systems and on balance, is supported by the evidence (see Rae 1971; Lijphart 1994a). Aside from these two 'laws' of political science, the bulk of comparative research eschews making such strong claims.

What then are the main conclusions about comparative politics that can be drawn from this cursory comparison to natural science? First, for practical and ethical reasons, comparative politics relaxes some of the rigours of natural science, but still employs the same logic of inference. Second, comparative politics is a non-experimental (or quasi-experimental) social science that seeks to make generalizations based on the best available evidence (Campbell and Stanley 1963; Lijphart 1975: 162; Lieberson 1987). Third, as a substitute for experimentation, comparison allows for *control* (Sartori 1994: 16), holding certain things constant while examining and accounting for observed differences (see Chapter 2). Fourth, while not seeking ironclad laws, comparative politics seeks clarity, understanding, and explanation of political phenomena about which it can be reasonably certain. The goal of this book therefore, is to provide the necessary tools for students of politics to achieve this clarity, understanding, and explanation while avoiding the pitfalls and obstacles that limit such an enterprise.

Scientific terms and concepts

Before concluding this chapter, it is necessary to define and clarify terms that have been used thus far, as well as terms that will be encountered throughout the book. These are general terms used throughout the social sciences that all students of politics ought to know if they aspire to a more scientific approach to understanding the political world. These terms include theory and method; ontology, epistemology, and methodology; cases (or countries), units of analysis, variables, and observations; levels of analysis; and quantitative and qualitative methods. Throughout the discussion every effort is made to show how the book uses these terms and concepts of social science.

Theory and method

There are two basic types of theory in political science, normative and empirical. Normative theory specifies how things in society *ought to be*, given a desired set of outcomes and philosophical position. Empirical theory seeks to establish causal relationships between two or more concepts in an effort to explain the occurrence of observed political phenomena. Theories in political science can also be deductive or inductive. Deductive theories arrive at their conclusions by applying reason to a given set of premises (Stoker 1995: 17; Lawson 1997: 16–19; Couvalis 1997). For example, the rational choice perspective in political science assumes that all political actors maximize their own personal utility, or self-interest, when choosing between alternatives. From that basic assumption, the scholar logically deduces the range of possible outcomes (Ward 1995: 79; Levi 1997). Inductive theories arrive at their conclusions through observation of known facts (Couvalis 1997). For example, a scholar observing higher instances of peasant rebellion in geographical areas with higher levels of land and income inequality will arrive inductively at the conclusion that inequality is related to rebellion. Comparison of evidence from other countries or geographical regions would seek to confirm this generalization.

Method, on the other hand, is the means by which a theory is derived and tested, including the collection of evidence, formulation and testing of hypotheses, and the arrival at substantive conclusions. Evidence can be collected, for example, through the examination of historical records, the collation and analysis of open-ended interviews of political activists, the systematic reporting of the participant observation of social movement activities, or the construction and analysis of mass surveys of a sample of the population. In formulating and testing hypotheses, method makes the decision rules and the rejection of rival hypotheses explicit. Finally, substantive conclusions are drawn from the theories and the evidence. As the preceding discussion in this chapter suggests, this book, although not primarily concerned with different theories of comparative politics, seeks to demonstrate the different ways in which comparative methods can be used to test deductive and inductive empirical theories of politics.

Ontology, epistemology, and methodology

Ontology, epistemology, and methodology are terms that occur in the discussion of the philosophy of science and the distinctions between them often become blurred in the comparative literature. Ontology is, quite literally, the study of being, or the metaphysical concern with the essence of things, including the 'nature, constitution, and structure of the objects' of comparative inquiry (Lawson 1997: 15). Epistemology is the study of the nature of knowledge, or how scholars come to know the world, both through a priori means and through a posteriori means of observation, sense impression, and experience. Methodology, as its name suggests, is the study of different methods or systems of methods in a given field of inquiry. Having defined these terms, it is helpful for the reader to know how the discussions throughout the rest of this book are grounded in certain ontological, epistemological, and methodological assumptions.

Without entering a philosophical debate, this book is grounded in the ontological belief that animate and inanimate objects in the world exist in and of themselves, and by extension observable events exist in and of themselves. The object of political science is to account for and understand these events in terms of why they happened, how they happened, and the likelihood of them happening again in the future, as well as in different parts of the world. While adhering to the notion that history is 'open ended' (Popper 1997), this book accepts that there are certain 'event regularities' (Lawson 1997) in the world that political science seeks to describe and explain. Epistemologically, comparative politics inhabits a broad spectrum. One end of the spectrum contends that all things political and social are knowable through the process of deduction based on indisputable assumptions about human nature. The other end of the spectrum claims that all knowledge is culturally bound and relative, suggesting that it is impossible to know anything beyond the strict confines of the local cultural context (Kohli *et al.* 1995).

In an effort to be inclusive of different methods of comparison, this book is located somewhere in between these two extremes. On the one hand, it accepts that certain deductive theories of politics can be tested in the real world and that generalizations about the world of politics are possible given the proper adherence to rules of inquiry. On the other hand, it recognizes that knowledge of the political world cannot be 'value-free' and that the processes of theory generation and observation may not be mutually exclusive (Feyerabend 1993: 27; Sanders 1995: 67–68; Couvalis 1997). Methodologically, the book is concerned with the application of comparative methods to real research problems in comparative politics in an effort to help students make more valid generalizations about the political world they observe.

Cases, units of analysis, variables, and observations

These four terms are vital aspects of systematic research in comparative politics. Cases are those countries that feature in the comparative analysis. For example, in *States and Social Revolutions* (1979), Theda Skocpol examines the cases of France, Russia, and China. Units of analysis are the objects on which the scholar collects data, such as individual people, countries, electoral systems, social movements, etc. Variables are those concepts whose values change over a given set of units, such as income, political party identification, propensity to join a protest movement, etc. Observations are the values of the variables for each unit, which can be numeric, verbal, or even visual. For example, a hypothetical study of social movements in Britain, France, The Netherlands, and Germany may have a variable entitled 'strategy', which has categories denoted 'political lobbying', 'peaceful demonstration', 'violent direct action', 'grass-roots organizing', and 'consciousness-raising'. In this hypothetical study, the cases are the countries, the units of analysis are the movements, the variable is 'strategy', and the observation is the value of the strategy variable for a given movement in a given country.

In addition to the different values that variables assume, they can either be *dependent* or *independent*. Dependent variables (alternatively referred to as outcome variables, endogenous variables, or the explanandum) are those political outcomes that the research is trying to explain. An independent variable, on the other hand, is that which explains the dependent variable (and is alternatively labelled a causal variable, an explanatory variable, an exogenous variable, or the explicandum). The distinction between dependent and independent variables is derived from the specific research question of a comparative project and the particular theoretical perspective that has been adopted. Since most political events have multiple explanations, it is possible to have more than one independent variable for a given dependent variable. In formal models of politics, the dependent variable is often depicted by a y, and the independent variable is often depicted by an x.

For example, a dependent variable may include vote for a leftist party, military coups, revolutions, or transitions to democracy. Independent variables to account for each of these dependent variables may include, respectively, social class, economic crisis, the commercialization of agriculture, or elite bargaining. In his study of guerrillas and revolution in Latin America, Wickham-Crowley (1993) seeks to explain the occurrence of successful social revolutions. In this case, successful social revolution is the dependent variable. The independent variables include the presence of a guerrilla group, the support of workers and peasants, sufficient guerrilla military strength, the presence of a traditional patrimonial regime, and the withdrawal of US military and economic support for the incumbent regime (Wickham-Crowley 1993: 312; see Chapter 5 in this volume).

Levels of analysis

Levels of analysis in political science are divided between the micro, or individual level, and the macro, or system level. Micro-political analysis examines the political activity of individuals, such as respondents in a mass survey, elite members of a political party or government, or activists in a protest movement. Macro-political analysis focuses on groups of individuals, structures of power, social classes, economic processes, and the interaction of nation states. As in other divisions in political science, there are those who believe all of politics can be explained by focusing on micro-level processes, and there are those who believe that all of politics can be explained by a focus on macro-level processes. This is sometimes called the 'structure-agency' problem of politics (see Hay 1995). Micro-analysts believe that the world of politics is shaped by the actions of 'structureless agents', while macro-analysts believe that that world is shaped by the unstoppable processes of 'agentless-structures'.

The comparative politics literature is rich with examples of these different levels of analysis. In *The Rational Peasant*, Samuel Popkin (1979) argues that revolutionary movements are best understood by focusing on the preferences and actions of individual peasants (a micro-level analysis). Support for this assertion comes from his intense study of peasant activity in Vietnam. In contrast to Popkin, Jeffrey Paige (1975) in *Agrarian Revolution*, demonstrates that revolutions are most likely in countries with a particular structural combination of owners and cultivators. This macro-level analysis is carried out through comparing many countries at once, and then verifying the findings in the three countries of Vietnam,

Angola, and Peru (see Chapter 2). In *Liberalism, Fascism, or Social Democracy*, Gregory Luebbert (1991) claims that the types of regime that emerged in inter-war Europe had nothing to do with 'leadership and meaningful choice' (ibid.: 306), but were determined structurally by mass material interests, social classes, and political parties (a macro-level analysis). Finally, in the *Breakdown of Democratic Regimes*, Stepan (1978) finds the middle ground in accounting for the 1964 breakdown of democracy in Brazil, where he suggests that macro-political conditions at the time of breakdown certainly limited but did not determine the actions of individual leaders. This present book remains agnostic on the question of which level of analysis is best. Rather, it merely demonstrates the ways in which different levels of analysis can fit into the different comparative methods.

Quantitative and qualitative methods

Simply put, quantitative methods seek to show differences in number between certain objects of analysis and qualitative methods seek to show differences in kind. Quantitative analysis answers the simple question, 'How many of them are there?' (Miller 1995: 154), where the 'them' represents any object of comparison that can either be counted or assigned a numerical value. For example, it is possible to count the number of protest events or assign values to different social movement strategies (see above). Quantitative data can be official aggregate data published by governments on growth rates, revenues and expenditures, levels of agricultural and industrial production, crime rates and prison populations, or the number of hectares of land devoted to agrarian reform. Quantitative data can also be individual, such as that found in the numerous market research surveys and public opinion polls. Quantitative methods are based on the distributions these data exhibit and the relationships that can be established between numeric variables using simple and advanced statistical methods.

Qualitative methods seek to identify and understand the attributes, characteristics, and traits of the objects of inquiry, and the nature of the method necessarily requires a focus on a small number of countries. In comparative politics, there are three types of qualitative methods: macro-historical comparison (and its three subtypes) (Skocpol and Somers 1980; Ragin *et al.* 1996); in-depth interviews and participant observation (Devine 1995); and what is variously called interpretivism, hermeneutics, and 'thick description' (Geertz 1973; Fay 1975). In none of these types of method is there an attempt to give numerical expression to the objects of inquiry, and in all of them, the goal is to provide well-rounded and complete discursive accounts. These more complete accounts are often referred to as 'ideographic' or 'configurative', since they seek to identify all the elements important in accounting for the outcome.

Through focus on a small number of countries, comparative macro-history allows for the 'parallel demonstration of theory', the 'contrast of contexts', or 'macro-causal' explanation (Skocpol and Somers 1980). Parallel demonstration of theory tests the fruitfulness of theory across a range of countries. The contrast of contexts helps to identify unique features of countries in an effort to show their effect on social processes, while bringing out the richness of the individual countries and aspiring to 'descriptive holism'. Macro-causal analysis seeks to explain observed political phenomena through the identification and analysis of 'master' variables (Luebbert 1991: 5). In-depth interviews and participant observation strive to uncover a deeper level of information in order to capture meaning, process, and context, where explanation 'involves describing and understanding people as conscious and social human beings' (Devine 1995: 140). Similarly, interpretivism, hermeneutics, and 'thick description' are concerned with interpretation, understanding, and the deeper structures of meanings associated with the objects of inquiry.

Over the years a division in political science has developed between those who use quantitative methods and those who use qualitative methods; however, it seems that this division is a false one if both methods adhere to the goal of making inferences from available evidence (Foweraker and Landman 1997: 48–49). In other words, this book is grounded in the belief that the same logic of inference ought to apply equally to quantitative and qualitative methods (see King *et al.* 1994). Perhaps more importantly, the qualitative distinction made among categories in comparative classification schemes necessarily precedes the process of quantification (Sartori 1970, 1994). And, as the ensuing chapters will demonstrate, it is clear that the field of comparative politics is richly populated with studies that use quantitative and qualitative methods (or both) at all levels of analysis, as well as across all methods of comparison.

Summary

This chapter has outlined the four main objectives of comparative politics and argued further that all co-exist and are necessary for systematic research. Predictions cannot be made without well-founded theories; theories cannot be made without proper classification; and classification cannot be made without good description. The chapter has shown how comparative politics is scientific if it aspires to making inferences about the political world based on the best available evidence. Finally, it defined the key terms that will be used throughout the book. The next chapter examines the different methods of comparison that are available to students, all of which can be used to make larger inferences about the political world that we observe.

Note

1 A slightly more cumbersome definition is offered by Goodin and Klingemann (1996a: 9): 'science . . . [is] systematic enquiry, building toward an ever more highly differentiated set of ordered propositions about the empirical world.'

Further reading

Chilcote, R. H. (1994) *Theories of Comparative Politics: The Search for a Paradigm Reconsidered*, 2nd edn, Boulder, CO: Westview.

An overview of the main theories of comparative politics, including system theory, state theory, political culture theory, modernization theory, dependency theory, and class theory.

Dogan, M. and Pelassy, D. (1990) *How to Compare Nations: Strategies in Comparative Politics*, 2nd edn, Chatham, NJ: Chatham House.

A review of why and how to compare countries as well as a brief overview of popular concepts in comparative politics.

Hague, R., Harrop, M., and Breslin, S. (1992) *Political Science: A Comparative Introduction*, New York: St Martin's Press.

A textbook on political science written from a comparative perspective.

King, G., Keohane, R. O., and Verba, S. (1994) *Designing Social Inquiry: Scientific Inference in Qualitative Research*, Princeton: Princeton University Press.

Demanding but worthwhile effort to unify qualitative and quantitative research methods under one logic of inference.

Lichbach, M. and Zuckerman, A. (eds) (1997) *Comparative Politics: Rationality, Culture, and Structure*, Cambridge, Cambridge University Press.

Advanced text on rational, cultural, and structural theories and how they are used in comparative politics.

Marsh, D. and Stoker, G. (eds) *Theories and Methods in Political Science*, London: Macmillan.

Excellent reader on the main theories and methods of political science.

Chapter 2

How to compare countries

Introduction

As the last chapter made clear, there are different strategies of comparative research in political science, including comparing many countries, comparing few countries, and single-country studies. In contrast to some comparativists (Lijphart 1971; Peters 1998) and in agreement with Mackie and Marsh (1995: 177), this book argues that all three of these strategies of research are subsumed under the broader umbrella of comparative politics, which can be unified under one logic of inference. The comparative literature is replete with examples of all these methods, but why have they come about and what are the advantages associated with each? This chapter demonstrates that these methods are a function both of the explanatory aspirations of the researcher and the level of conceptual abstraction contained within a given study. The chapter outlines each method and discusses how each is useful for drawing inferences. In no way is one method privileged over another, as each has different advantages and disadvantages.

Methods of comparison

The distinction between different comparative methods should be seen as a function of the particular research question, the time and resources of the researcher, the method with which the researcher is comfortable, as well as the epistemological position he or she adopts. Different research questions require different methods. For example, someone wanting to know why Tony Blair and New Labour won the 1997 General Election in Britain will necessarily focus on that one country, but someone interested in the electoral support for reformed left-of-centre political parties may choose all countries in the European Union. Second, the time and resources of researchers are often constrained, and this limits the number of countries that can be feasibly researched in any one project. Third, some are comfortable using quantitative methods while others are not. Some enjoy large comparisons while others enjoy researching the fine details of particular countries. Finally, researchers who adhere to deductive theory may use different methods to those adhering to inductive theory. Those seeking more universal generalizations may use different methods from those that seek more contextually specific levels of explanation.

The central distinction between different comparative methods depends on the key trade-off between the *level of abstraction* and the *scope of countries* under study (Mair 1996). In general, the higher the level of conceptual abstraction, the more potential there is for the inclusion of a large number of countries in a study, where political science concepts 'travel' across different contexts (Sartori 1970; 1994). Alternatively, focus on one country or a few countries means that the researcher can use less abstract concepts that are more grounded in the specific contexts under scrutiny. For example, in the study of democratic institutions, a comparison of many countries may use a simple dichotomy between 'presidential' or 'parliamentary' political systems (Stepan and Skach 1993). A comparison of Latin American political systems, however, would have to adopt more refined categories of presidentialism since all the countries in the region are presidential (Jones 1995;

Foweraker 1998). Finally, further refinements of the concept of presidentialism could be made in order to fit the nuances of a particular country, such as the United States.

Figure 2.1 summarizes these methods of comparison by showing this trade-off between the level of abstraction and the scope of countries. The cells identifying each method are determined by the intersection between the level of abstraction (high, middle, and low) and the scope of countries (one, few, and many). The figure is a heuristic device to illustrate this trade-off in stark terms. In reality, the lines of distinction between the various methods are more blurred, and there are studies that use several different methods at once. For example, Paige's (1975) *Agrarian Revolution* compares many countries at once to uncover the structural determinants of revolution in the world, and then compares the specific countries of Angola, Vietnam, and Peru to see if the cross-national findings hold at the local level.

This representation of comparative methods differs slightly from that outlined in previous work on comparative politics (Lijphart 1971; Collier 1991: 9–12). First, it includes all three methods under the comparative umbrella. In the past, Lijphart (1971) called comparing many countries using quantitative analysis the 'statistical' method and comparing few countries using qualitative analysis the 'comparative method'. For many, single-country studies are by their nature not comparative but may have comparative merit. Many such studies either use concepts that are applicable in other countries, develop new concepts that may become applicable in other countries, and/or embed their studies in a comparative context (Sartori 1994: 15). This book argues that if the research strives to make larger inferences about politics through some form of comparison and uses concepts applicable to more than the country under study, then it is comparative (Lichbach and Zuckerman 1997: 4). Thus, all three methods are deemed comparative.

Second, comparing many countries is commonly referred to as 'large-*n*' comparison, and comparing few countries 'small-*n*' comparison, where *n* is the number of countries. This nomenclature tends to confuse the terminology. As Eckstein (1975: 85) rightly observes, it is possible to have a single-country study with many observations, such as six general elections, or 2,000 respondents in a national survey. Putnam's (1993) *Making Democracy Work* compares many regions

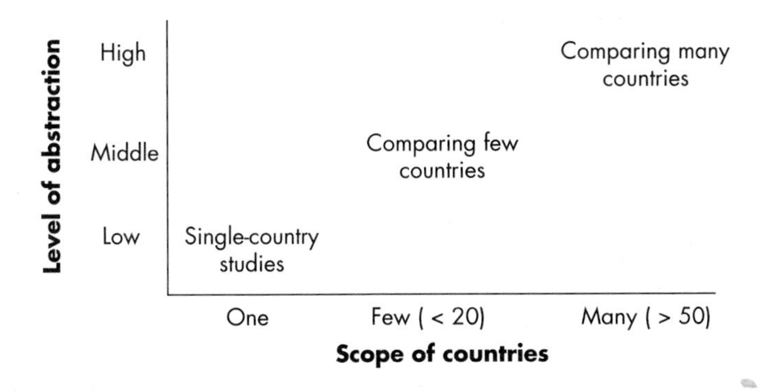

Figure 2.1 Methods of comparison
Sources: Based on Sartori (1970) and Mair (1996)

within Italy, which in this case, is a single-country study drawing inferences from a large-*n*. To prevent confusion in this book, *n* is always used to denote the number of observations (King *et al.* 1994: 51–52). For example, Burkhart and Lewis-Beck (1994) compare 131 countries from 1972–1989 ($n = 2,358$), and Foweraker and Landman (1997) compare Brazil (1964–1990), Chile (1973–1990), Mexico (1963–1990), and Spain (1958–1983), producing $n = 99$ (four countries times the total number of years compared). While the former study compared many countries and the latter a few countries, both could be considered 'large-n' comparative studies. Thus, this book divides the three methods into comparing many countries, comparing few countries, and single-country studies.

Comparing many countries

Comparing many countries most closely approximates the experimental method of science, since it is particularly suited to quantitative analysis through measurement and analysis of aggregate data collected on many countries (Lijphart 1971). Although there are examples of qualitative comparisons of many countries, such as Huntington's (1996) *The Clash of Civilizations* and Finer's (1997) *History of Government*, the majority of studies that compare many countries simultaneously use quantitative methods. This method of comparison requires a higher level of abstraction in its specification of concepts in order to include as many countries as possible. Its main advantages include statistical control to rule out rival explanations, extensive coverage of countries, the ability to make strong inferences, and the identification of 'deviant' countries or 'outliers'.

Comparing many countries is referred to as 'variable-oriented', since its primary focus is on 'general dimensions of macro-social variation' (Ragin 1994: 300) and the relationship between variables at a global level of analysis. The extensive coverage of countries allows for stronger inferences and theory-building, since a given relationship can be demonstrated to exist with a greater degree of certainty. For example, Gurr (1968: 1015) demonstrates that levels of civil strife across 114 countries are positively related to the presence of economic, political, short-term, and long-term deprivation. His analysis also explains that this relationship holds for roughly 65 per cent of the countries (see Chapter 5 and Sanders 1995: 69–73). More recently, Helliwell (1994) has shown that for 125 countries from 1960–1985, there is a positive relationship between per capita levels of income and democracy. After controlling for the differences between OECD countries, Middle Eastern oil-producing countries, Africa, and Latin America, this relationship is demonstrated to hold for about 60 per cent of the countries.

A second advantage of comparing many countries lies in the ability to identify so-called 'deviant' countries or 'outliers'. These are countries whose values on the dependent variable (levels of civil strife or democracy in the examples above) are different than expected, given the values on the independent variables (levels of deprivation or per capita income). In testing for the positive relationship between income inequality and political violence in sixty countries, Muller and Seligson (1987: 436) use a simple scatter plot to identify which countries fit their theory and which do not. For example, Brazil, Panama, and Gabon were found to have a lower level of political violence than was expected for the relatively high level of income inequality. On the other hand, the UK was found to have a particularly high level of political violence given its relatively low level of income inequality. By identifying these 'outliers', scholars can look for other explanations that account for their deviance, and they can remove them for their analysis to make more accurate predictions for the remaining countries. Thus, in this case the unexpected level of political violence observed for the UK was due to the Northern Ireland conflict.

Quantitative studies of many countries help in building general theories of politics since they allow other scholars to replicate their findings. The data sets for these studies can be read and analysed by a variety of statistical software packages. Scholars doing this kind of research often deposit their data in national data archives, such as the UK Data Archive at the University of Essex, the Roper Center at the University of Connecticut, and the Inter-university Consortium for Political and Social Research (ICPSR) at the University of Michigan. More recently, these data sets have been made available in files that can be downloaded from the World Wide Web. In this way, new measures and new methods of analysis can be applied to these data to test the same theories or develop new theories. As a general rule, all scholars should strive to make their data public in an effort to keep a record of the progress of research, as well as help develop new understandings of politics.

Qualitative comparison of many countries is more difficult for two reasons. First, qualitative analysis generally requires a richer level of information, such as deep history of all the countries, which is often difficult to collect and synthesize. Indeed, Finer's (1997) attempt to compare regime types over 5,000 years and across the globe represents a monumental task that occupied all the years of his retirement and produced a three-volume study with 1,700 pages. Second, it is more difficult to draw strong inferences from these data since they cannot be subjected to statistical analysis. Thus, Finer is able to describe and analyse different regime types as they have appeared in history to show how those in existence today are products of innovations from the past, but he is unable (or unwilling) to make any larger causal inferences. Even though he 'privilege[s] those governmental innovations that are still relevant today', he is adamant in stating that these regime types are not the product of a process of 'linear evolution' (ibid.: 88–89).

Despite the advantages of comparing many countries, there are some distinct disadvantages, including the availability of data, the validity of measures, and the mathematical and computing skills needed to analyse data. First, collecting relevant data on the independent nation states of the world can be difficult and time-consuming. Aggregate data are often published only for selected years or selected countries, making comprehensive comparison difficult. In the past, students had to rely on statistical abstracts and yearbooks produced by governments and international organizations, but the advent of the World Wide Web has made the search for data much easier. By using careful search terms on any of the search 'engines' on the Web (e.g. Lycos, Excite, Magellan), students can locate official statistics produced all over the world that can be downloaded quickly.

Second, measuring concepts from political science is difficult and can affect the validity of the measures. Valid measures closely approximate the true meaning of a concept, or what the researcher thinks he or she is measuring (King *et al.* 1994: 25). For example, the literature on economic development and democracy (see

Chapter 4) tends to measure economic development with a country's level of per capita gross domestic product. But some argue that this measure does not take into account the distribution of income, which is also needed in order to capture the nature of a country's level of development. Democracy is also measured in a variety of ways. Freedom House (e.g. 1995) uses abstract scales that measure the degree to which political and civil liberties are protected. Vanhanen (1997: 35) measures democracy with an index that combines the vote share of the smallest party with the level of electoral turnout. Banks (1994) measures the presence of democratic institutions, including the competitiveness of the nomination process, executive effectiveness, legislative effectiveness, legislative selection, and party legitimacy. Many argue that this plethora of democratic measures highlights problems of validity.

Many students eschew quantitative comparison of many countries since it requires mathematical and computing skills. Statistical analysis of data requires an understanding of basic four-figure maths, algebra, probability theory, and calculus. It also requires knowledge of computers, spreadsheets, and statistical software packages. In response to these worries of students, there are several important things to consider. First, many undergraduate and most graduate programmes in political science require their students to take courses in statistics and political explanation, and some universities offer intensive data analysis training. Second, the development of computer technology combined with the availability of data makes this type of analysis much easier than in the past, and it is not unreasonable to assume that it will continue to do so. Third, a large portion of published literature in comparative politics uses quantitative analysis. Students who avoid learning even the basics can shut themselves off from important sources in the field. Thus, all students of comparative politics ought to achieve a basic understanding of the principles of quantitative analysis in order to evaluate studies that use it and employ it when appropriate (Collier 1991: 25).

An underlying assumption of statistical analysis is that events and facts in the world exhibit certain distributions, which can be described, compared, and analysed. But scholars compare and analyse these distributions of data, which are collected from a sample of countries during specific periods of time. The comparison of the distributions is carried out in an effort to see if a relationship exists between them, and whether this relationship would hold for all countries in all periods of time. This basic practice of making inferences from a *sample* (some countries over one period) to a *population* (all countries in all time) lies at the heart of statistical analysis in comparative politics.

This basic principle of statistical analysis can be demonstrated using a deck of playing cards (see Knapp 1996). A deck of playing cards has a known population of fifty-two cards. Each card has known characteristics, including the four suits (clubs, hearts, spades, and diamonds), the two colours (red and black), and the different values (Ace through King). There is thus a distribution of suits (thirteen cards in each), colours (twenty-six red cards and twenty-six black cards), and values (four cards of each value). Using a sample of twenty cards from a well-shuffled deck, a student could get a first approximation of any of these distributions. Replacing the sample, drawing repeated samples, and noting the distributions of the various characteristics would allow the student to get a more accurate picture of the whole deck. This process of sampling and inference is precisely what comparativists are trying to do when they collect and compare aggregate statistics from many countries.

Comparing few countries

Variously called the comparative method, the 'comparable cases strategy' (Lijphart 1975), or 'focused comparison' (Hague *et al.* 1992), comparing few countries achieves control through the careful selection of countries that are analysed using a middle level of conceptual abstraction. Studies using this method are more intensive and less extensive since they encompass more of the nuances specific to each country. The political outcomes that feature in this type of comparison are often seen to be 'configurative', i.e. the product of multiple causal factors acting together. This type of comparison is thus referred to as 'case-oriented' (Ragin 1994), since the country is often the unit of analysis, and the focus tends to be on the similarities and differences among countries rather than the analytical relationships between variables. Comparison of the similarities and differences is meant to uncover what is common to each country that accounts for the observed political outcome.

The method of comparing few countries is divided primarily into two types of system design: 'most similar systems design' and 'most different systems design' (Przeworski and Teune 1970; Faure 1994). Most similar systems design (MSSD) seeks to compare political systems that share a host of common features in an effort to neutralize some differences while highlighting others. Based on J. S. Mill's (1843) method of difference, MSSD seeks to identify the key features that are different among similar countries and which account for the observed political outcome. Most different systems design (MDSD), on the other hand, compares countries that do not share any common features apart from the political outcome to be explained and one or two of the explanatory factors seen to be important for that outcome. This system is based on Mill's method of agreement, which seeks to identify those features that are the same among different countries in an effort to account for a particular outcome. In this way, MDSD allows the researcher to distil out the common elements from a diverse set of countries that have greater explanatory power (Collier 1993: 112).

Table 2.1 clarifies the distinction between these two systems and shows to which of Mill's methods they adhere. For MSSD on the left-hand side of the figure, the countries share the same basic characteristics (*a*, *b*, and *c*), and some share the same key explanatory factor (*x*), but those without this key factor also lack the outcome which is to be explained (*y*). Thus, the presence or absence of the key explanatory factor is seen to account for this outcome, a state of affairs that complies with Mill's method of difference. For MDSD on the right-hand side of the figure, the countries have inherently different features (*a* through *i*), but share the same key explanatory factor (*x*) as well as the presence of the outcome to be explained (*y*). In this system, the outcome to be explained is due to the presence of the key explanatory factor in all the countries (*x*), and thus adheres to Mill's method of agreement. In both systems, the presence of *x* is associated with the

Table 2.1 Most similar systems design (MSSD) and most different systems design (MDSD)

	MSSD Difference[†]			*MDSD Agreement*[†]		
	Country 1	*Country 2*	*Country Φ*	*Country 1*	*Country 2*	*Country Φ*
Features	a b c	a b c	a b c	a b c	d e f	g h i
Key explanatory factor (s)	*x*	*x*	not *x*	*x*	*x*	*x*
Outcome to be explained	*y*	*y*	not *y*	*y*	*y*	*y*

Source: Adapted from Skocpol and Somers (1980: 184)
Note: † Based on J. S. Mill's (1843) method

presence of *y*, and some would argue that *x* actually causes *y*. The difference between the two systems resides in the choice of countries.

Most similar systems design is particularly well suited for those engaged in area studies (Przeworski and Teune 1970: 33). The intellectual and theoretical justification for area studies is that there is something inherently similar about countries that make up a particular geographical region of the world, such as Europe, Asia, Africa, and Latin America. Whether it is common history, language, religion, politics, or culture, researchers working in area studies are essentially employing most similar systems design, and the focus on countries from these regions effectively controls for those features that are common to them while looking for those features that are not. For example, Jones (1995) compares the institutional arrangements of Latin American countries, which not only share the same cultural and historical Iberian legacies, but also share the same basic form of presidentialism. Similarly, Collier and Collier (1991) compare the experiences of eight Latin American countries to uncover the 'critical junctures' during which labour movements were incorporated into the political system.

Where quantitative analysis requires mathematical and computer skills, area studies require language training and extensive field research. Thus, some see these requirements as distinct disadvantages to comparing countries from a given region. It can take years to learn the languages needed to compare countries in Asia or Africa. Even within Latin America, students must learn Spanish and Portuguese, let alone the various dialects of each that are spoken in different parts of the region. Extensive field research can mean long periods living under adverse conditions to which the researcher is unaccustomed. Moreover, funding organizations may be less inclined to support projects that envision long periods of field research. These problems represent the practical considerations that all researchers confront, and

Briefing box 2.1 Most similar and most different systems design

Both system designs appear in comparative politics, particularly by those who compare few countries. Both these examples show how Mill's methods of agreement and difference can be applied to research questions. The first example shows how the most similar systems design is applied to six Latin American countries in an effort to uncover the sources of peasant support for revolutionary activity. The second example shows how the most different systems design is used to account for different regime types in fourteen European countries during the inter-war period.

Most similar systems design (MSSD): sources of peasant support for guerrillas

As part of a more comprehensive effort to account for revolutionary activity in Latin America between 1956 and 1970, Wickham-Crowley (1993: 92–117) uses the most similar systems design to examine the type of peasants that are most likely to support guerrillas in the region. Drawing on the work of Jeffery Paige (1975), he argues that guerrilla strongholds and support for revolutionary behaviour ought to be higher in rural areas in which there are peasants whose livelihood is the most vulnerable to negative influences from the structure of the agricultural system of production. His hypothesis is stated as follows:

> If the guerrillas gain support in an area with a relatively high prevalence of sharecroppers, squatters, or perhaps tenants, my working assumption is that there is an 'elective affinity' between the two, and that guerrillas would not have received such support in more ordinary agricultural regions.
>
> (Wickham-Crowley 1993: 95)

To test the hypothesis, he compares the regional breakdown of Cuba, Venezuela, Guatemala, Colombia, Peru, and Bolivia to determine whether such a relationship

Table 2.2 Most similar systems design

Case	*Cuba*	*Venezuela*	*Guatemala*	*Colombia*	*Peru*	*Bolivia*
Key peasant groups	Squatters	Share-croppers	Tenants	Share-croppers	Serfdom	Small-holders
Outcome to be explained	Guerrilla support	Guerrilla support	Guerrilla support	Guerrilla support	Guerrilla support	No guerrilla support

Source: Adapted from Wickham-Crowley (1993: 92–117)
Note: Cases cover the period 1956–1970

Table 2.3 Most different systems design

	Group 1				
Cases	*Britain*	*France*	*Switzerland*	*Belgium*	*The Netherlands*
Class alliance	Middle class vs. working class	Middle class vs. working class	Middle class vs. working class	Middle class vs. working class	Middle class vs. working class
Outcome	Liberalism	Liberalism	Liberalism	Liberalism	Liberalism
	Group 2				
Cases	*Denmark*	*Norway*	*Sweden*	*Czechoslovakia*	
Class alliance	Working class + middle peasantry	Working class + middle peasantry	Working class + middle peasantry	Working class + middle peasantry	
Outcome	Social democracy	Social democracy	Social democracy	Social democracy	
	Group 3				
Cases	*Germany*	*Italy*	*Spain*		
Class alliance	Middle class + middle peasantry	Middle class + middle peasantry	Middle class + middle peasantry		
Outcome	Fascism	Fascism	Fascism		

Source: Adapted from Luebbert (1991)

exists. Table 2.3 summarizes the comparison and shows that in all the cases except Bolivia, there is the presence of both the specified types of peasants and the outcome to be explained. Bolivia has a prevalence of smallholders, who according to the theory are not likely to support guerrilla activity, and in this case, do not. Thus, across similar cases, the presence of the key explanatory factor is associated with the presence of the outcome to be explained.

Most different systems design: the origins of regimes in inter-war Europe

In seeking to account for the different regime types that emerged in twelve countries in Europe during the inter-war period, Luebbert (1991) claims that the key explanatory variable is the particular class alliance that formed within these countries. The three regime types include liberalism, social democracy, and fascism. The twelve countries are grouped according to these three outcomes and within each group, the countries share few features in common apart from the same class alliance and the same outcome. Thus, Luebbert matches the presence of a particular class alliance to a particular regime type. Table 2.3 summarizes this analysis, and shows that liberalism is the product of a strong middle class versus a weak working class. Social democracy is seen to be a product of an alliance between the working class and the middle peasantry. And fascism is seen to be a product of an alliance between the middle class and the middle peasantry. In this example, the most different systems design is applied to each group of countries.

they highlight the different ways in which comparative methods can be seen to be a function of the training and disposition of the researcher.

Most different systems design is typical of comparative studies that identify a particular outcome that is to be explained, such as revolutions, military coups, transitions to democracy, or 'economic miracles' in newly industrialized countries (Geddes 1990: 134–141). The countries that comprise these types of comparative studies are all instances in which the outcome occurs. For example, Wolf (1968) compares instances of revolutionary movements that had significant peasant participation in Mexico, Russia, China, North Vietnam, Algeria, and Cuba. Though these countries share few common features, Wolf argues that the penetration of capitalist agriculture is the key explanatory factor common to each that accounts for the appearance of the revolutionary movements and their broad base of peasant support. As the next chapter will show, this kind of intentional choice of countries based on the presence of the same outcome constitutes one form of 'selection bias' (Geddes 1990; King *et al.* 1994), which necessarily limits the types of inferences that can be drawn from comparison.

Some comparativists use both system designs. In *Problems of Democratic Transition and Consolidation*, Linz and Stepan (1996) use MSSD to compare the experiences of democratic consolidation within the separate regions of South America, Southern Europe, and Eastern Europe; and then use MDSD to compare across these three regions. Similarly, Rueschemeyer *et al.* (1992) use MSSD to examine the relationship between capitalist development and democracy within

Latin America, and MDSD to compare Latin America and the advanced industrial world. De Meur and Berg-Schlosser (1994) employ both designs to analyse the conditions of survival or breakdown of democratic systems in inter-war Europe. What remains important to all these methods of comparing few countries is the proper specification of the outcome that is to be explained, the reason for adopting either system design, as well as the choice of the particular countries under scrutiny (see Chapter 3).[1]

Single-country studies as comparison

This final section of the chapter considers single-country studies as a method of comparison. As outlined above, a single-country study is considered comparative if it uses concepts applicable to other countries, develops concepts applicable to other countries, and/or seeks to make larger inferences. What should be recognized is that inferences made from single-country studies are necessarily less secure than those made from the comparison of several or many countries. Nevertheless, such studies are useful for examining a whole range of comparative issues. For Eckstein (1975), single-country studies are the equivalent of clinical studies from medicine, where the effects of certain treatments are examined intensively. Beyond this, however, single-country studies provide contextual description, develop new classifications, generate hypotheses, confirm and infirm theories, and explain the presence of deviant countries identified through cross-national comparison. This section of the chapter will consider these in turn.

As outlined in Chapter 1, one of the goals of comparison is contextual description. Single-country studies that merely describe or interpret political phenomena have been variously referred to as 'atheoretical' and 'interpretative' (Lijphart 1971: 691), or configurative-idiographic (Eckstein 1975: 96). Strictly speaking, these types of studies are not comparative but are useful for comparison purely for their information. But single-country studies that provide new classifications are useful for comparison. For example, in describing the Franco regime in Spain, Juan Linz (1964) identified a new form of authoritarianism that was different from personalistic dictatorships and totalitarian states. The regime institutionalized representation of the military, the Catholic Church, and the Falange, as well as the Franco loyalists, monarchists, and technocrats. Unlike totalitarian states, the regime relied on passive mass acceptance rather than popular support (Linz 1964; Carr and Fusi 1979: 31–5; Foweraker and Landman 1997: xxiii). Similarly, Guillermo O'Donnell (1973) established the concept of the 'bureaucratic authoritarian state' in his examination of Argentine politics, a concept which would later be applied not only to other authoritarian regimes in Latin America but also to those in Southeast Asia.

Single-country studies are also useful for generating hypotheses for theories that have yet to be specified fully. As 'plausibility probes' (Eckstein 1975: 108), they either explicitly or implicitly suggest that the generated hypothesis be tested in a larger selection of countries (Lijphart 1971: 692). Again, O'Donnell's (1973) work on authoritarianism is illustrative. To account for the 1966 military coup and subsequent authoritarian regime in Argentina, O'Donnell posited a relationship between a particular stage of dependent capitalist development and the advent of the bureaucratic authoritarian state. This hypothesis was subsequently tested in other Latin American countries and was found wanting on many grounds (see Collier 1979). The point remains, however, that the hypothesis generated from the Argentine case was stated in such a way that other scholars could test it for other countries, and its rejection led to the search for rival explanations (see Cohen 1987; 1994).

When someone gives a lecture using comparative evidence from many countries, a member of the audience may exclaim, 'But in my country, things are different!' This is undoubtedly true, but more importantly the comment illustrates how single-country studies can be used to confirm and infirm existing theories, or illuminate known deviant countries. Theory-confirming and theory-infirming studies are conducted within the confines of known generalizations (Lijphart 1971: 692) and they often adopt the 'least likely' or 'most likely' method of comparison (Eckstein 1975:118). Least likely studies find a country where the theory suggests the outcome is not likely to occur. If the outcome is not observed, then the theory is confirmed. Most likely studies are conducted in countries where the theory suggests the outcome is definitely meant to occur. If the outcome is not observed, then the theory is infirmed. These crucial country studies do not definitively prove or disprove a theory, but merely confirm or infirm its applicability to other countries.

Finally, deviant country studies are particularly useful for theory generation. As outlined above, comparison of many countries often reveals a host of deviant countries that do not conform to the theoretical expectations of the researcher. This deviance invites further research of the countries to establish which rival explanations had not been considered, and it forces the re-evaluation of how the key variables of the study were originally operationalized. Deviant country studies can weaken existing theories as well as further refine the concepts and measures used in the original comparative analysis (Lijphart 1971: 692). The United States, China, and Brazil represent excellent examples of deviant countries for different research questions. For the United States, comparativists seek to explain the absence of a large socialist party; for China, the survival of the communist regime after the 1989 'velvet revolutions' in Central and Eastern Europe (Hague *et al.* 1992: 37–38); and for Brazil, the absence of a social revolution given its poor distribution of income. All three countries represent a state of affairs that defies predominant theories in comparative politics.

Conclusion

This chapter has shown that all three methods – comparing many countries, comparing few countries, and single-country studies – should be grouped under the umbrella of comparative politics if they seek to make generalizations through explicit comparison, or if they use and develop concepts applicable to other countries through implicit comparison. Comparing many countries is the best method for drawing inferences that have more global applicability. Through use of the method of difference and method of agreement, comparing few countries can lead to inferences that are better informed by the contextual specificities of the countries under scrutiny. Single-country studies can provide contextual description, generate hypotheses, confirm and infirm theories, and enrich our understanding of deviant countries identified through other comparisons. Finally, the chapter has made it clear that different strategies of comparison should be seen as the product of the trade-off between the level of conceptual abstraction and the scope of countries, as well as the arbitrary and practical factors surrounding any comparative research project. The next chapter examines the process of choosing countries, the main problems associated with comparison, and summarizes the main arguments of the first three chapters.

Note

1 Despite the prevalence of such comparisons in the field, there are four underlying assumptions to these two methods, which if violated, reduce their ability to make valid inferences. The research must assume: (1) a deterministic explanation, rather than a probabilistic one, (2) no errors in measurement, (3) the existence of one cause, and (4) the absence of interaction effects (see Lieberson 1991, 1994; Savolainen 1994).

Further reading

Collier, D. (1991) 'New Perspectives on the Comparative Method', in D. A. Rustow and K. P. Erickson (eds) *Comparative Political Dynamics: Global Research Perspectives*, New York: Harper Collins, 7–31.

An excellent review of comparative methods.

Eckstein, H. (1975) 'Case-study and Theory in Political Science', in F. I. Greenstein and N. S. Polsby (eds) *Handbook of Political Science, Vol. 7: Strategies of Inquiry*, Reading, MA: Addison-Wesley, 79–137.

The most comprehensive review of the scientific value of single-country studies.

Faure, A. M. (1994) 'Some Methodological Problems in Comparative Politics', *Journal of Theoretical Politics*, 6(3): 307–322.

This essay outlines the most similar and most different systems design as well as their 'mirror images'.

Lijphart, A. (1971) 'Comparative Politics and Comparative Method', *The American Political Science Review*, 65 (3): 682–693.

The original statement about comparative method, locating it as a non-experimental and non-statistical social science.

—— (1975) 'The Comparable Cases Strategy in Comparative Research', *Comparative Political Studies*, 8 (2): 158–177.

This essay presents further reflections on comparative method.

Mackie, T. and Marsh, D. (1995) 'The Comparative Method', in D. Marsh and G. Stoker (eds) *Theory and Methods in Political Science*, London: Macmillan, 173–188.

A brief overview of comparative methods.

Ragin, C. C. (1994) 'Introduction to Qualitative Comparative Analysis,' in T. Janoski and A. Hicks (eds) *The Comparative Political Economy of the Welfare State*, Cambridge: Cambridge University Press, 299–320.

This essay distinguishes between 'variable-oriented' and 'case-oriented' approaches and proposes a way to unify them.

Sartori, G. (1970) 'Concept Misinformation in Comparative Politics', *American Political Science Review*, 64: 1033–1053.

The classic statement on 'conceptual stretching' and the 'ladder of abstraction'.

—— (1994) 'Compare Why and How: Comparing, Miscomparing and the Comparative Method', in M. Dogan and A. Kazancigil (eds) *Comparing Nations: Concepts, Strategies, Substance*, London: Basil Blackwell, 14–34.

A restatement of the main claims in 1970 and that 'to compare is to control'.

Skocpol, T. and Somers, M. (1980) 'The Uses of Comparative History in Macrosocial Inquiry', *Comparative Studies in Society and History*, 22: 174–197.

This essay outlines the uses of comparative history as well as Mill's methods of agreement and difference.

Chapter 3

Choosing countries and problems of comparison

The preceding two chapters made it clear why and how to compare countries. Scholars compare to provide context, make classifications, test hypotheses, and make predictions. They do this by comparing many countries, few countries, or they provide in-depth studies of single countries. As there are many trade-offs associated with these different goals and methods of comparison, there are also important fundamental problems, which if not addressed explicitly can limit the types of generalizations that can be drawn from any study. While not representing insurmountable obstacles to comparison, it is important to address these problems and outline the strategies for overcoming them. This chapter discusses six complementary problems of comparison, which are associated with the choice of countries, the manner in which they are compared, the structure of the research design, and the nature of the evidence.

The first is the problem of *too many variables and not enough countries* (Collier 1991; Dogan and Pelassy 1990; Hague *et al.* 1992), also known more generally as 'too many inferences and not enough observations' (King *et al.* 1994: 119). This problem arises when more factors of explanation for the observed outcome have been identified than there are countries (or observations) in the study, leading to an indeterminate research design. Clearly this problem tends to be associated more often with single case studies and those that compare few countries than with those studies that compare many countries. The second problem is one of *establishing equivalence* both in the theoretical concepts that are used and the operational indicators of those concepts as they are applied in multiple contexts (Sartori 1970; Macintyre 1971; Mayer 1989). For example, the concept of political participation may mean very different things across different contexts, such as voting in one country, or mobilizing activists against nuclear power in another.

The third problem of *selection bias* arises from the intentional choice of countries (Lieberson 1987; Geddes 1990; Collier 1995; King *et al.* 1994), as well as the use of historical accounts and sources that favour the particular theoretical position of the comparativist (Lustick 1996). The fourth problem is *spuriousness*, or the omission of key variables that may account for both the outcome and other explanatory factors already identified. The fifth problem – *ecological and individualist fallacies* – arise when a study seeks to make inferences about one level of analysis using evidence from another (Robinson 1950; Scheuch 1966, 1969; Miller 1995). For example, a theory of revolution may concentrate on individual psychological factors that account for rebellious behaviour, but the comparison to test the theory may use aggregate statistics on levels of inequality and instances of political violence. The final problem for all comparativists to consider is that of *value bias*, where the particular cultural, political, and philosophical predisposition of the researcher necessarily biases the conduct and conclusions of the enquiry.

Too many variables and too few countries

This problem of comparison is illustrated initially with two simple examples, one from simple algebra and one from introductory economics. It is then illustrated using a hypothetical example from political science. Algebra courses often present simple equations that take the following form:

$$x + 5 = 10 \quad [1]$$

In this equation, x is some unknown, whose value is solved by subtracting 5 from 10. A slightly more complicated problem would include *two unknowns* and takes the following form:

$$y = x + 10 \quad [2]$$
$$2x = y + 35 \quad [3]$$

In equations [2] and [3], the values of x and y are not immediately known; however, by combining the two equations through substitution, it is possible to solve for both x and y. Once the value of x has been determined, the value of y can be determined. The steps for this process are as follows:

$$2x = (x + 10) + 35 \quad [4]$$
$$2x = x + 45 \quad [5]$$
$$\therefore \; x = 45; y = 55$$

Similarly in economics, the price and quantity of any good in a market at equilibrium is a function of its supply and demand. Goods in short supply fetch a higher price than goods in abundance, and goods in high demand are more expensive than goods in low demand. If there is an upward shift in demand for a product, then a firm raises the price until it can produce more. Similarly, if a firm produces too much of a good, it is forced to lower its price until the excess supply is sold. Knowing only the supply or demand function for a particular good could not allow the market price or quantity to be determined. As in the algebra example above, the supply and demand curves can be approximated using equations for straight lines. The market price and quantity of a good are determined by setting the two equations equal to one another, which is the same thing as saying that they intersect. Thus, given specific demand and supply equations, the market price and quantity can be derived.

In both the algebra and economic examples, the idea of a system of two equations is similar to the problem of two many variables (or inferences) and not enough countries (or observations). On its own, equation [2] above is meaningless, and x and y can have any number of values that would satisfy it. Similarly, a demand equation without its complementary supply equation is equally meaningless if one wants to know both the quantity and price at market equilibrium. In comparative politics, if a study has too many unknowns (i.e. inferences or possible explanations) and not enough equations (i.e. countries or observations), then solving for the unknowns is problematic. Consider the following hypothetical example from political science. A scholar wants to know which factors are crucial for explaining high public expenditure. After reviewing the relevant literature, it is posited that public expenditure is high in wealthy countries controlled by left-of-centre governments. In this example, there is one dependent variable, public expenditure, and two independent variables, partisan control of government and wealth of the country. Logically, there are four possible combinations of the two independent variables (Figure 3.1). It would be impossible for a scholar to know the effects of

		Wealth of country	
		Poor	Rich
Partisan control of government	Left	Country A Left-poor	Country B Left-rich
	Right	Country C Right-poor	Country D Right-rich

Figure 3.1 Logical combination of two variables in four countries

these variables on the level of public expenditure if the comparison only looked at two countries or less. For example, if a left-poor country is compared to a left-rich country, partisanship is not allowed to vary. Similarly, if a left-rich country is compared to a right-rich country, then wealth is not allowed to vary. Adding a third case to either comparison (e.g. a right-poor country), allows both variables to vary, and the hypothesis can be tested with a determinate research design.

In extending this logic to an example from the last chapter (Table 2.2), Wickham-Crowley (1993) could not know the explanatory relevance of the type of peasant if he only looks at peasants in one country. Similarly, Luebbert (1991) could not know the likely outcome of class alliances if he limited his study to Britain. In general, a study that has too many variables and not enough countries makes explanation of the outcome problematic. Although this problem is more frequent in single case studies and those studies that compare few countries, it can also arise in those that compare many countries since there is a relatively small and finite number of them in the world (Hague *et al.* 1992: 27).

There are three solutions to the problem of too many variables and not enough countries, all of which are based on the principle that the number of variables (or inferences) must be less than the number of countries (or observations) (King *et al.* 1994: 119–122). The first solution is to *raise the number of observations* to allow the key factors of the study greater overall variation, sometimes referred to as 'degrees of freedom'. This can be achieved by comparing instances of the political phenomenon and its hypothesised explanatory factors over time, by adding more countries to the study, or by comparing sub-units of the nation under scrutiny. Recent work in comparative politics has sought to compare many countries over many years using new techniques in so-called 'pooled cross-section time series analysis' (see Stimson 1985; Beck and Katz 1995). In studies that compare few countries, more instances of the phenomenon are drawn from history to increase the number of observations, and in single case studies, sub-units or regions within the nation are compared, such as Putnam's (1993) study of Italy or Hagopian's (1996) study of Brazil.

The second solution to the problem is to use the most similar systems design (MSSD) to achieve focused comparison of few countries. As was outlined in the last chapter, the MSSD framework seeks to control for those factors that are similar across the countries in the study, while focusing on only those factors that are different that account for the outcome. Again, this strategy of comparison underlies the justification for area studies, but some argue that the MSSD framework simply provides 'overdetermined' outcomes (Przeworski and Teune 1970; Collier 1991: 17), where many rival explanations are never truly eliminated. Another criticism of the MSSD framework involves one of perspective, in that similarities for one researcher may be differences for another, effectively lending little value to the approach (Collier 1991; King *et al.* 1994). Despite these criticisms, area studies continue to be carried out with the implicit or explicit reference to the MSSD framework.

The third solution is to reduce the number of variables by focusing on the key explanatory factors that are hypothesized for the outcome. This can be achieved either by using the most different systems design (MDSD) or by having stronger theoretical specifications. Recall that the MDSD framework intentionally compares a diverse set of countries, while concentrating on their key similarities. For example, Opp *et al.* (1995) compare the relationship between left–right ideological positions and support for social protest in Germany, Peru, and Israel. For them, the comparison of such different countries allows for a rigorous test of their main theoretical propositions (Opp *et al.* 1995: 71–72). Apart from comparing most different countries, a strong theory can highlight a parsimonious set of explanatory factors that can travel across space and over time. For example, the 'rational choice' perspective examines the role that 'selective incentives' play in the motivations of revolutionary peasants across the globe and over the centuries.

Establishing equivalence

The second problem confronting comparativists is the equivalence of both their theoretical concepts and the indicators for those concepts across multiple contexts. Mayer (1989: 57) argues that 'the contextual relativity of the meaning or the measures of indicators constitutes the most serious impediment to the cross-contextual validity of empirically testable explanatory theory.' In other words, is it possible to specify concepts and indicators that have shared meanings to allow valid comparisons? For example, does the concept of class apply equally in all societies? Does the idea of 'civic culture' (Almond and Verba 1963) mean the same thing in Brazil as it does in France? Is it possible to have 'new' social movements in Latin America (Fuentes and Frank 1989; Escobar and Alvarez 1992)? Does it mean the same thing when a British MP votes against his party as when a US Senator votes against his party (Hague *et al.* 1992: 29)? The crux of the problem is not specifying identical, or even similar concepts, but *equivalent* ones so that their comparison is meaningful (Dogan and Pelassy 1990; Sartori 1994).

There are three intellectual positions that offer insight into this problem. The 'universalist' position argues that if theoretical concepts and their indicators are to have any explanatory power, they must be able to travel to all parts of the globe. For example, rationalist, functionalist, and structuralist approaches take such a position. Rationalists argue that all individuals maximize their own personal utility given a set of preferences and confronting a range of choices (Ward 1995). Functionalists argue that 'certain vital functions', such as interest articulation and interest aggregation, are 'fulfilled everywhere' (Dogan and Pelassy 1990: 42). Structuralists argue that macro-structures such as the state, economic development, and social classes are omnipresent, but exist in varying degrees which are responsible for determining political outcomes.

The 'relativist' position argues that all meaning is locally determined, and that a general 'science' of comparative politics is necessarily limited if not impossible (Macintyre 1971). Ethnographic, interpretivist, and anthropological approaches take this position (see Geertz 1973; Scott in Kohli *et al.* 1995). In a critique of Almond and Verba's (1963) study of political culture in Italy, Germany, Britain, the United States, and Mexico, Macintyre (1971:173) argues that indicators of commitment to government were never sufficiently examined to account for their cross-cultural differences in meaning. Thus, substantive comparison of these countries and the generalizations about civic culture must be treated with suspicion. Although not an extreme relativist, Sartori (1970, 1994) argues that 'stretching' a concept too far dilutes its meaning and precision, suggesting, that once defined and operationalized, certain concepts can only travel so far.

The middle position argues that comparativists must not abandon all their concepts, but should *modify* them to be more sensitive to the cultural specificities of the contexts they are studying. In *Theorizing Social Movements*, Foweraker (1995) seeks to modify the North American rationalist and European culturalist perspectives on social movements to explain the patterns of social mobilization in Latin America. Key factors of explanation from the rationalist perspective (interests, strategies, micro-mobilization, and political opportunity structure) are combined with culturalist concerns of identity and expression in discussing the various origins, trajectories, and outcomes of Latin American social movements. Some comparativists consider themselves 'opportunists' as they modify, combine, and reconstitute concepts to fit the cases under study (Przeworski on Kohli *et al.* 1995: 16), and argue that wilful sacrifice of insights from different perspectives may obscure important explanatory factors (Katzenstein in Kohli *et al.* 1995: 15).

Since the relativist position obviates the reason for comparative politics, this chapter provides common solutions for those seeking to make larger inferences through comparison (i.e. those adhering to the universal and middle positions). These solutions include raising the level of abstraction (Sartori 1970), focusing on smaller numbers of countries for which the comparativist has thorough substantive knowledge (Sanders 1994), using 'specialist teams' in compiling cross-national data sets (ibid.), and specifying the functional equivalence between concepts or indicators (Dogan and Pelassy 1990). As in the solutions to the problem of 'too many variables not enough countries', there are trade-offs associated with each of these solutions. The key to all is careful specification of concepts, thoughtful construction of indicators that operationalize them, careful application of them to multiple contexts, and recognition of their limitations.

In returning to the distinctions made in Chapter 1, raising the level of abstraction allows a study to be more inclusive, while lowering the level of abstraction makes it more exclusive. For example, in the comparative study of public administration, Sartori (1970: 1042) argues that the term 'staff' is abstract enough to travel universally, 'administration' to all societies that have the presence of some form of bureaucracy, and 'civil service' to all societies with a fully developed modern state. Finer (1997: 78) adopts terms that will travel through space and over time. His 'master variables' for classifying the world's regimes include territory (city, country, or empire), type of regime (palace, forum, nobility, church, and hybrids), the presence or absence of a standing military or civil bureaucracy, and the substantive and procedural limitations on the activities of rulers. Inglehart (1997) seeks to apply two value continua to forty-three countries, which range on the one hand from citizens' concerns with 'survival' vs. 'well-being' and, on the other, from 'traditional' vs. 'legal-rational' forms of authority. In the latter two examples, important concepts are specified in such a way as to incorporate many countries.

The second solution – focusing on a small set of countries for which the comparativist has thorough substantive knowledge – suggests that the analyst be 'extremely cautious about engaging in cross-national comparative research' (Sanders 1994: 43). The explanatory power of concepts can be enhanced if they are applied in contexts with which the comparativist is most familiar. Thus, those who engage in area studies spend many years studying the history, economics, politics, and culture of a regional sub-set of countries in an effort to make more meaningful explanations of political phenomena. This 'local' knowledge can identify gaps between theoretical concepts and their application, and result in more meaningful comparison. Sanders (1994: 48) summarizes this point precisely:

> It is only with detailed substantive knowledge that analysts can make informed judgements either about the relevance of the characterizations that they make of particular systems or about the identity of meaning attached to the questions that they pose to people living in different countries.

The third solution necessarily follows from the second. If truly informed comparison of many countries is limited, then those seeking to compare many countries 'should venture out of the security of the familiar if they are prepared to collaborate with other scholars' who possess specialist knowledge of the countries under scrutiny (Sanders 1994). This solution was used by Fitzgibbon (1967), who sought to measure democratic change in Latin America by using a questionnaire to measure general social and political factors he believed were both preconditions and manifestations of democracy. The questionnaire was sent to leading academics working in specific countries and regions in Latin America and was repeated at five-year intervals between 1945 and 1985. The resulting 'image index' is highly correlated with similar such measures (Foweraker and Landman 1997: 61 fn. 14; Chapter 4). Another example that follows Sanders' prescription is Inglehart's (1997) *World Values Survey*, which uses local specialist teams to implement a similar survey in forty-three countries. It is also common practice in the human rights community to produce world reports on human rights protection such as the Amnesty International *Annual Reports*, the US State Department *Country Reports*, or *The Freedom of Religion and Belief: A World Report* (Boyle and Sheen 1997). These reports can then be used for secondary analysis, such as Poe and Tate's (1994) global analysis of the repression of human rights (see Chapter 10 below).

The final solution is the identification of 'functional equivalence' of concepts and indicators. This solution does not envisage concepts as identical or even similar, but functionally equivalent. If two entities share exactly the same qualities, properties, and characteristics, they are considered identical (apples are apples). If they share some qualities, properties, or characteristics, then there are said to be similar (apples and pears are fruit). If they share the same *function*, however, they are said to be functionally equivalent. For example, leaders of countries can serve three functions: symbolic representation of the nation, chief executive of state authority, and party leader. The French president embodies all three while the British monarch embodies the symbolic role and the British prime minister embodies the executive and party leader roles (see Dogan and Pelassy 1990: 37). Depending on the functional focus and political systems of the comparison, the study may include an examination of one, two, or three individuals. Thus, functional equivalence allows entities with seemingly dissimilar characteristics to be grouped into useful and exclusive categories. In general, the analyst must specify clearly in which respect the concept is comparable.

Selection bias

A crucial scientific principle frequently violated by comparative politics is the principle of selection. Comparison seeks to achieve experimental simulation, but experiments and mass attitudinal surveys in political science use *random selection* of individual respondents, while the essence of much of comparative politics is the *intentional selection* of countries. The basic experimental form has an experimental group and a control group. The experimental group receives the 'treatment' (stimulus, drug, or exposure to some independent factor), and the control group does not. The outcome of both groups after treatment is then compared. If the experimental group exhibits a different outcome than the control group, it is attributed to the treatment, given that all else is equal (known as the *ceteris paribus* condition). In mass attitudinal surveys, a completely random sample of individuals is selected and the subsequent data analysis of responses yields substantive inferences about the whole population from which the sample is drawn (see de Vaus 1991). In studies of electoral behaviour, a frequent finding is that those from a lower social class tend to vote for left-of-centre political parties while those of higher social class tend to vote for right-of-centre parties. The analysis of the survey data *compares* groups of individuals from each social class and determines the effects of that difference on their preference for particular political parties.

In both these examples, *the selection of individuals or units of analysis is not related to the outcome to be explained.* Selection bias in comparative politics occurs through the non-random choice of countries for comparison, or the deliberate selection by the comparativist (Collier 1995: 462). Though selection of countries lies at the heart of comparison, selection without reflection may lead to serious problems of inference. The most blatant form of selection occurs when a study includes only those cases that support the theory. More subtle forms of selection bias, however, occur when the choice of countries relies on values of the dependent variable (Geddes 1990; King *et al.* 1994) and for qualitative studies, the use of certain historical sources (Lustick 1996).

The problem of selection does not affect studies that compare many countries as much as studies that compare few countries, and it is a major problem for single case studies. Studies that compare many countries usually have a sufficient number of observations to avoid the problem of selection, and quantitative studies of many countries can use a number of statistical techniques to eliminate the problem (see Gujarati 1988; Fox 1997). For studies that compare few countries and single case studies, however, selection can seriously affect the type of inferences that are drawn. Frequently in these types of studies, countries are chosen because they exhibit only the outcome the comparativist seeks to explain, such as a social revolution, a military coup, a transition to democracy, the failure of deterrence, or high economic growth rates (Geddes 1990; Collier 1995). Selecting on the dependent variable in this way can lead either to an overestimation of effects that do not exist, or to an underestimation of effects that do exist (Geddes 1990: 132–133).

Recall O'Donnell's (1973) study of the bureaucratic authoritarian state (see Chapter 2). O'Donnell tried to explain the advent of the bureaucratic-authoritarian state based on the case of Argentina in 1966. O'Donnell argued that the presence of key independent factors – a collapse of a certain mode of dependent capitalist industrialization, economic stagnation, and an increase in popular demands – led the military to overthrow the democratic government, implement economic plans for recovery, and repress popular mobilization against the Argentine state. Subsequent research tested this theory both in Latin American countries that had similar experiences of authoritarianism and in countries that did not (Collier 1979). These studies showed that countries with similar authoritarian experiences did not share the same antecedent factors, while countries that sustained democracy did share these factors. Moreover, when the Latin American economy took another downturn in the early 1980s, no new instances of the bureaucratic-authoritarian state arose. Thus, the comparison across cases and time revealed that the strong connection between these independent factors and authoritarianism could not be upheld (Cohen 1987). O'Donnell's single case study overestimated the effect of the antecedent factors on the political outcome he observed (see Briefing Box 3.1).

In a less obvious but equally problematic example of selection bias, Skocpol (1979) compares countries that experienced social revolutions (Russia, China, and France) to contrasting countries where revolution did not occur (Japan, Prussia, and Britain) in an effort to demonstrate the explanatory relevance of certain structural factors to these revolutions. These structural factors include external military threats, regime reform, dominant class opposition, and state collapse (see Chapter 5). The contrasting cases did not share these factors and did not experience social revolutions. Geddes (1990) argues that the comparison to these contrasting cases is good but still limited, since these countries represent the other extreme of her dependent variable. The comparison confirms Skocpol's theory, but Geddes (1990: 143) asks, 'would a differently selected set of cases do so?' Comparison to the cases of Mexico, Guatemala, El Salvador, Honduras, Nicaragua, Ecuador, Peru, Bolivia, and Paraguay, which have similar structural factors and varying experiences with social revolution, would reveal the limits to the inferences about structures that Skocpol draws (ibid.: 144–145).

In both the O'Donnell and Skocpol examples, selection on the dependent variable led to an overestimation of the importance of certain explanatory factors. In general, there are three solutions to the problem of choosing on the dependent variable. The first solution is to have a dependent variable that *varies*; i.e., countries

Briefing box 3.1 The problem of selection bias

The rise of the bureaucratic-authoritarian state

In explaining the rise of the bureaucratic authoritarian state in Argentina, O'Donnell (1973) focused on two key explanatory factors: (1) the stagnation of the economy as measured by balance of payments deficits, low growth rates, rising inflation, and (2) the inability of the country to make the necessary transition from the 'easy phase' to the 'hard phase' of import-substitution-industrialization (ISI).

Under the easy phase of ISI, the state provided protection of the local economy with high tariffs and import quotas to allow new industries to develop the capacity to produce domestically what used to be imported from abroad. The policy included credit at concessionary rates, high wages for labour, and artificially high prices for traditional exports through manipulation of exchange rates. The hard phase of ISI, on the other hand, saw a shift to the domestic production of all intermediate goods necessary for finished capital goods, which was known as 'deepening' or 'vertical integration'. This phase required the attraction of foreign investment from multinational corporations, the loosening of tariff and quota restrictions, a reduction in wages, and a readjustment of exchange rates.

In the Argentine case, economic stagnation preceded the military overthrow in 1966 and 'deepening' of the economy occurred after the coup. From this chain of events, O'Donnell theorised a connection between the antecedent factors, the advent of the bureaucratic state, and the subsequent economic policy of deepening. This reasoning is depicted in column three of Table 3.1. Subsequent comparison to the cases of Brazil, Colombia, and Venezuela revealed that while all three experienced economic stagnation, two (Colombia and Venezuela) *did not* experience military coups, and one (Brazil) had *already* started a process of deepening *before* the military overthrew the democratic government in 1964. These contrasting cases are listed in columns four, five, and six of Table 3.1. Thus, by relying on only the case of Argentina, O'Donnell's theoretical conceptualization and explanation suffered from selection bias.

Table 3.1 Explaining the bureaucratic-authoritarian state in Latin America

		Argentina	*Brazil*	*Venezuela*	*Colombia*
Explanatory factor 1	Economic stagnation	Yes	Yes	Yes	Yes
Explanatory factor 2	Failure to make transition to hard phase of ISI	Yes	No	Yes	Yes
Outcome 1	Military coup and implementation of BA state	Yes	Yes	No	No
Outcome 2	Deepening of domestic economy	Yes	Yes (pre-coup)	Yes	Yes

Source: Adapted from O'Donnell (1973); Serra (1979)

in which the outcome has occurred and those in which it has not. Only by comparing across the presence and absence of outcomes can the importance of explanatory factors be determined. Second, when comparing few countries, the choice of countries ought to reflect substantive knowledge of parallel cases (Laitin 1995: 456). Third, stronger theory may specify more accurately a range of countries in which certain outcomes and their explanations would obtain (ibid.). Fourth, and related to the third solution, strong theory will also identify which countries represent 'least likely' (cf. Chapter 2) instances of the phenomenon under investigation (Caporaso 1995: 458). All four solutions demand close attention to the types of inferences that are being drawn when intentionally choosing countries for comparison.

A second form of selection bias arises in qualitative studies that rely on historical sources, where the analyst chooses historical accounts either intentionally or unintentionally whose description of events fits the particular theory being tested. As Lustick has pointed out, 'the work of historians cannot be legitimately treated as an unproblematic background narrative from which theoretically neutral data can be elicited for the framing of problems and the testing of theories' (Lustick 1996: 605). Historiography varies in its description of how the past actually unfolded, which events receive emphasis, as well as the different theoretical dispositions of the historians themselves. Thus, inferences drawn from studies using descriptive historical accounts that 'are organized and presented according to the categories and propositions of theories they are testing' will necessarily be biased (ibid.: 610). Solutions to this form of selection bias include using multiple sources to arrive at a 'mean' account of the events and identifying the tendencies within each source to acknowledge possible sources of bias.

Spuriousness

A spurious explanation is one in which some unidentified factor is responsible for the outcome, while the identified factor is mistakenly attributed to having an effect on the outcome. Also known as omitted variable bias (King *et al.* 1994: 168), this problem frequently arises in comparative politics and is related to selection bias since the choice of cases may overlook an important underlying factor that accounts for the outcome. Consider the following example. An industrious graduate student spends the summer holidays working in resorts around the United States. Over the years, the student recognizes that wherever he works, there appears to be both a high number of flamingos and retired people. He decides to spend his leisure time collecting data on the geographical distribution of flamingos and retired people. Cognisant of the problem of selection bias, the student extends the collection of data to include all the states in the US. After the data are collected, the student finds a positive correlation between the number of flamingos and the number of retired people. From these robust statistical results, he concludes that flamingos *cause* retired people. It is clear that the unidentified factor in this example is climate. On balance, both flamingos and retired people in the United States 'flock' to those areas with warmer climates. Thus, the mistaken connection between the two is due to the unidentified factor (see Briefing Box 3.2). By omitting the variable

Briefing box 3.2 Spuriousness

Simple explanations of events often take the form 'if event *x* then event *y*' (Sanders 1994, 1995; Lawson 1997), which can be depicted graphically as follows:

In this example, *x* and *y* are the only variables that have been identified. Suppose data collected on the occurrence of *x* and *y* shows that whenever (or wherever) *x* occurs, *y* also occurs. The regular and concomitant occurrence of both would lead to either the weak conclusion that *x* and *y* are *associated* with each other, or the strong conclusion that *x* actually causes *y*. But what if some other factor *z* also occurs regularly with *x* and *y*? The analyst risks specifying a relationship between *x* and *y* that may actually be the result of *z* acting on *x* and *y* independently. This situation is depicted as follows:

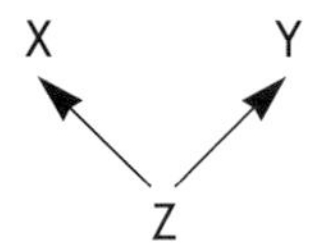

In this case, there is no direct relationship between *x* and *y*, but a common underlying factor to both, which explains their occurrence. Failure to specify this third variable and its effects on *x* and *y* constitutes the problem of spuriousness. The assertion that authoritarian regimes (*x*) are better at promoting economic development (*y*), failed to identify that authoritarian regimes tend to collapse in times of economic hardship (*z*).

In another example, Lieberson and Hansen (1974) found a negative relationship between language diversity (*x*) and development (*y*), when they compared a sample of countries at one point in time. Had they stopped there, they would have concluded that language diversity inhibits development. Further analysis showed, however, that for a given nation *over time*, there was no relationship between language diversity and development. What they did find, however, was that the *age of a nation* (the previously unspecified *z*) was negatively related to language diversity and positively related to development. Thus, the original relationship between language diversity and development was spurious (see Firebaugh 1980). This example of spuriousness is summarized as follows:

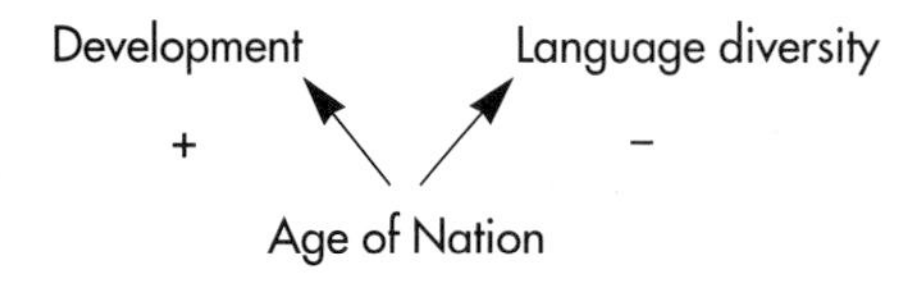

In both these examples, failure to identify the common underlying factor can lead to a false inference regarding the relationship between the two variables specified originally.

of climate, the student mistakenly concluded that flamingos cause retired people. If the student had only collected data in Florida, he may have reached the same conclusion, but one that was additionally influenced by selection bias.

In comparative politics, it has been frequently asserted that authoritarian regimes are better at promoting economic development than democratic regimes, since their 'relative autonomy' from society allows them to control more easily instances of political dissent. Global analysis of the relationship compares indicators of authoritarianism and economic performance and finds a strong positive association between the two. What these studies fail to identify, however, is that authoritarian governments tend to fall during periods of economic downturn, since much of their legitimacy rests on their ability to deliver economic benefits (Przeworski and Limongi 1993). Once discredited in economic terms, authoritarian regimes tend to lose their grip. Democracies, on the other hand, endure through periods of thick and thin. In terms of the overall relationship, this fact means that authoritarian regimes are only in power during times of good economic performance. Thus, by ignoring the important factor of regime 'attrition', the original finding in support of the connection between authoritarian regimes and economic performance is spurious (Przeworski and Limongi 1993, 1997).

As above, the solutions to the problem of spuriousness are related to the number of countries in a comparative study; moreover the trade-offs associated with these solutions can often be a source of frustration. The easiest solution for spuriousness is to specify all the relevant variables that may account for the observed outcome. This solution is fine if the comparison is across many countries or many observations, but if the study is one of few countries or one country, specifying additional variables can overlap with the first problem identified in this chapter (too many variables, not enough countries). It is important not to specify irrelevant variables as they may simply cloud the analysis. The second solution is to select countries that fit the criteria of the theory that has been specified, but this solution overlaps with the problem of selection bias. Thus, the comparativist is forced to recognize these various trade-offs while maximizing the types of inferences that can be made given the countries and the evidence in the study.

Ecological and individualist fallacies

There are two types of data in the social sciences: *individual* data and *ecological* data. Individual data, as the name suggests, comprise information on individual people. Ecological data comprise information that has been aggregated for territorial units, such as voting districts, municipalities, counties, states, and countries (Scheuch 1969:136). Individual data are collected through the use of periodic censuses carried out on the whole of a particular population, through other 'official' means, or through surveys carried out on a representative sample of the population. The twin problems of ecological and individualist fallacies occur when inferences are drawn about one level of analysis using evidence from another. An ecological fallacy occurs when results obtained through the analysis of aggregate-level data are used to make inferences about individual-level behaviour. Alternatively, an individualist fallacy occurs when results obtained through analysis of individual-level data are used to make inferences about aggregate-level phenomena. For example, claiming that women support the right to abortion by correlating the percentage of women in electoral districts with votes in support of an abortion measure is an ecological fallacy. Claiming that Germany is a more 'authoritarian' society than Britain by comparing responses to standardized survey questions is an individualist fallacy.

Both fallacies are a problem since analysis carried at one level may over-estimate relationships at another level (Robinson 1950: 353), and both fallacies originate from the same sources, namely, the ontological predispositions of the researcher and data availability. In the first case, some scholars may assume that data at one level represent a higher degree of reality that data at another level. As Scheuch (1969: 134) argues, 'individual behaviour may be treated as being the only real phenomenon, while system properties are abstractions, or individual behaviour may be viewed as mere reflection of the only reality, namely structural properties'. In either case, the source of the fallacy is due to a certain ontological predisposition that serves as the starting point of the inquiry. As outlined in the previous chapter, rationalist explanations see collective behaviour as having no particular status other than the individuals who comprise it (Lichbach 1997: 245). Structuralist explanations, on the other hand, focus on the political, social, and economic connections among people, such as '[h]istorically rooted and materially based processes of distribution, conflict, power, and domination, thought to drive social order and social change' (ibid.: 247–248). Thus, a rationalist may collect information on individuals to make larger claims about groups, while a structuralist may collect information on groups of people to make larger statements about individuals.

Data availability is the second source of ecological and individualist fallacies, since scholars may be forced to substitute data from one level to examine a research question specified at another level. For example, Gurr (1968) posited that a sense of relative deprivation was the prime motivating force behind rebellious activity. Relative deprivation is a psychological condition that obtains when individuals perceive that those 'goods and conditions of life to which they are rightfully entitled' fall short of those they are actually capable of achieving, given the social means available to them (Gurr 1970: 13). Gurr (1968) posited that high levels of relative deprivation ought to be related to high levels of political violence. Since individual-level data on relative deprivation were unavailable, Gurr tested this hypothesis using aggregate data on 114 countries (see Chapters 2 and 5), which showed a positive association between his measures of relative deprivation and political violence. In this case, aggregate data were used to falsify a hypothesis at the individual level (Sanders 1981: 30–31).

Similarly, in *Modernization and Postmodernization*, Inglehart (1997) commits an individualist fallacy in his study of values in forty-three societies. Using a standard battery of questions ranging from the importance of God to protection of the environment, Inglehart constructs 'clusters' of values that cohere into distinct geographical patterns. These patterns, Inglehart argues, are meaningfully distributed around the globe according to general cultural groups, including Latin America, Northern Europe, Eastern Europe, Catholic Europe, South Asia, Africa, and North America. In this study, Inglehart is aggregating individual-level responses to questions to establish simplified classifications of countries based on culture. Grouping percentages of individuals who responded similarly to a battery of survey questions and ascribing cultural 'types' to them is a clear illustration of the individualist fallacy, which confuses systemic properties with individual characteristics. As Scheuch (1966: 158–159) argues, a democratic system may be comprised of many individuals who respond positively to a series of questions probing their authoritarian tendencies, none the less the system is still democratic. Similarly, an authoritarian system may be comprised of individuals who respond positively to a series of questions probing their democratic tendencies or 'civic culture' (Almond and Verba 1963). In short, to ascribe a certain cultural or systemic trait to a country based on a sample of the population is to draw an incorrect inference about that system based on an incorrect level of analysis.

The solution for avoiding both fallacies is straightforward. The data used in any research ought to minimize the chain of inference between the theoretical concepts that are specified and the measures of those concepts that are ultimately adopted in the analysis. Known as the 'principle of direct measurement' (Scheuch 1969: 137), the solution means that research that specifies questions at the individual level ought to use individual data, and vice versa for research questions that specify systemic relationships. For quantitative analysis, Miller (1995: 155–156) argues that 'analysis of individuals can only lead to precise quantitative conclusions about individuals; an analysis of places to precise conclusions about places; and analysis of times only to conclusions about times'.[1] The pragmatic aspects of research may not allow the direct measurement of the phenomena, but the overall point remains that this measurement must be as close to the level of the phenomena being examined as possible.

Value bias

The final problem of comparison is one of value bias, a problem which depends upon the perspective from which one sees the world. Over the course of the last century, social science has come to recognize that knowledge is not 'value-free'. Classification, analysis, and substantive interpretation are all subject to the particular perspective of the researcher. Modern empirical analysis accepts that to some degree 'what is observed is in part a consequence of the theoretical position that the analyst adopts in the first place' (Sanders 1995: 67), but the quest to 'separate fact and value' is still considered worthwhile (Hague *et al.* 1992: 30). The key to making valid comparisons is to *be as public as possible* (King *et al.* 1994: 8) in terms of the judgements that have been made in the overall construction of the comparative study. These judgements include the theoretical perspective upon which the study is based, the identification of its key variables, the specification of its research design, and the limits to the type of inferences that can be drawn from it.

Conclusion

This chapter has identified six key problems of comparative method. It has also made clear that these problems are embedded in the overall trade-offs between the various methods of comparison. Specifying too many inferences without having enough observations constitutes an indeterminate research design that often affects single case studies and those that compare few countries. Establishing cross-cultural equivalence in terms of theoretical concepts and their operational indicators is a constant worry for studies that compare many countries, since the global travel of concepts may undermine the precision of their meaning. The intentional selection of countries that support the theory being tested and that represent one or opposite values on the dependent variables can lead to an overestimation of a relationship that does not exist or the underestimation of a relationship that does. Failing to specify important 'control' or other relevant variables can lead to the overestimation of relationships. Transcending different levels of analysis can also affect the type of inferences. Finally, ignorance of the cultural and theoretical perspective that underlies a study can colour its substantive conclusions.

These problems were outlined not to paralyse comparative researchers, but to highlight possible sources of bias in drawing valid inferences. Careful attention to these problems at the outset of any comparative inquiry will maximize the types of inferences that can be drawn. Acceptance of the natural limits of comparative inquiry is a healthy step along the winding road to the production of knowledge. Taken together, the three chapters in Part I have identified why political scientists compare countries, how they compare countries, and the types of problems they frequently encounter along the way. Table 3.2 summarizes the methods of comparison and assesses their strengths and weaknesses both in terms of their ability at arriving at valid inferences and the trade-offs for the researcher that are associated with each.

Comparing many countries is susceptible to statistical analysis, which helps eliminate possible sources of selection bias and spuriousness. The large number of observations means that these types of studies are good at making strong inferences, which in turn contribute to theory-building. The comparison of many countries is good for identifying deviant cases that invite closer scrutiny both of the cases as well as of the theory that is being tested. On the other hand, comparison of many countries can rely on measures that are invalid owing to the limitations of available data. The connections established between variables may be considered too abstract and simplistic. The collection and analysis of the data may be time-consuming and may require mathematical and computing training, which many comparativists are not willing to undertake.

Comparing few countries achieves control through the careful selection of countries that fit within either the most similar systems design (MSSD) or the most different systems design (MDSD). These types of studies are intensive and are good for theory generation. They avoid conceptual stretching since they rely on specialist knowledge of a few cases. These studies tend to see their objects of analysis as a configuration of multiple explanatory factors that depend on the careful comparison of history of the chosen countries. Alongside these benefits,

Table 3.2 Comparative methods: an assessment

Method	*Strengths*	*Weaknesses*
Comparing many countries	Statistical control Limited selection bias Extensive scope Strong inferences and good for theory-building Identify deviant countries	Invalid measures Data availability Too abstract/high level of generality Time-consuming Mathematical and computer training
Comparing few countries	Control by selecting 1 Most similar systems design (MSSD) 2 Most different systems design (MDSD) Good for theory-building Intensive, less variable-oriented Avoid 'conceptual stretching' Thick description Areas studies Configurative analysis Macro-history	Less secure inferences Selection bias: 1 Choice of countries 2 Choice of historical account Language training Field research
Case study	Intensive, ideographic, path-dependent, and configurative analysis Six types: 1 Atheoretical 2 Interpretive 3 Hypothesis-generating 4 Theory-confirming 5 Theory-infirming 6 Deviant countries	Insecure inferences Selection bias: 1 Choice of countries 2 Choice of historical account Language training Field research

studies that compare few countries are not able to draw strong inferences owing to problems of selection bias both in terms of the choice of countries and the choice of the historical accounts used for evidence. Finally, many comparativists who consider themselves 'generalists' do not want to spend their time and energy learning the languages and conducting the field research in the countries that comprise these types of studies.

Studies of single countries constitute the most intensive of the comparative methods and still make up a large proportion of research in the field of comparative politics. Single case studies useful for comparison are those that generate hypotheses, confirm and infirm theories, and elucidate deviant cases identified through other modes of comparison. Since they are the least extensive, single case studies are most susceptible to problems of selection bias, too many variables and not enough observations, and indeterminate research designs that yield less secure inferences than the other modes of comparison. As with area specialists, 'country specialists' invest a tremendous amount of their time learning the local language and culture of their particular country, a commitment that other comparativists may find too demanding. Having outlined these methods of comparison, the logic that underpins them, and the problems that are associated with them, the chapters in Part II interrogate popular topics of comparative politics using the 'architecture' established in these first three chapters. Part II is primarily concerned with how different methods have been applied to different research questions, and whether these methods have produced consistent answers to these problems. In this sense, Part II *compares comparisons* in an effort to illustrate the practical implications of different comparative methods as they are applied to real research problems. The topics in Part II include economic development and democracy (Chapter 4), violent political dissent and revolution (Chapter 5), non-violent political dissent and social movements (Chapter 6), transitions to democracy (Chapter 7), and institutional design and democratic performance (Chapter 8).

Note

1 Recent work in this area claims to have resolved the problem of ecological fallacy using advanced statistical techniques and the creation of specific software (King 1997), which is available for those wanting to pursue this line of research. Thus far, the new technique has been applied to voting rights cases in the United States in which aggregate data is used to make inferences about individual voting behaviour based on categories of race and social class. The extension of the method to aggregate data on nation states will certainly follow, but will involve more complicated techniques. For those not willing to pursue this line of work, however, theories that posit relationships to exist at the individual levels ought to be tested with data at the individual level, and the same rule of thumb should apply for theories that posit relationships at the aggregate level.

Further reading

Collier, D. (1991) 'New Perspectives on the Comparative Method', in D. A. Rustow and K. P. Erickson (eds) *Comparative Political Dynamics: Global Research Perspectives*, New York: Harper Collins, 7–31.

This essay addresses the problems of too many variables and not enough countries.

Dogan, M. and Pelassy, D. (1990) *How to Compare Nations: Strategies in Comparative Politics*, 2nd edn, Chatham, NJ: Chatham House.

This book provides a good discussion of establishing functional equivalence in comparative politics.

Geddes, B. (1990) 'How the Cases You Choose Affect the Answers You Get: Selection Bias in Comparative Politics', *Political Analysis*, 2: 131–150.

An excellent article on selection bias using real examples from the comparative literature.

Hague, R., Harrop, M., and Breslin, S. (1992) *Political Science: A Comparative Introduction*, New York: St Martin's Press.

Chapter 2 makes brief statements about value bias, too many variables not enough countries, and equivalence.

Lieberson, S. (1987) *Making It Count: The Improvement of Social Research and Theory*, Berkeley: University of California Press.

Chapter 2 provides an exhaustive review of problems with selection bias.

Lustick, I. (1996) 'History, Historiography, and Political Science: Multiple Historical Records and the Problem of Selection Bias', *American Political Science Review*, 90 (3): 605–618.

A good review of historical sources of selection bias.

Sanders, D. (1994) 'Methodological Considerations in Comparative Cross-national Research', *International Social Science Journal*, 46.

This article presents a strong argument in favour of using only those countries with which the comparativist has good substantive knowledge.

Part II

COMPARING COMPARISONS

Part I established why countries are compared and how comparison helps generate, test, and refine theories of politics. It established a general 'architecture' of comparative methods that includes the comparison of many countries, few countries, and single-country studies. It demonstrated how these three types of comparison use quantitative and qualitative techniques at different levels of analysis. Finally, it highlighted the key problems associated with comparison and suggested how best to overcome them. Throughout the chapters, concrete examples from the comparative literature were used to demonstrate these points. The chapters that make up Part II of this text use these different methods to interrogate popular research topics in comparative politics. The topics chosen have received wide attention in the comparative literature, are attractive to students of comparative politics, and are well suited to examine the different ways in which comparative methods can be applied to real world problems. In essence, the chapters in this part of the text *compare comparisons* in an effort to demonstrate the utility of different methods of comparison.

The post-war period brought a whole range of new research questions and political problems to the field of comparative politics. The initial years of the period witnessed: the rise of communism; an end to colonial rule and birth of new nation states; the appearance of new forms of political conflict from peasants, workers, and other subordinate groups; military coups and the rise of authoritarianism; and new experiences with democracy. The latter part of the period saw transitions to democracy in Latin America, Southern Europe, Africa, Asia, and (with the collapse of the Soviet Union) Central and Eastern Europe. These events raised intriguing questions for comparativists as they focused on global, regional, and local aspects of political change, and many of these studies were motivated by the concern for achieving political stability in the short term and promoting democratic rule in the long term (Valenzuela and Valenzuela 1978: 535). In this sense, comparative political inquiry has responded to contemporary issues (Lichbach 1997: 4), and has been motivated by a concern for the well-being of the people who comprise the modern world.

The chapters that comprise this section of the book reflect in part these challenges and concerns of comparativists. Chapter 4 examines the efforts to uncover the social and economic 'preconditions' (Karl 1990) for healthy democracy. Chapter 5 looks at attempts to explain violent political dissent and the surge of revolutionary movements. Chapter 6 compares efforts to explain the origins, characteristics, and impact of non-violent political dissent and social movement activity. Chapter 7 traces the comparative work that seeks to explain the 'third wave' (Huntington 1991) of democratic transitions that began in Portugal 1974. Finally, Chapter 8 examines the comparative work on democratic institutions and democratic performance. The discussion in each chapter is concerned primarily with the hypothesis-testing and theory-building functions of comparison (see Chapter 1), while the focus is on method and not on the theories themselves.

Each chapter begins with a statement of the basic research question and what motivated its emergence in the comparative literature, followed by a comparison of the attempts to investigate the problem using the methods outlined in the first part of the book. This comparison seeks to answer several important questions. First, do the different comparisons (i.e. many countries, few countries, case studies) arrive at the same conclusion about the research question? If not, why not? Second, for those studies that compare few countries, is the most different systems design or most similar systems design used? And, by extension, does the choice of research design make a difference to the substantive results? Third, are the various studies cognisant of the problems of comparison outlined in the first part of the book? For example, are there enough countries in the analysis? Do the comparisons establish equivalence? Is there a problem of selection bias? Are the relationships established spurious or not? Are there value biases that taint the analysis? Are there problems with ecological or individualist fallacies? Each chapter ends with a methodological discussion and summary table that includes the method of comparison, the exemplars used in the chapter, and their main findings with regard to the research question.

Chapter 4

Economic development and democracy

The scholarly attention devoted to the relationship between economic development and democracy was initially motivated by the search for the 'preconditions' (Karl 1990: 2–3) of democracy. Focusing on both the 'old' democracies in the northwest triangle of Europe and North America and the 'new' democracies in the rest of the world, this research seeks to identify the key factors that help explain both the *emergence* and *maintenance* of democracy. Among the many factors that have been identified to account for democracy, the level of economic development continues to intrigue comparativists. This chapter compares the key efforts that examine this link between economic development and democracy to demonstrate whether or not different methods lead to the same result. It examines studies that compare many countries, those that compare few countries, and single-country studies. The discussion of each method of comparison focuses on how different theories specify the dependent and independent variables and nature of the relationship, how the analyses measure the concepts, the different problems that the analyses encounter, and the different results they obtain.

The research problem

Are wealthy countries more democratic? If they are, why are they? Does economic development create favourable conditions for the emergence of democracy? Once democracy is established, does continued economic performance help maintain democratic institutions? The model depicted in Figure 4.1 is a simple graphical representation of this research problem. It shows that democracy is the dependent variable and economic development is the independent variable. The arrow in the figure has both a plus and minus sign above it to indicate that economic development may have either a positive or negative effect on democracy. Over the years, this model has changed very little in terms of its basic concepts and the relationship between them.

What has changed, however, are the ways in which democracy and economic development are measured, the different forms the relationship takes, the selection of countries used as evidence (Landman 1999),[1] and the methods of comparison employed to support different theories about the relationship (Rueschemeyer *et al.* 1992). In terms of the concepts, some scholars argue that democracy is an all or nothing affair. Either a country is democratic or it is not. Others argue that it is possible to have degrees of democracy (Przeworski and Limongi 1997). Similarly, there have been different views on what constitutes economic development. Some authors argue that economic development is best understood as economic growth, while others claim it has more to do with the distribution of income and other economic resources (Todaro 1994: 14–20), or overall levels of human development (Ersson and Lane 1996: 59). The relationship between the two has been variously specified as linear, curvilinear, and as a 'step' function (see Briefing Box 4.1).

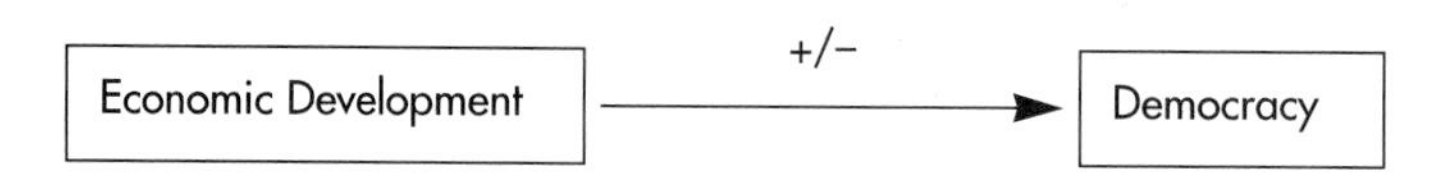

Figure 4.1 Economic development and democracy

Briefing box 4.1 Possible relationships between economic development and democracy

The relationship between economic development and democracy can assume different *functional forms*, the most common of which include linear, curvilinear, and a 'step' function.

Linear relationship

A positive linear relationship between economic development and democracy suggests that as the level of economic development increases, the likelihood that a country will be democratic also increases. Thus, if a scholar measures both concepts and plots them on a graph, the scatter of points would be around a line that rises from the lower left-hand corner to the upper right-hand corner of the graph, as depicted in Figure 4.2. Moving along the line in the figure shows that a rise in one variable is associated with a rise in the other.

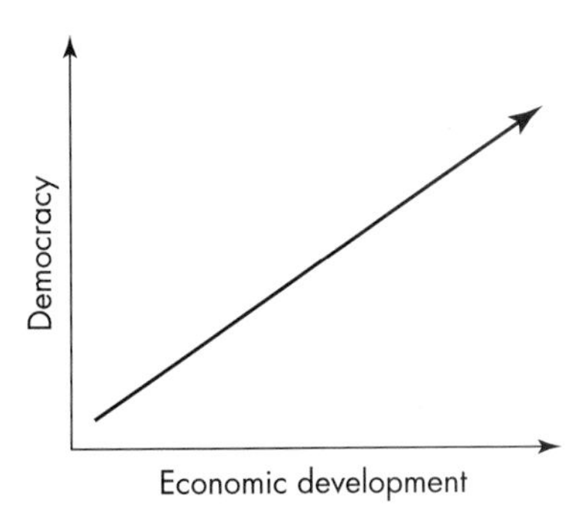

Figure 4.2 A linear relationship between economic development and democracy

Curvilinear relationship

A curvilinear relationship between economic development and democracy suggests that a positive change in economic development is accompanied by a positive change in democracy, but unlike a linear relationship, the degree to which democracy increases tapers off with higher levels of economic development. In this case, there is a distinct range of economic development after which the likelihood a country becomes democratic does not change. This relationship is depicted in Figure 4.3, where this range, or 'threshold of democracy', is evident. A scatter of data points on this graph would group around the line, but it is clear from the figure that after a certain level of economic development, the level of democracy does not increase.

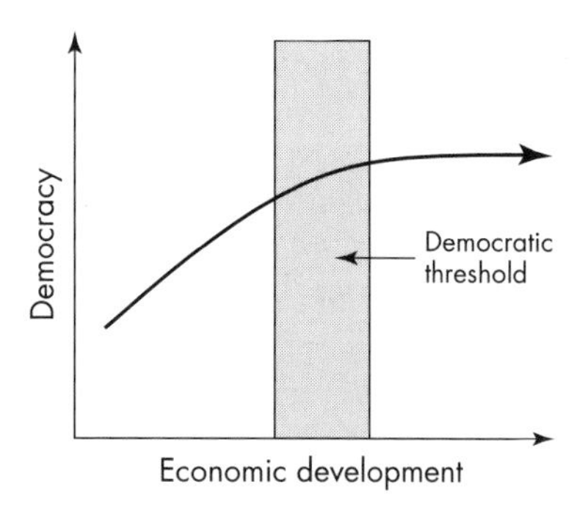

Figure 4.3 A curvilinear relationship between economic development and democracy

A 'step' relationship

A step-function is most different from the first two relationships. In this case, there is a distinct level of economic development after which the likelihood of country being democratic does not change. Figure 4.4 shows that the democratic threshold is not a range of economic development, but a distinct 'take-off' point for democracy (Rostow 1961; Landman 1999).

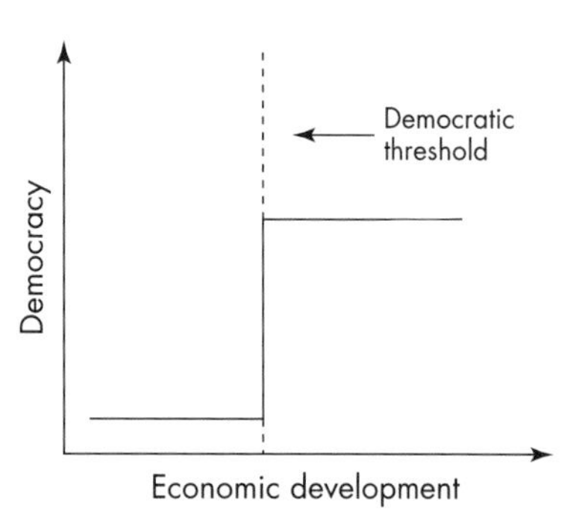

Figure 4.4 A step relationship between economic development and democracy

Finally, different methods of comparison focus on different aspects of the relationship. Studies that compare many countries tend to use quantitative techniques to uncover uniform patterns of variation in a small number of variables. Studies that compare few countries and single-country studies use both quantitative and qualitative techniques to uncover the more historically contingent factors that intervene between processes of economic development and democracy (see Chapter 2), and tend to couch their arguments in more 'path-dependent' language (see Briefing Box 4.2).

Briefing box 4.2 Path-dependent arguments

A path-dependent argument focuses on the sequence of events in any given historical account. Its basic assumption is that once a particular event transpires, be it a war, election, revolution, or important decision, the course of events that succeeds it is altered forever. Consider the following two examples: an abstract example called the 'urn problem' (Jackson 1996: 723) and one from political science concerning democratic consolidation (Burton *et al.* 1992).

First, consider an urn containing one red ball and one white ball. In the first instance, a ball is selected from the urn, then it and a ball of the same colour are placed back into the urn. If this operation is repeated a second and third time (or infinitely), the urn will develop a distribution of red and white balls that is highly dependent on the first few choices that are made. This situation is illustrated in Figure 4.5. The various possible distributions of red and white balls multiply rapidly with each successive round, but it is clear from the figure that each succeeding distribution is highly dependent on the previous round. For example, the left side of the figure shows that if a red ball is chosen on the first round, then two reds and white are in the urn. If a red is chosen again, the urn will have three reds and a white, and so on. The bottom of the figure shows how many different types of distributions are possible, but what is clear is that the first two choices have a dramatic effect on the subsequent distributions.

Begin		R		W		
1		RRW			WWR	
2	RRRW	RRRW	WWRR	WWWR	WWWR	WWRR
3	RRRRW	WWWRR	RRRWW	WWWWWR	WWWRR	RRRWW
	(× 6)	(× 2)	(× 2)	(× 6)	(× 2)	(× 2)

Figure 4.5 The urn problem and path-dependence
Source: Adapted from Jackson (1996: 723)

In the second example, Burton *et al.* (1992: 23) develop a path-dependent argument to account for different types of democratic consolidation in Latin America and Southern Europe, which is illustrated in Figure 4.6.

For countries that experienced democratic transitions accompanied by popular mobilization, the figure shows initially two paths: elite settlement and mass mobilization, or no elite settlement and mass mobilization. The first path leads to stabilization, institutionalization, and consolidated democracy. The second path leads to a state of polarization between elites and masses, which in turn can lead to unconsolidated democracy, pseudo-democracy, or a reversion to authoritarianism. Crucial to their argument is that once a country reaches one of the nodes in the path,

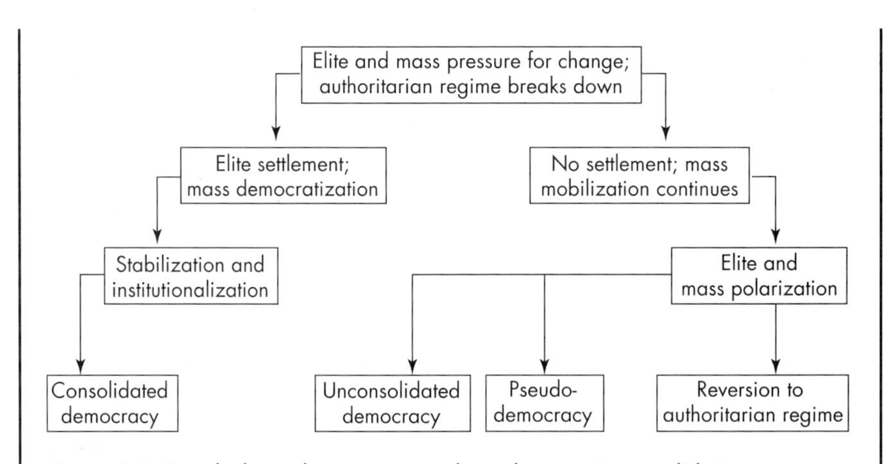

Figure 4.6 A path-dependent argument about democratic consolidation
Source: Adapted from Burton *et al.* (1992: 23)

certain outcomes are no longer available, suggesting that without an elite settlement and mass democratization, democratic consolidation is not likely. Macro-historical studies on economic development and democracy use path-dependent arguments (Moore 1966; Rueschemeyer *et al.* 1992), and such arguments can be found throughout political science, such as Collier and Collier's (1991) study of labour incorporation and regime formation in Latin America, or the historical analysis of war between countries (e.g. de Mesquita *et al.* 1997: 17–19).

Comparing many countries

The initial efforts to identify a simple set of democratic preconditions compared many countries at one point in time. Seymour Martin Lipset (1959, 1960) carried out the seminal study on these preconditions by comparing twenty-eight European and English-speaking countries with twenty Latin American countries (Lipset 1959: 74). His definition of democracy is as follows:

> a political system which supplies regular constitutional opportunities for changing the governing officials. It is a social mechanism for the resolution of the problem of societal decision-making among conflicting interest groups which permits the largest possible part of the population to influence these decisions through their ability to choose among alternative contenders for political office.
>
> (Lipset 1959: 71)

Using this definition, Lipset then divides his sample of countries into various groups. The European and English-speaking countries include stable democracies on the one hand and unstable democracies and dictatorships on the other. The Latin American countries include democracies and unstable dictatorships on the one hand and stable dictatorships on the other. For the first group, those countries that had an 'uninterrupted continuation of political democracy since World War I, and the absence over the past twenty-five years of a major political movement opposed to the democratic "rules of the game"' were considered to be democracies (ibid.: 72, emphasis in original). The Latin American countries were classified as democratic if they 'had a history of more or less free elections for most of the post-World War I period' (ibid.: 72–73).

The comparison provides indicators of economic development for this sample of countries, including wealth, industrialization, education, and urbanization. Wealth is measured by per capita income, thousands of persons per doctor, persons per motor vehicle, telephones per 1,000 people, radios per 1,000 people, and newspaper copies per 1,000 people. Industrialization is measured by the percentage of males employed in agriculture and the per capita consumption of energy. Education is measured by the percentage of the population that is literate and enrolment in primary school, post-primary school, and higher education. Urbanization is measured by the per cent of cities with populations over 20,000, percentage of cities with populations over 100,000, and the percentage of metropolitan areas (ibid.: 76–77). These various measures are seen as objective indicators of socio-economic development, where higher values indicate more development.

To demonstrate the relationship between the level of economic development and democracy, the study compares the averages of these indicators across both groups of countries. On all these indicators, the European and English-speaking stable democracies and the Latin American democracies and unstable dictatorships score higher (or better) than their non-democratic counterparts, which means, on average, that democracies tend to have higher levels of socio-economic development than non-democracies. This pattern of results leads Lipset (ibid.: 80) to claim that all the factors 'subsumed under economic development carry with [them] the political correlate of democracy'. While not saying that economic development actually *causes* democracy, his study is the first to establish a correlation, or probable association, between the two, and thus paves the way for a succession of studies that seek to build on this original comparison.

Following Lipset, Cutright (1963) compares seventy-seven countries in North America, South America, Asia, and Europe using scales of communications development, economic development, and political development. Unlike Lipset, however, he considers political development (or democracy) to exist on a continuum based on the prolonged presence of viable legislative and freely elected executive branches for the period 1940–1961. The correlation between communications development and political development is higher than that between economic development, yet both are high enough for Cutright (ibid.: 571) to conclude that there is an interdependence between political institutions and the level of social and economic development (see also Rueschemeyer *et al.* 1992: 15). The overall confidence in his results leads him to predict the level of political development for the individual countries that comprise his sample based on the individual values of the various independent variables.

In responding to criticism that initial comparative efforts to examine the relationship were 'snapshot analyses', Cutright and Wiley (1969) compare forty 'self-governing' countries using data from before and after the Second World War to examine whether it can be sustained over time. Their dependent variable is political representation, which is defined as 'the extent to which the executive and legislative branches of government are subject to the demands of the non-elite population' (ibid.: 23–24). Annual scores on an index of political representation were compiled for each of four decades: 1927–1936, 1937–1946, 1947–1956, and 1957–1966. They also measure the difference between the scores for the successive decades to capture the change in political representation. Economic development is measured using the amount of energy consumed in any given year. The comparison of the forty countries over the four decades reveals a significant and stable relationship between the level of economic development and political representation. Moreover, since the analysis uses four different time periods, Cutright and Wiley (ibid.: 29) conclude that the level of political representation is causally dependent on the level of economic development.

In *Polyarchy*, Robert Dahl (1971) seeks to formulate a classification of political forms of which democracy is one type, and then use the typology to examine the conditions that foster democracy. He conceives of democracy as having two critical dimensions: contestation and participation (ibid.: 4–9). Countries that have high levels of contestation (i.e. the degree to which members of a political system are free to contest the conduct of government) and participation (i.e. the proportion of the population entitled to participate in controlling the conduct of government) are considered 'polyarchies', or democracies. Using per capita GNP as a measure of economic development, his comparison of 118 countries and 33 polyarchies and near-polyarchies reveals a weak threshold effect (see Briefing Box 4.1). In other words, countries that achieve a certain level of economic development (between 700 and 800 1957 US dollars) tend to be polyarchies. Dahl (ibid.: 68–69, 74) is cautious about this finding, since there are many deviant cases that have low levels of development and are polyarchies (e.g. India), or that have high levels of development and are not polyarchies (e.g. the Soviet Union and East Germany).[2] Moreover, history shows that the United States, Australia, New Zealand, Canada, Britain, Norway, and Sweden, among others, were polyarchies long before they achieved high levels of economic development (Dahl 1971: 69–70; see also Rueschemeyer *et al.* 1992).

Jackman (1973: 611) concentrates his comparison of sixty non-communist countries on the relationship between economic development and democracy, as well as the 'definition of democratic political development itself'. Drawing on the earlier studies conducted by Lipset (1959) and Cutright (1963), Jackman (1973) argues that democracy is best understood as a continuous rather than a dichotomous concept, and that both the linear and curvilinear forms of the relationship ought to be tested. His measure of democracy combines four indicators, including voter turnout, the competitiveness of the party voting system, the degree of electoral irregularity, and relative freedom of the press. Like Cutright and Wiley (1969), his measure of economic development is the level of energy consumption. His statistical analysis reveals that the curvilinear relationship is more significant than the linear relationship, effectively adding comparative evidence to the idea of a democratic threshold in line with Dahl (1971).

Bollen (1979) represents the last study in this earlier sample of comparative efforts that examine the relationship between economic development and democracy. In addition to focusing on the level of economic development, Bollen is also interested in the timing of development. It is possible that the countries that have developed long after those in Europe and North America may have had more difficulty in establishing democratic forms of governance (see below). For example, Britain's model of rapid economic development had profound effects on those countries that developed after it, such as France, Belgium, or the United States (ibid.: 573). When the so-called 'late developers' seek to 'catch up' to other countries in the world economy (Gerschenkron 1962), their efforts to do so may put undue pressure on their burgeoning political systems and thus lead to democratic breakdown. This type of argument suggests that countries that developed early are more likely to be democratic than those countries that developed later.

Thus, Bollen's comparison of ninety-nine countries seeks to examine whether the level of democracy is higher in countries that developed early, whether it is higher in countries that have simply achieved better levels of economic development, or both. His index of democracy includes three indicators of popular sovereignty and three indicators of political liberties (Bollen 1979: 580). Like Jackman (1973) and Cutright and Wiley (1969), the level of development is measured using energy consumption. The timing of development is measured by subtracting the starting year of development from 1966 (Bollen 1979: 577). His statistical analysis reveals that the timing of development is not significant, but that the level of development has a significant and positive effect on democracy. In other words, for this sample of countries, a country's level of development, regardless of when it actually started developing, has an effect on the degree to which it is democratic.

Since this first phase of comparative work, new studies have been published that use increasingly sophisticated statistical techniques that allow scholars to compare many countries over time, thereby increasing the number of observations (see Chapter 1). There are three notable studies that use this method of comparison. Helliwell (1994) compares 125 countries over the period 1960–1985 (N = 1,250); Burkhart and Lewis-Beck (1994) compare 131 countries from 1972–1989 (N = 2,096); and Przeworski and Limongi (1997) compare 135 countries between 1950 and 1990 (N = 4,126). The first two studies find significant statistical evidence in support of a relationship between economic development and democracy. The third study casts serious doubt on these findings, and a comparison of all three reveals that their different results depend largely on their conceptualization of democracy and their specification of the relationship. This section of the chapter considers them in turn.

Helliwell (1994: 226) selects a sample of countries for which 'it is possible to obtain comparable measures of per capita income and regular assessments of the extent of political and civil rights'. His index of democracy (or 'probability of political freedom') combines two separate measures of the protection of political and civil liberties[3] and ranges from low (no democracy) to high (full democracy). In addition to his measure of economic development, Helliwell (ibid.: 228–229) controls for different regional effects, including the OECD countries, the oil-producing countries of the Middle East, African countries, and Latin American countries. His statistical analysis reveals a strong positive effect of per capita income on the level of democracy. In addition, his analysis shows positive effects for the OECD countries and Latin America, and negative effects for Africa and the Middle East. Overall, the statistical results confirm the relationship between economic development and democracy established by the comparative studies in the earlier phase.

Burkhart and Lewis-Beck (1994) use a slightly more robust collection of data than Helliwell (1994) and a similar measure of democracy ranging from low (no democracy) to high (full democracy). They use energy consumption to operationalize economic development and control for the effects of 'other social forces' and the 'world position' of the countries in the study. Other social forces are represented by past values of democracy, and the identification of a country's world position (core, semi-periphery, or periphery) is made on the basis of nine other studies (Burkhart and Lewis-Beck 1994: 904–995). The results of the statistical analysis show that economic development and other social forces are positively associated with democracy, while both peripheral and semi-peripheral world positions detract from these positive effects. In other words, the effect of economic development on democracy is lower in newly developed and developing countries. By using more advanced statistical techniques than those employed by Helliwell (1994), they are able to claim with confidence that economic development *causes* democracy (Burkhart and Lewis-Beck 1994: 907).

The final study in this section is that of Przeworski and Limongi (1997), who are sceptical of the findings of earlier comparative work. They do not dispute the fact that the relationship between economic development and democracy has been demonstrated empirically, but they do object to the way in which the results have been interpreted. Przeworski and Limongi classify countries according to strict rules of assessment, which include the election of the executive, the legislature, a competitive party system, and the alternation of power over time (ibid.: 178). Simple analysis reveals that the relationship between levels of economic development and democracy is strong. Rather than immediately proclaiming that economic development fosters democracy, however, they argue that 'either democracies may be more likely to emerge as countries develop economically, or they may be established independently of economic development but more likely to survive in developed countries' (ibid.: 156). Further analysis of the data that tests the likelihood of democratic transition, given levels of development, shows that 'democracies are almost certain to survive once they are established in rich countries' (ibid.: 166). Thus, a slightly different analysis/interpretation of the empirical data avoids the strong causal language of the other two studies.

This review of studies that compare many countries reveals that there is a 'stable positive relationship between socio-economic development and democracy' (Rueschemeyer *et al.* 1992: 26). The repeated empirical verification of the relationship, however, leads to two conclusions in the comparative literature. For the majority of studies, robust evidence in support of the relationship has led many to conclude that economic development causes democracy, a finding that has helped develop the 'modernization' perspective in comparative politics. In this perspective, it is argued that the development of social institutions enhances the level of education of the population, improves its social and spatial mobility, and promotes the political culture that supports liberal democratic institutions (Lipset 1959; Valenzuela and Valenzuela 1978: 538; Karl 1990: 3; Inglehart 1997: 5). The theory assumes that the process of socio-economic development is 'a progressive accumulation of social changes that ready a society to its culmination, democratization' (Przeworski and Limongi 1997: 158). On the other hand, an emerging minority of scholars point to the fact that while the relationship appears to hold over time and space, it may be spurious, since rich democracies tend not to collapse.

Comparing few countries

As outlined in Chapter 2, studies that compare few countries use both quantitative and qualitative techniques. However, common to both is the intentional selection of countries for comparison based on criteria including theory, regional focus, data availability, and resources. As the review of the comparisons in this section will demonstrate, the choice of countries can affect the inferences that are drawn concerning the relationship between economic development and democracy (see also Chapter 3). This section first examines three studies that use quantitative techniques to compare few countries, namely Lerner's (1958) study of modernization in the Middle East, Neubauer's (1967) comparison of democratic development in twenty-three countries, and my own work on economic development and democracy in Latin America (Landman 1999). It then examines three qualitative studies that compare several countries, including de Schweinitz's (1964) study of industrialization and democracy in Britain, the US, Germany, and Russia, Moore's (1966) study of the 'three routes to modernity', and Rueschemeyer *et al.*'s (1992) comparison of developmental paths in advanced capitalist countries, Latin America, and the Caribbean.

Comparing few countries quantitatively

One year before Lipset (1959) provided the first cross-national study of economic development and democracy, Daniel Lerner (1958) published an ambitious study that examined patterns of modernization in the Middle East. His study starts with a comparison of seventy-three countries, which shows a high level of association across a range of indicators of modernity, including urbanization, literacy, media participation, and political participation. This initial evidence leads him to establish such associations across a much smaller sample of countries, including Turkey, Lebanon, Jordan, Egypt, Syria, and Iran using surveys of individuals carried out by a team of country specialists. An initial combined comparison of these six countries is then followed by individual case studies of each country to identify particularities associated with each while remaining sensitive to the overall regularities that exist among them.

For Lerner (1958: 89), modernization is a 'secular trend unilateral in direction – from traditional to participant lifeways'. This secular trend is characterized by physical, social, and psychic mobility whose culmination is a modern participant society with high levels of urbanism, literacy, media consumption, and an empathic capacity. While not directly assessing the connection between economic development and democracy, the study implies that democracy is the end-state for modernization and that for two of his most 'modern' societies – Turkey and Lebanon – the control of political power is decided by elections (ibid.: 84–85). Initial comparisons of the six countries using aggregate data lead to the following ranking from low to high levels of modernization: Iran, Jordan, Syria, Egypt, Lebanon, and Turkey. This comparison is then followed by an analysis of the individual-level data from the six national surveys. Among the strongest regularities associated with modernity, Lerner (ibid.: 398–412) finds consistent patterns of happiness among urban dwellers, a decline in traditional forms of rule, increasing opportunities for both genders, and high levels of empathy, or willingness to tolerate the views of others. In the end, Turkey and Lebanon are viewed as having achieved balanced modernization, Egypt and Syria are considered to be 'out of phase', and Jordan and Iran as exhibiting no process of modernization.

The importance of Lerner's study for the comparative method is that he uses aggregate-level data and global comparisons to establish basic associations between important variables. He then uses individual-level data that measure what he believes are key characteristics of modernity to allow intensive examination of six countries. This use of data at two levels of analysis seeks to minimize the problem of ecological fallacy. His analysis has not 'proved' the theory of modernization, but has 'only explained and exemplified the regularities it posits', which for him are 'only more plausible hypotheses than they were before' (ibid.: 398). As the comparisons of many countries outlined above have demonstrated, considerable scholarly effort has been devoted to examining more fully the implications of these hypotheses. And as the comparisons of few countries reviewed below will demonstrate, the verification of these hypotheses is by no means a settled matter.

Drawing on the insights of the comparison of many and few countries, Neubauer (1967) compares twenty-three countries using an index of democratic development and indicators of economic development. The index of democratic development combines four indicators 'which measure the relative amount of *electoral equality* and *competition* present in a given political system' (ibid.: 1004–1005). He uses the same indicators of economic development as those employed by Cutright. The main difference between his study and those that compare many countries is the size of his sample. Neubauer (ibid.: 1006) argues that the 'data necessary for the democratic performance indicator come only from democratic countries', and that the findings of the comparison of many countries ought to hold for his smaller sample. His comparison of the twenty-three democracies reveals that there is 'simply no relationship between [the] level of democratic performance and measures of socio-economic development' (ibid.: 1007). His only significant correlation is between the level of communication and democratic performance. Overall, he concludes that there may be some threshold effect between economic development and democracy, but that for democratic countries, higher levels of economic development do not lead to improved democratic performance (ibid.: 1007).

My own work in this area also examines the relationship using a small sample of countries confined geographically to Latin America (Landman 1999). Using seven different measures of democracy and three different measures of economic development, seventeen Latin American countries are compared over the period 1972–1995 (408 total observations). Like Neubauer (1967), I argue that the findings of the global comparisons ought to hold for smaller groups of countries, particularly those with great variation in both economic development and democracy. Unlike Neubauer's study, the countries in the sample are geographically proximate and culturally similar, therefore fitting squarely in the most similar systems design (see Chapter 2). The comparison controls for the cultural commonality of the region (similar Iberian heritage and patterns of economic development), and the model specifies further controls for sub-regional differences between the Southern Cone and Central America, both of which had somewhat different patterns of development and democracy during the period. The statistical analysis tests for both the linear and non-linear forms of relationship, and finds no significant results.[4]

Taken together, these three studies use the quantitative techniques of those studies that compare many countries, but confine their comparisons to a smaller universe of countries. It is clear that the comparison over a smaller selection of countries produces different results. Lerner (1958) uses his initial extensive comparison as a preliminary guide to his more intensive inquiry into the six case studies, but he maintains a large number of observations by using individual-level data. Neubauer's (1967) comparison across democracies and my own time-series comparison of Latin American countries reveal no relationship between economic development and democracy. But are these results simply a product of the sample size, or are there theoretical and historical reasons for raising doubts about the association between economic development and democracy? The review of studies that compare few countries qualitatively seeks to provide some answers to this important question.

Comparing few countries qualitatively

The starting point for this group of qualitative macro-historical studies is to uncover the causal factors inside the 'black box' of the relationship between economic development and democracy (Rueschemeyer *et al.* 1992: 29). While accepting some of the theoretical assumptions of the global comparisons, and arguing that at best the positive and significant statistical results they obtain are empirical generalizations (ibid.: 30), these studies seek to identify key intervening variables that help 'unpack' the relationship. These variables include the timing and nature of economic development, the strength and coalitions of different social classes, the strength and nature of the state, and important transnational factors in the form of wars and economic depressions. In this way, these studies emphasize the processes involved in the development of democracy over the *longue durée* (Rustow 1970). As these studies necessarily develop more complex and less parsimonious explanations than the global comparisons, they are discussed at greater length.

In *Industrialization and Democracy*, de Schweinitz (1964: 7) argues that 'the rise of the democratic political community has been associated with industrialization and economic growth'; however, these must be seen as 'necessary but not sufficient' conditions for the emergence of democracy. For him democracy is 'a system in which the problems of government are resolved on the basis of an appeal to the preferences of autonomous individuals', through periodic use of a majority voting mechanism open to the adult population (ibid.: 14–15). This democratic system requires rational individuals capable of making appropriate choices and a general consensus on fundamental values in society (ibid.: 23), the cultivation of which depends highly upon high levels of education and income. The key question for de Schweinitz (ibid.: 34) is 'How may economic growth which is a process by which an economy passes from a subsistence to a high-income status economy democratize political systems which initially are nondemocratic?' The answer to this question lies in comparing the historical experiences with economic development and democratization in Britain, the US, Germany, and Russia.

The comparison begins with Britain, since it is seen as the first country to have undergone rapid industrialization and the development of democratic political institutions. Implicit throughout the comparisons is that the British experience somehow radiates out across Europe and North America, effectively offering the countries that comprise these regions a model for growth and governance. The key to explaining British success is the fact that the process of economic development was achieved autonomously, as opposed to a state-led process. This process of autonomous growth resulted in the rise of the middle class, a well-tamed and well-managed and organized labour force, and the piecemeal installation of democracy, which 'did not have to be sacrificed at the altar of economic growth' (ibid.: 128). What is clear in the British case is that it was not fully democratic before the industrial revolution in the middle of the eighteenth century, but that the process of industrialization unleashed the necessary social forces to realize democracy by the middle of the nineteenth century.

The establishment of democracy in the United States had many factors in its favour that were absent in Britain. It possessed vast amounts of space, a favourable climate, and abundant natural resources, and perhaps most importantly, the American Revolution meant that those pro-democratic forces in this new country did not have the vestiges of a feudal order with which to contend (de Schweinitz 1964: 130 *après* Hartz 1955). In contrast to Britain, where democratization of the political process grew out of industrialization, the political institutions in the United States had to be created to restrain the democratic impulse while unleashing the forces of economic growth (de Schweinitz 1964: 142). Like Britain, however, economic growth in the United States was produced autonomously and the period of rapid industrialization did not occur until after the Civil War. For de Schweinitz (ibid.: 148–152), there are several other conditions favourable to the establishment of democracy in the United States, including better working conditions for labourers, lower economic expectations and ethnic differentiation of immigrant groups, a strong political culture of individualism, and the overall size of the continental land mass, all of which helped overcome the 'welfare problem' created by the process of industrialization.

In contrast to the gradual installation of democracy in Britain and the relatively 'easy history' of the United States, de Schweinitz (ibid.: 159) argues that the German experience bore the heavy weight of history, which had created the need for a strong centralized state to unify its diverse political units in the latter half of the nineteenth century. By the First World War, Germany's rapid industrialization had outpaced that of Britain, but both the war and the subsequent rise to power of Hitler appear to have confounded the hypothesis about autonomous economic growth and democracy (ibid.: 184). This apparent deviant case is explained away with reference to a certain British 'exceptionalism'. At a comparable stage of development, Britain was not fully democratic but had over half a century of peace for the democratic practices to flourish. Germany had a different historical legacy than Britain, which had created more formidable obstacles to democratization, and Britain was not as susceptible to political developments and crises on the continent. It is important to note that global comparisons treat deviant cases as a normal occurrence where they simply are outliers to a standard distribution of outcomes. In this comparison, de Schweinitz (1964) is at pains to explain why Germany did not achieve stable democracy by the dawn of the twentieth century. The difference between these two styles of analysis will be addressed further in the summary that follows.

The final case in this study is Russia, which was more underdeveloped and had less access to natural resources than the other cases, did not experience spontaneous and autonomous development, and was more open to foreign invasion. Moreover, the lack of growth of a middle class and the persistence of a system of serfdom further hindered any moves toward democracy. Although Russia achieved rapid industrialization toward the end of the nineteenth century, de Schweinitz (1964) argues that Marxist ideology became an important factor in shaping its subsequent history. Ultimately Russia forms a one-party state with no legitimate opposition. Paradoxically, there is no explanation for the Russian Revolution of 1917. Rather, it becomes a new factor that helps explain its lack of democracy. In the end, Russia and Germany had both late and less autonomous economic development, and either limited or no experience with democracy, while Britain and the US experienced autonomous economic development and the development of fundamental values that fostered the growth of democracy. These comparisons are summarized in Table 4.1.

Such qualitative comparison of a few countries allows de Schweinitz to concentrate on historical sequences and factors unique to the individual cases while drawing larger inferences about the more general relationship between development and democracy. He stresses that his research design and method 'raise the possibility that a unique configuration of historical conditions relating to the availability of natural resources, the mobility of the population, ideology, and the locus and sequence of development, accounted for the emergence of the democratic political order' (ibid.: 269). Overall, the key obstacles to successful democratization are late development and state-centred growth. In drawing inferences beyond the confines of his four-country comparison, de Schweinitz (ibid.: 11) argues that the 'Euro-American route to democracy is closed' and that countries developing in the twentieth century must find other means for establishing democratic political institutions.

Table 4.1 A summary of de Schweinitz's (1964) *Industrialization and Democracy*

Case	*Britain*	*US*	*Germany*	*Russia*
Character of economic development	Early autonomous economic development	Autonomous economic development	Late industrialization, partly state-led	Late industrialization, not autonomous
Unique features	Isolated geographically	Space, climate, natural resources	Heavy weight of history	Limited access to natural resources
	Peaceful half century	No feudal past	Strong centralized state	Centralized state and persistence of serfdom
Social class development	Large middle class	Large middle class	Large but alienated middle class	No large middle class
	Strong labour movement	Weak labour movement	Strong labour movement	Small working class
Political culture	Liberal individualism	Rugged individualism	Lack of individualism	Marxist ideology
Outcome	Democracy	Democracy	Unstable democracy	No democracy

In *The Social Origins of Dictatorship and Democracy*, Barrington Moore (1966) extends the comparison of democratic and non-democratic outcomes found in de Schweinitz (1964) to a larger group of countries, including Britain, France, the United States, Japan, India, and China; he also makes implicit comparisons with Germany and Russia. Like de Schweinitz, Moore seeks to understand the relationship between processes of economic development and political form through comparing few countries. These comparisons 'serve as a rough negative check on accepted historical explanations. And a comparative approach may lead to new historical generalizations' (ibid.: xiii). Like de Schweinitz (1964), he believes that certain political outcomes are the product of discrete historical configurations, which may not be repeated. His comparisons reveal three 'routes to the modern world': (1) bourgeois revolutions and democracy, (2) revolution from above and fascism, and (3) revolution from below and communism. The central categories of comparison include economic development, state structures, and social classes.

The democratic route to modern society was achieved in Britain, France, and the United States. The Puritan Revolution (English Civil War), the French Revolution, and the American Civil War are seen as events that dramatically altered the developmental paths these three countries would take. The process of economic development was accompanied by a balance of power between the crown and the landed nobility. The development of commercial agriculture weakened the role of the landed upper classes, while building the ranks of the bourgeoisie, which for Moore (1966: 418) was critical for the development of democracy: 'No bourgeois, no democracy.' There was no coalition between the landed upper classes and the bourgeoisie against the interests of peasants and workers. Finally, all three cases had a *revolutionary break with the past* (ibid: 431). The Puritan Revolution altered forever the role of the monarchy in Britain, while the French Revolution abolished royal absolutism and established the political rights of modern citizenship.[5] While the American Revolution initially removed the role of the British crown, the American Civil War broke the landed upper classes and so paved the way for the continued growth of industrial capitalism. In this way, Moore (1966) argues that all three historical events were bourgeois revolutions, the conditions of which were made possible by economic development, and the resolution of which ultimately led to the establishment of liberal democracy.

The fascist and 'top-down' route to modern society is illustrated through a detailed analysis of Japanese history that is compared implicitly to that of Germany. In both countries, Moore (ibid.: 437) argues that the development of the commercial and industrial class was too weak and dependent to take power on its own and it therefore forged coalitions with the landed upper classes and royal bureaucracy, 'exchanging the right to rule for the right to make money'. This coalition against the interests of peasants and workers was supported by a strong state that provides trade protection and labour control. Any experiments with democracy soon disappeared as they were ultimately not to the liking of the landed upper classes and 'fascist repression is the final outcome' (Rueschemeyer *et al.* 1992: 24).

The communist route in both Russia and China has four main causal factors. Both countries had a highly centralized state and a landed upper class, both of which repressed the labour force, which was the essential means of economic development at that time. The lack of commercial agriculture meant that only a weak bourgeoisie developed, which was not strong enough either to confront the strong land-owning class or the crown (as in Britain and France). Both societies had a mass peasantry that showed great potential for collective action. Thus, the 'absence of a commercial revolution in agriculture led by the upper classes and the concomitant survival of peasant social institutions' provided the social and political backdrop for communist revolution (Moore 1966: 477). The failure of the landed upper classes to maintain institutional links with the peasantry and their continued exploitation of the peasants created the conditions by which the agrarian bureaucracies in Russia and China were ultimately overthrown.

Table 4.2 summarizes Moore's (1966) three routes to modernity, including the character of economic development, the nature of the emergent class coalitions, the role of the state, and the different political outcomes. Most striking is the fact that democracy is seen to be the product of a violent break with the past, not a gradual installation of a political form as the result of incremental advances in the process of economic development. The beheading of Charles I in Britain, the execution of Louis XVI in France, and the Union Army's defeat of the Confederates in the United States all serve as radical events that fundamentally altered the social, economic, and political conditions that made democracy possible. Like de

Table 4.2 Moore's (1966) three routes to modern society

	I *Britain, France, United States (India)*	II *Germany, Italy, Japan*	III *Russia, China*
Character of economic development	Development of commercial agriculture	Development of commercial agriculture	No development of commercial agriculture
Class development and coalitions	Weakening of landed aristocracy	Strong land-owning class	Strong land-owning class
	Balance of power between crown and landed aristocracy (in Britain, France, and India)	Coalition of powerful land-owning class and weak, dependent bourgeoisie	Weak bourgeoisie
	Absence of aristocratic–bourgeois coalition against peasants and workers		Mass peasantry with capacity for collective action
Role of the state		Strong state that provides trade protection, manages industrialization, and controls labour	Centralized state and labour repression
	Revolutionary and violent break with the past		
Outcome	Capitalist parliamentary democracy	Capitalist fascism	Communism

Source: Adapted from Moore (1966)

Schweinitz (1964), Moore (1966) is keen to point out that the constellation of events that led to these democratic outcomes was by no means inevitable, and that any one of these three societies (given a slightly different set of events), could have ended up taking one of the other two routes to the modern world.

In response to some of the limitations of both these two key qualitative studies and the quantitative global comparisons, Rueschemeyer *et al.* (1992) extend the analysis of the relationship between economic development and democracy. They accept that the global comparisons yield empirical generalizations, but like de Schweinitz (1964) and Moore (1966), they seek to examine the historical sequences that comprise the links between development and democracy. In contrast to de Schweinitz and Moore, they expand the number of countries to include smaller advanced countries of Europe, Britain's settler colonies, and countries in Latin America and the Caribbean. In contrast to Moore (1966), they emphasize the role of the working class and the importance of international factors, which they claim are lacking from his analysis. They thus focus on the meaning of democracy and its relation to social inequality, social class divisions, the role of the state, and transnational power constellations (Rueschemeyer *et al.* 1992: 40). Due to the length and complexity of their study, the following review will sketch out in skeletal fashion the main points of the comparative analysis and subsequent argument.

The first part of the study compares the experiences with development and democracy in seventeen advanced countries, including Sweden, Denmark, Norway, Switzerland, Belgium, The Netherlands, France, Britain, the United States, Australia, Canada, New Zealand, Austria-Hungary, Spain, Italy, and Germany. The goal of the comparison is to identify the key variables that help explain prolonged periods of democracy, unstable periods of democracy, and authoritarianism in all these countries. All of them underwent some form of capitalist development, and most experienced the rapid development of industrial capitalism in the latter half of the nineteenth century. Despite this similar set of starting conditions, some countries (Austria-Hungary, Spain, Italy, and Germany) were unable to sustain democracy through the inter-war years. Thus, the comparisons seek to explain these differences in outcome.

Like Moore (1966), the analysis stresses the importance of the strength of different social classes, including the agrarian elite, the bourgeoisie, and the working class. Except for Britain, the United States, and Australia, a strong agrarian elite stood as a key obstacle to democratization. In these exceptional cases, other important factors such as an autonomous state, a strong working class, and the legacy of British institutional practices in its former colonies helped attenuate this anti-democratic tendency within the agrarian elite. Elsewhere, a weak agrarian elite coupled with the presence of a strong bourgeoisie meant that the chances for sustaining democracy remained very high. The comparisons also reveal that historically it has been the working class that has been the main agent of democratization in the advanced countries. While certain elements in the middle class have supported democratic ideals, it has been the push for inclusion through the extension of rights by the working class that has made the key difference to the realization of liberal democracy in these countries (Rueschemeyer *et al.* 1992: 97–98). Moreover, the inclusion in the comparison of the smaller democracies demonstrated that democracy is not dependent on a revolutionary break with the past as Moore (1966) maintained.

The authoritarian countries had a different set of experiences. They industrialized later than the democratic countries and had a strong agrarian elite. This elite formed a coalition with the bourgeoisie and the state that oversaw labour-repressive agricultural practices and the establishment of a certain authoritarian ideological hegemony, which manifested itself in fascist tendencies inimical to the development of democracy. Like Moore (1966), Rueschemeyer *et al.* (1992) suggest that the conditions for authoritarianism existed in countries that managed to avoid it. They insist that the United States was not fully democratic until the passage of the 1965 Voting Rights act, which extended suffrage to African-Americans in the former Confederate states. In contrast to Moore (1966), they argue that the Civil War helped establish democracy in the north and the west, but the south was characterized by the re-institution of authoritarian practices dominated by a strong agrarian elite (Rueschemeyer *et al.* 1992: 122–132, 148). These different historical trajectories are summarized in Table 4.3, including the nature of development, the strength of classes and class alliances, and the role of the state.

The comparison of the Latin American countries begins with the basic premise that they developed differently than the advanced countries in two major respects. The process of development was initiated much later than the advanced countries and succeeded a period of growth that was highly dependent on the export of primary products particularly vulnerable to changing market conditions. The key determinants for the emergence of democracy in the first half of the twentieth century include the consolidation of state power, the nature of the export economy (mineral vs. agricultural), the strength and timing of the process of industrialization, and the agent of political articulation of the subordinate classes. Early consolidation of state power institutionalizes contestation among competing groups and ends overt challenges to the authority of the state. Mineral and agricultural export expansion developed different sets of social classes, which articulated their demands in different types of political party organizations; clientelistic parties developed in the agricultural countries while mass radical parties developed in the mineral countries. An early initialization of the process of industrialization breaks the landed classes and produces an active and strong subordinate class that can attract some middle-class support. The presence of two powerful political parties that seek to mediate competing interests in society helps foster democracy (Kueschemeyer *et al.* 1992: 197–199). Clientelistic parties that help channel the demands of the subordinate classes are seen as less threatening to elites. Taken together (see Table 4.4), these factors greatly enhance the chances of democratization in the region.

After the period of initial democratization, all of the countries in the comparison experienced breakdowns of democracy in one form or another. Some saw a collapse into civil war (Colombia and Venezuela), while others saw the rise of military authoritarianism (e.g. Brazil 1964–1985; Argentina 1966–1973, 1976–1983; Uruguay 1973–1984; and Chile 1973–1990). For Rueschemeyer *et al.* (1992: 216) the key to maintaining democracy and political stability is an institutionalized party system that protects the interests of elites (see Chapter 8). In addition to the weakness of party systems and the breakdown of democracy, they also stress the fact that the nature of the military and its relationship to the civilian world are different for Latin America, leading to frequent, and in some cases, long interventions into the political sphere. In sum, if the social and political forces unleashed by economic development are not channelled in such a way that the threat to elites is sufficiently minimized, the likelihood of democracy surviving during this period is very limited indeed.

This basic explanation for democracy holds in the comparisons of Central America and the Caribbean, with the added effects of the British colonial

Table 4.3 Conditions for democracy and authoritarianism in advanced countries

	Sweden, Denmark, Norway, Switzerland, Belgium, The Netherlands, France	*Britain*	*United States, Australia*	*Canada, New Zealand*	*Austria-Hungary Spain Italy Germany*
Development	Rapid development of industrial capitalism in latter half of 19th cent.	Rapid development of industrial capitalism in latter half of 19th cent.	Rapid development of industrial capitalism in latter half of 19th cent. in US only		Late industrialization
Classes	Weak agrarian elite Strong bourgeoisie	Strong agrarian elite Strong bourgeoisie	Strong agrarian elite Strong bourgeoisie	Weak agrarian elite Strong bourgeoisie	Strong agrarian elite Strong bourgeoisie (except Germany)
	Strong working class	Strong working class	Weak working class Autonomous state	Autonomous state	Agrarian elite–bourgeoisie–state alliance
	No labour-repressive agriculture	No labour-repressive agriculture	Labour-repressive agriculture	No labour-repressive agriculture	Labour-repressive agriculture
History			Vast supplies of cheap land British colonial influence: representative government & suffrage	Vast supplies of cheap land British colonial influence: representative government & suffrage	Authoritarian ideological hegemony
	Revolutionary break from the past only in France	Revolutionary break from the past	Revolutionary break from the past (except Australia)	No revolutionary break from the past	No revolutionary break from the past
Outcome	Democracy	Democracy	Democracy	Democracy	Authoritarianism

Source: Rueschemeyer *et al.* (1992: 79–154)

Table 4.4 Development and initial democratization in Latin America

	Uruguay, Argentina	*Colombia, Ecuador*	*Brazil*	*Bolivia, Venezuela*	*Chile, Peru*	*Mexico*	*Paraguay*
Development	Export expansion	Export expansion	Export expansion	Export expansion	Export expansion	Export expansion	No export expansion
	Agriculture	Agriculture	Agriculture	Mineral	Mineral	Mineral	Agriculture
	Non labour-intensive	Labour-intensive	Labour-intensive				Labour-intensive
Mobilizing agent	Clientelistic parties	Clientelistic parties	State	Radical mass parties	Radical mass parties	Revolution	State
Industrialization	Before 1930	After 1945	1930–1945	After 1945	After 1945	Before 1930	After 1945
Initial democracy	Before 1930	1930–1945 Ecuador after 1945	1945–1964	1930–1945 Bolivia after 1945	1930; 1930–1945 for Peru		
Outcome	Full stable democracy	Restricted stable democracy	Restricted stable democracy	Full unstable democracy	Restricted unstable democracy	Authoritarianism	Authoritarianism
	> 12 yrs	> 12 yrs	> 12 yrs	< 12 yrs	< 12 yrs		

Source: Rueschemeyer *et al.* (1992: 159–199)

experience. Except for Costa Rica, the Central American cases have had difficulty in establishing organizations within civil society and representatives of the subordinate classes that are strong enough to counter an elite-dominated state, leading to a history of civil war, political instability, and repression (Rueschemeyer *et al.* 1992: 259). Moreover, the heavy presence of US intervention has tended to strengthen the repressive apparatus of the state in these countries. In the Caribbean countries, the agrarian elite did not control the state during the period in which groups in civil society were forming, and by the time these countries achieved independence, both political parties and unions were well established (ibid.: 260).

It is clear from the examination of these various studies that the comparison of few countries offers different analytical opportunities for scholars. This method of comparison allows the intensive examination of individual countries and more focus on the differences between countries in order to explain the ways in which economic development may or may not foster democracy. A small number of countries allows the comparison to highlight historical sequences, and the importance of specific historical events on the subsequent chances of establishing democracy, including wars, revolutions, and economic crises. The difference in results between these studies and those that compare many countries regarding the relationship between economic development and democracy awaits final discussion, as it is important to consider a few single-country studies on this topic from the field.

Single-country studies

Clearly, there are likely to be as many (if not more) single-country studies as there are countries in the world that seek to explain paths of development and their relationship to democracy. From Tocqueville's classic study of democracy in the United States to the latest single-country studies of democratization, the field of comparative politics is replete with examples of such studies. As outlined in Chapter 2, single-country studies can confirm existing theories, infirm existing theories, or generate new hypotheses. Thus, this section presents some recent efforts to relate economic development and democracy at the single-country level that serve any or all of these comparative purposes. Moreover, they all in some way use the comparative categories and explanation found in the preceding studies. The studies in this section include Putnam's (1993) study of democratic institutional performance in Italy, Waisman's (1989) study of Argentina, and three case studies on Botswana, South Korea, and India found in Leftwich's (1996) *Democracy and Development*.

In *Making Democracy Work*, Putnam (1993) offers a single-country study of Italy that compares democratic institutional performance across its twenty administrative regions using quantitative and qualitative research techniques. Since Italy is democratic for the initial period of his study (1970–1989), Putnam (1993: 63–82) establishes a measure of democratic institutional performance, which is an index at the regional level that combines twelve indicators of policy processes, policy pronouncements, and policy implementation. These indicators include cabinet stability, budget promptness, statistical and informational services, reform legislation, legislative innovation, the provision of daycare centres, the number of family clinics, industrial policy instruments, agricultural spending capacity, local health unit expenditures, housing and urban development, and bureaucratic responsiveness (ibid.: 65–73). This combined index then serves as the key dependent variable for the remainder of the study.

Geographically, the level of democratic institutional performance is higher in the northern regions of Italy than in the southern regions. Drawing on many of the same studies reviewed in this chapter, Putnam (ibid.: 83–86) initially posits that the level of socio-economic modernization accounts for the differences in institutional performance that he observes. A simple analysis that compares measures of economic development (per capita income, gross regional product, and agricultural and industrial shares of the workforce and value added) and institutional performance reveals that those regions with higher levels of economic development have higher levels of institutional performance (ibid.: 85). Moreover, these levels of economic development are higher in the north than in the south. Closer inspection of the figures, however, reveals that within either the north or the south, the relationship drops out. In other words, economic development goes some way towards explaining institutional performance, but it cannot account for differences within the north or the south.

Putnam suspects that the simple relationship between economic development and institutional performance is spurious, and the paradox identified for the north–south divide leads him to look for some other factor that may help explain institutional performance in Italy (see Briefing Box 3.2). The answer for Putnam lies in the history of civic involvement in Italy: a slow process of accumulation that begins in medieval times and extends to modern-day Italy (ibid.: 121–162). Civic involvement consists in active participation in public affairs, the development of ideas of political equality, solidarity, trust, tolerance, and the formation of voluntary associations (ibid.: 86–91). When the effects of this additional factor are analysed, the direct relationship between economic development and institutional performance disappears. In its place, Putnam (ibid.: 157) specifies a model (see Figure 4.7) that establishes a link between past civic involvement (1900s) to civic involvement and socio-economic development in the 1970s. The level of civic involvement in the 1970s is related to democratic institutional performance in the 1980s.

Waisman's (1989: 59) study of Argentina opens with a key question: 'Why did this country fail to become an industrial democracy?' He shows that between 1900 and the Great Depression, Argentina experienced growth rates in per capita GNP that were higher than growth rates in Sweden and France. On the eve of the Great Depression, per capita GNP was higher than that in Austria and Italy. And by the mid-1940s, the country had higher levels of urbanization than the United States and most of Europe (ibid.: 61–63). Throughout this period, Argentina saw the emergence of restricted liberal democracy with the beginnings of an institutionalized political party system, but by 1930 democracy collapsed and would only make fleeting returns from this year until its full re-emergence in 1983. Between 1930 and 1983, the country saw six major military coups, twenty-two years of military rule, and twenty-five presidents, eighteen of whom were elected and

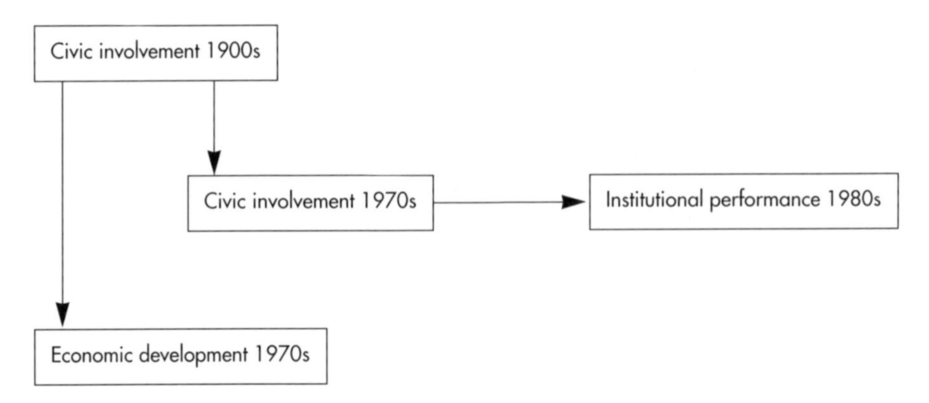

Figure 4.7 Explaining democratic institutional performance in Italy
Source: Adapted from Putnam (1993: 157)

subsequently overthrown between 1955 and 1983. The country's spectacular economic performance also collapsed by the middle of the century. Growth rates fell to 0.9 per cent in the 1950s, 2.8 per cent in the 1960s, 2.3 per cent in the 1970s, and negative levels in the 1980s, so that between 1950 and 1983, the country experienced only 1 per cent growth (ibid.: 62).

To explain the fluctuations in the experience of democracy in Argentina, Waisman (1989) uses similar analytical categories to those found in Rueschemeyer *et al.* (1992). He argues that the emergence and stability of democracy in the first period (1900–1930) were due first to a high and sustained rate of economic growth. The expansion during this period allowed for the 'absorption of mass immigration, rapid urbanization and industrialization, expansion of education, and high standards of living for the lower classes'. Second, middle-class demands for participation and intense labour mobilization were absorbed by elites through inclusionary strategies (Waisman 1989: 84). He argues that the subsequent periods of authoritarianism were largely due to the emergence of an autonomous developmental state and the presence of entrenched economic elites which opposed the interests of the subordinate classes as well as the representation of all interests through democratic political institutions (ibid.: 85–97).

The three separate case studies of Botswana (Holm 1996), India (Kaviraj 1996), and South Korea (Moon and Kim 1996) show great variation in both economic development and experiences with democracy. Holm (1996) argues that Botswana has had a developing economy and an emerging democracy for over thirty years. From 1965 onwards, the country has seen 10 per cent annual growth rates based on a mineral economy that has diversified into producing coal, soda ash, and manufactured products. It has a hybrid presidential-parliamentary democracy and well-developed bureaucracy (due to the British colonial experience 1885–1965). In terms of free elections and the protection of political liberties, Botswana meets the criteria of a democracy as found in the global comparisons reviewed above (Holm 1996: 103). Despite this seeming association between economic development and democracy, Holm is keen to point out that Botswana still only has formal democracy, and that the society remains characterized by government secrecy and low accountability, weak opposition parties, and an underdeveloped civil society. For Holm (ibid.: 98, 107) the key intervening variable that lies between economic development and democracy is Tswana political culture, which maintains authoritarian and hierarchical patterns of organization, and tends to separate the activities of civil society and politics.

Like Moore (1966), Kaviraj (1996) argues that the temporal sequence of the relation between economic development and democracy is different for India than for the patterns observed in Europe. The secularization of politics, the individuation of civil society, and the development of a modern capitalist economy preceded the development of democracy in the west. In India these processes all happened at the same time. Thus, the development of democracy has altered but not displaced traditional identities based on the caste system and religious divisions. A formalized and 'modern' redefinition of the caste system has profound implications for the distribution of the economic goods of development as well as the definition of the proper activities for political and economic actors in society (Kaviraj 1996: 132–133). Moreover, the case of India illustrates that both the process of economic development and democracy can raise expectations within a society as well as threaten political stability (ibid.: 133–134).

The final case of South Korea appears as the model of successful modernization. As in Botswana, it has maintained 10 per cent growth rates since 1965, a process of development which has also been accompanied by a reasonably equitable distribution of economic resources (Moon and Kim 1996: 139). Politically, however, the country has seen the repressive Yushin regime in the 1970s, the quasi-military rule of Chun Doo Hwan in the 1980s, a period of democratic transition between 1988 and 1992, and its first free and fair elections only in 1992 (ibid.: 140). Thus, the successful model of economic growth has been accompanied by a long period of non-democratic rule. Moon and Kim (ibid.: 148) attribute the transition to democracy and the subsequent period of democratic consolidation to sustained economic growth, which has been mediated by two further important factors. Economic development has altered the distribution of power in society and this has favoured the emergence of democracy. Following Inglehart (1990), they argue that economic development has changed Korean political culture by replacing traditional conservative and authoritarian values with modern and participant values.

Summary

Table 4.5 summarizes the 'comparison of comparisons' on the relationship between economic development and democracy presented in this chapter. There appears to be a contradiction between the main findings of those studies that compare many countries and those that either compare a few countries or those that study one country. On balance, the comparison of many countries at one time or over time reveals a strong positive effect between the level of economic development and democracy. Some of these comparisons claim that the two phenomena are associated with each other, while others argue that they are causally related. In contrast, the comparison of few countries and single-country studies claim that the

Table 4.5 Economic development and democracy in comparative perspective

Method of comparison	*Number of countries*	*Exemplars*	*Result*
Many countries	Between 48 and 135 either at one point in time or over time	Lipset 1959; Cutright 1963; Cutright and Wiley 1969; Dahl 1971; Jackman 1973; Bollen 1979; Helliwell 1994; Burkhart and Lewis-Beck 1994; Przeworski and Limongi 1997	Weak version: democracy is associated with development; Strong version: development causes democracy
Few countries (quantitative)	Between 6 and 23 either at one point in time or over time	Lerner 1958; Neubauer 1967; Landman 1999	For Lerner, modernity associated with democracy; for Neubauer and Landman, no relationship exists
Few countries (qualitative)	Between 4 and 37 countries over time	De Schweinitz 1964; Moore 1966; Rueschemeyer *et al.* 1992	Democracy is a product of discrete historical events that are not likely to be repeated in the future
Single-country studies	One country over time	Waisman 1989; Putnam 1993; Holm 1996; Kaviraj 1996; Moon and Kim 1996	Case-specific factors, particularly political culture, condition the relationship

relationship between economic development and democracy is mediated by other important factors, such as class structures, the nature of economic development, the role of the state, important historical events, political culture, and international factors.

The different conclusions reached by different methods raise an important question. Is there something wrong methodologically with each major type of comparison? The short answer is no. As Part I of this book argued, each method of comparison is useful for drawing inferences, and as the review of comparisons here demonstrated, scholars interested in this research question have used different methods precisely to redress problems of earlier studies, draw stronger inferences, and test different theories. A longer answer suggests that there are three factors inherent in these comparisons that account for the difference in result, including the role of historical time, the selection of cases, and the different emphasis put on similarities and differences between countries. This concluding section will discuss these in turn.

The global comparisons assume that all countries are on a common trajectory that extends from a 'traditional' end to a 'modern' one, which suggests that sooner or later, any country at any time will necessarily make this transition. Comparisons of many countries at one point in time imply this trajectory, since each country in their sample is located at a different point along this trajectory. Later global comparisons reacted to this criticism by comparing over time and space, and Bollen (1979) controlled for the effects of the timing of development. Studies that compare few countries argue that the inclusion of both time and the timing of development are not enough, since these factors still ignore the importance of history. These studies argue that specific historical events and the contingent concatenation of these events affect the nature of the traditional–modern trajectory implied by the global comparisons. In the 1960s, countries were undergoing the process of development *after* the Russian, Mexican, Chinese, and Cuban revolutions, all of which demonstrated different developmental trajectories than those assumed by the global comparisons.

The importance of historical time and the emphasis on historical sequences are necessarily related to the selection of cases, which is in turn related to the difference in results for the comparisons examined in this chapter. Thus, Neubauer (1967) compares *only* democracies, since he seeks to measure democratic development. Lerner (1958) and Landman (1999) compare countries that share geographical proximity and cultural similarities. Both de Schweinitz (1964), and Moore (1966) choose countries based on the key outcomes of democracy, fascism, and communism. Neubauer (1967), de Schweinitz (1964) and Moore (1966) all have problems with selection bias since the choice of cases is determined by the dependent variable (see Chapter 3). Lerner (1958) and Landman (1999) do not have problems with selection bias since their choice of countries is not related to the dependent variable. In similar fashion, Rueschemeyer *et al.* (1992) avoid selection bias by comparing all the countries in each of their clusters (i.e. advanced countries, Latin America, Central America and the Caribbean). Indeed, by looking at the smaller democracies of the advanced world, they rule out a revolutionary break with the past as a significant explanatory variable for democracy.

Even when selection bias is avoided, the selection of cases still helps explain the difference in results between the global comparisons and those that examine a smaller number of countries. The global comparisons concentrate their efforts on the regularities that hold across a large sample. Deviant cases are a natural occurrence in large samples, while the goal of the analysis is to demonstrate the commonality across the countries. In contrast, studies that compare few countries place more emphasis on the differences across the countries. These studies demonstrate that the relationship between economic development and democracy does not hold for all countries. The global comparativists would not disagree; they would merely reply that the relationship does hold more often than not. Thus, the differences in results lie as much in the nature of the comparison as in the interpretation of the evidence.

In sum, the different comparative methods should be seen as complements to one another. Global comparisons establish general patterns of co-variation, which can be examined further through the analysis of a smaller number of countries. Global comparisons allow for the specification of parsimonious explanations that are based on a small set of variables, while additional variables can be specified in studies that compare a few countries. Finally, both methods of comparison may identify deviant cases that can be examined further with a more intensive single-country study. In the case of the relationship between economic development and democracy, the evidence suggests that there is a stable positive association between the two, but as in many things, there are exceptions to the rule. The lesson for comparative politics is to determine whether these exceptions are important for the overall inferences that are drawn about the political world.

Notes

1 A corollary branch of comparative research inverts the relationship to examine whether democracies achieve better levels of economic development. See Helliwell (1994).
2 Since the comparison was made in 1971 with 1957 GNP per capita figures, both the USSR and GDR existed.
3 The separate scales were originally developed by Raymond D. Gastil and since then have been maintained on an annual basis by Freedom House (see Foweraker and Landman 1997: 55–56).
4 A similar style of analysis was carried out for Central America and arrived at similar results (see Seligson 1987).
5 Moore concedes that there were some conservative reversals with the Bourbon Restoration (1815–1848), but by 1830, the power of the old aristocracy had been effectively eliminated (Moore 1966: 106).

Further reading

Lipset, S. M. (1994) 'The Social Requisites of Democracy Revisited', *American Sociological Review*, 59 (February): 1–22.

This is a good overview of the entire topic of economic development and democracy.

Rueschemeyer, D., Stephens, E. H., and Stephens, J. (1992) *Capitalist Development and Democracy*, Cambridge: Polity Press.

Chapter 2 of this book reviews the different efforts to examine the relationship between economic development and democracy.

Chapter 5

Violent political dissent and social revolution

The quest to understand the individual, structural, and cultural motivations for domestic violent political dissent and the conditions for successful social revolution was in part stimulated by the process of decolonization in the post-war period. Concern over political violence and political instability is directly related to the establishment and maintenance of democracy. Seeking first to understand the origins of political violence and the conditions for revolution, scholars in this field ultimately hope to promote peace (Lichbach 1989: 470) and democratic stability (Huntington 1968; Sanders 1981: 1–21; Cammack 1997). As in the many comparisons reviewed in the last chapter, this chapter compares the research design and substantive findings of studies of many countries, few countries, and single countries in an effort to understand and explain this important research question. The 'comparison of comparisons' in this chapter examines the choice and number of cases, the time period of the studies, the types of measures and indicators each study uses to operationalize the theoretical concepts, and the different types of qualitative and quantitative techniques contained in each study.

The research problem

There are three interrelated research questions that form the basis for this field of inquiry in comparative politics:

1 Why do people rebel?
2 Which sectors of society are more likely to rebel?
3 What factors contribute to successful social revolution?

The first question concerns the individual, structural, and cultural factors that motivate people to rebel. These factors include 'relative deprivation' (Gurr 1968, 1970), general levels of inequality (e.g. Muller and Seligson 1987; Lichbach 1989), rational response to changing economic conditions (e.g. Popkin 1979; Lichbach 1994), moral outrage at injustice (Scott 1976; Moore 1978), and the structural composition of primary export economies (Paige 1975; Wickham-Crowley 1993). The second question concerns the types of groups most likely to comprise the largest support for violent rebellions or revolutionary movements. Since many of the successful revolutions during the twentieth century occurred in countries whose economies were largely based on agriculture (Midlarsky and Roberts 1985: 163–164), much comparative attention has been focused on the role peasants play in overall levels of political violence and revolutionary movements. Finally, the third question concerns the key explanatory factors for successful revolution (Goodwin and Skocpol 1989).

Those studies that compare many countries tend to focus on the motivational aspects of political violence, while those that compare few countries and single-country studies tend to concentrate on identifying the key groups and the necessary conditions for successful revolution while remaining cognisant of the individual motivations for rebellious activity. While the many-country studies focus most of their attention on the relationship between changing socio-economic conditions and political violence, few-country and single-country studies extend their analyses to examine the role of rebellious elites, revolutionary coalitions, the strength of guerrilla groups, the strength of the state, and other factors. Moreover, the many-country studies imply a link with revolution, while the few-country and single-country studies are more explicit in their attention to revolution. Thus, as in the comparisons that examine the relationship between economic development and democracy, the comparisons in this chapter show great variance in the factors that account for political violence and successful revolution. The discussion now turns to key examples from comparative politics that have examined these important questions.

Comparing many countries

As in the comparisons for economic development and democracy, the studies that compare many countries in this field of inquiry seek to discover the universal factors that account for political rebellion and political violence. They thus remain relatively high on the level of abstraction in order to include as many countries as possible (see Chapter 2). In this way, these studies identify a parsimonious set of factors that ought to explain 'why [individuals] rebel' (Gurr 1970). These studies assume that individuals and groups of individuals experience some form of grievance, and that this grievance ultimately manifests itself in violent political behaviour. Based on this assumption, these studies look for the micro and macro factors that may or may not lead to increased levels of grievance as manifested in political conflict.

This section considers six important studies from the literature that demonstrate the methodological issues encountered in the comparison of many countries. These studies include the comprehensive attention to general levels of political dissent found in Gurr's (1968) work on civil strife and Hibbs's (1973) *Mass Political Violence*; the examination of rural rebellion in Paige's (1975) *Agrarian Revolution*; and a sub-set of studies that focus primarily on the relationship between inequality and political violence, including Sigelman and Simpson (1977) and Muller and Seligson (1987). All five studies use quantitative methods to analyse a global sample of countries ($49 \leq N \leq 114$) in order to identify the factors that account for political violence. The differences among them reside in the number of countries and time periods that each includes, the types of measures and indicators each employs, and the types of model each specifies.

As foreshadowed in the methodological discussions in Chapters 2 and 3, Gurr's (1968) search for conditions that cause 'civil strife' draws on a field of empirical inquiry in comparative politics that began with the publication of *Internal War* (Eckstein 1964). Gurr (1968: 1109–1110) operationalizes the notion of relative deprivation through separate measures and indicators of persisting deprivation, short-term deprivation, the coercive potential of states, levels of institutionalization, the degree of political legitimacy, and general socio-structural conditions of facilitation. His variable for political dissent is the magnitude of civil strife, which is a combined measure of demonstrations, political strikes, riots, local rebellions, assassinations, coups, mutinies, plots, purges, and widespread revolts for the years 1961–1965. The data were coded from various primary news sources and individual country reports, yielding a total of 1100 strife 'events' (ibid.: 1109). Through correlation and regression analysis, Gurr shows that all his indicators of deprivation are positively related to the magnitude of civil strife, even after controlling for the mediating effects of coercion, institutionalization, legitimacy, facilitation, and past levels of civil strife (ibid.: 1116–1117). His final model of civil strife is depicted in Figure 5.1.

The indices in this study operationalize the main theoretical concepts and the quantitative analysis shows how the variation in the magnitude of civil strife across 114 countries is explained by these different measures of relative deprivation. Figure 5.1 demonstrates that the two key independent variables (persisting and short-term deprivation) show significant positive effects on the magnitude of civil strife while the analysis controls for the effects of the other independent variables. This study also shows that the comparison of many countries is an appropriate method with which to identify universal factors that account for civil strife. The large number of countries means that there are plenty of degrees of freedom to include the seven independent variables in the model. In other words, *there are enough countries to allow the variables to vary*. Moreover, the selection of countries was not determined by the outcome to be explained and thus *does not suffer from selection bias*. This study stands as one of the earliest and most comprehensive analyses of this research question using this particular comparative method.

Like Gurr (1968), Douglas Hibbs (1973: ix), in *Mass Political Violence*, seeks to examine the 'causal processes underlying differences across nations in levels of mass political violence during the post-World War II period'. He is quite clear in stating that he is willing to sacrifice both an examination of micro-political factors and the study of single countries in an effort to make generalizations based on global evidence. He develops two main indicators of mass political violence (the dependent variable). The first is *collective protest*, which comprises riots, armed

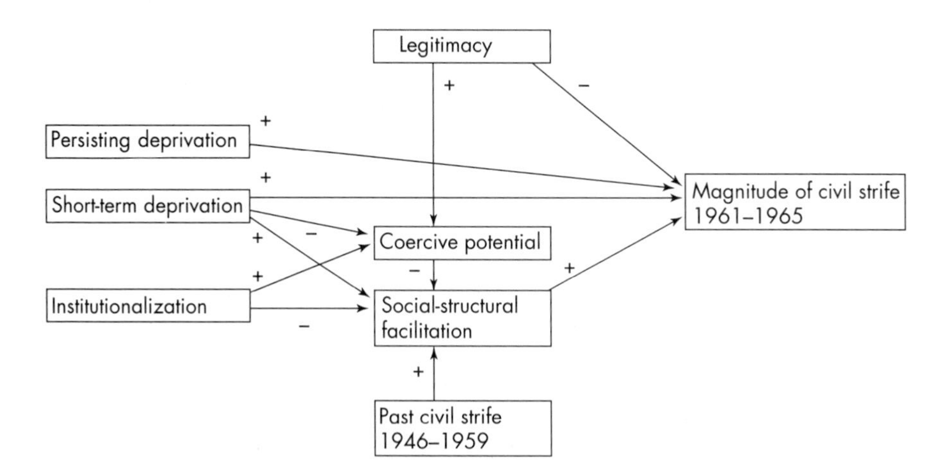

Figure 5.1 A causal model of civil strife

Sources: Adapted from Gurr (1968: 1121) and Sanders (1995: 71)

Note: Plus signs show positive effects and minus signs show negative effects attacks, political strikes, political assassinations, deaths from political violence, and anti-government demonstrations. The second is *internal war*, which comprises armed attacks, deaths from political violence, and political assassinations. The components of each of these index variables were coded from newspaper sources and are reported in the *World Handbook of Political and Social Indicators* (Taylor and Hudson 1972). Both indices serve as the dependent variables used throughout the statistical analysis and serve as checks on each other as there is some overlap in their composition. The data are available for 108 countries and are grouped into two separate decades, viz. 1948–1957 and 1958–1967.

Rather than establishing a well-developed theory of mass political violence, Hibbs (1973) engages in a comprehensive exercise of generating and testing hypotheses (see Chapter 1) before specifying a complex causal model. In testing hypotheses, Hibbs specifies over twenty-five different linear and non-linear relationships between his independent variables and his two indices of mass political violence. These relationships are grouped together in general categories including economic development, societal cleavages and separatism, state coercion and repression, and domestic politics. Table 5.1 summarizes in non-quantitative fashion the main findings of this hypothesis-testing exercise. Overall, Hibbs finds very little support for direct bivariate relationships between the various independent variables and his two dependent variables, although some of his findings are in the expected direction. For example, the level of political separatism in a society appears to be related to the level of internal war. Past levels of repression in the previous decade appear to inhibit mass political violence, while levels of repression in the same decade appear to encourage it. Finally, the presence of a communist totalitarian regime discourages political violence.

While direct bivariate relationships are by and large not supported by the data, Hibbs proceeds to use these findings to construct an elaborate multivariate causal model of political violence that takes into account the causal primacy of certain factors, which in turn determine the subsequent outcomes. Since the data are divided into two decades (1948–1957 and 1958–1967), Hibbs is able to construct models that examine the effects of values of some variables from the first decade on the same variables in the second decade, while estimating their overall effects on political violence. This complex model is depicted in Figure 5.2, from which it is possible to discuss the main conclusions of the study and highlight its strengths and weaknesses. Overall, Hibbs (1973) reports over thirty substantive findings from his statistical analysis, most of which refute popular propositions in the literature (Sanders 1981: 19), and some of which are important for the present discussion. The key variables that emerge in the analysis to account for increased levels of political violence include past levels of political violence, the presence of societal cleavages, low levels of repression, and the absence of a communist totalitarian regime. Thus, deeply divided societies tend to have higher levels of political violence either in the form of collective protest or internal war. Both forms of violence in the second decade are in part due to levels of violence in the previous decade. Violence also tends to be higher in countries without high levels of repression and in countries that are not controlled by a communist regime.

The strength of the study is that Hibbs (1973) seeks to avoid the problem of 'omitted variable bias' (King *et al.* 1994: 168–182) through the inclusion of a

Table 5.1 Exploring the causes of political violence: A summary of hypothesis-testing in Hibbs (1973)†

	Independent variables	*Dependent variables*	
		Collective protest (1948–1957)	*Internal war (1958–1967)*
Economic development hypotheses	Population	Positive linear	Positive linear
	Economic development 1 (static)	Inverted-U shape	Inverted-U shape
	Economic development 2 (dynamic)	Not significant	Not significant
	Urbanization	Not significant	Not significant
	Education	Not significant	Not significant
	Urbanization/development	Not significant	Positive linear
	Social mobility	Not significant	Negative linear
	Social mobility/expenditure	Not significant	Not significant
	Social mobility x expenditure	Negative linear	Negative linear
	Social mobility/welfare	Positive linear	Not significant
	Social mobility x welfare	Not significant	Negative linear
Cleavage hypotheses	Ethnic cleavages x social mobility	Not significant	Not significant
	Group discrimination	Positive linear	Positive linear
	Political separatism		Positive linear
	Post-war independence		Positive linear
Repression hypotheses	Internal security forces	Not significant	Inverted-U shape
	Repression (1958–1967)	Positive linear	Positive linear
	Repression (1948–1957)	Not significant	Negative linear
	Military coups	Positive linear	Positive linear
	Social mobility/institutionalization	Not significant	Not significant
Domestic politics hypotheses	Elite accountability	Not significant	Not significant
	Electoral turnout	Not significant	Not significant
	Political development (i.e. democracy)	Not significant	Negative linear
	Communist regime	Negative linear	Negative linear
	Left in parliament (% seats)	Negative linear	Not significant

Source: Adapted from Hibbs (1973: 21–131)

multitude of variables he thinks may (or may not) be related to political violence. Since he has two separate decades of indicators, he effectively doubles his sample size to 216 countries (108 x 2), which provides adequate degrees of freedom for the analysis; however, the use of ten-year aggregates has led some commentators to question his conclusions (see Sanders 1981: 41–43). His conclusions adhere very closely to the statistical results and he is careful in specifying which effects are causally prior to others. Despite these strengths, no overarching theory of political

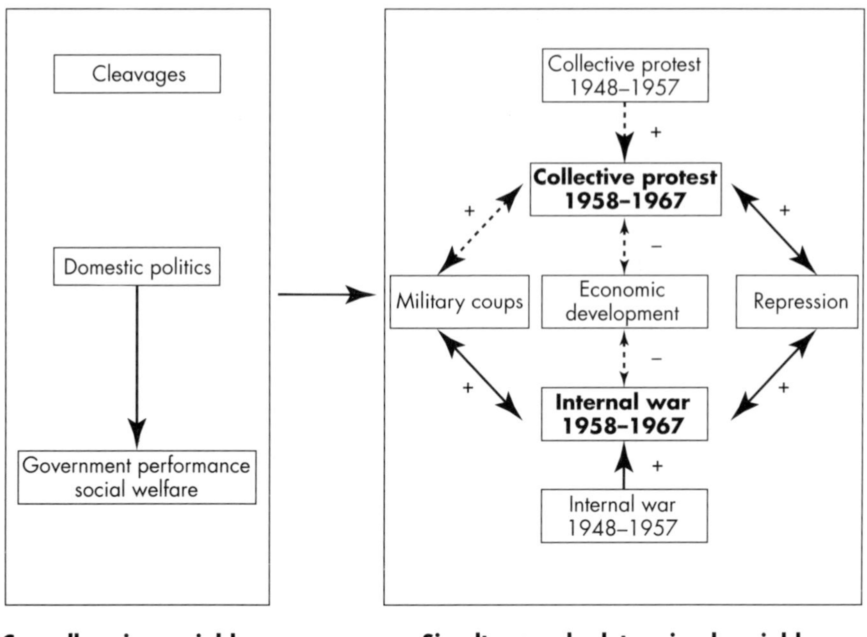

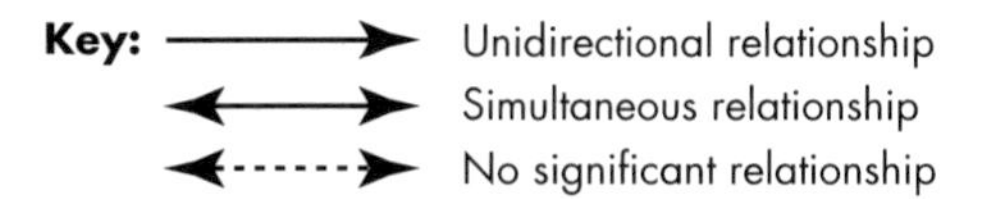

Figure 5.2 A causal model of political violence
Source: Adapted from Hibbs (1973: 135–153)

violence is developed in the study; rather a series of interesting hypotheses are tested and separate models are variously constructed, effectively 'losing the forest for the trees'. In all the models, past levels of violence are taken as given, or *exogenous* to the overall system, and the significant effect these past levels have on current levels of political violence begs the question as to what accounts for the earlier levels of political violence. Finally, apart from one small reference, the analysis never examines the relationship between collective protest and internal war. Hibbs claims they are highly associated with one another, but neither is included as an independent variable in any of the models. Overall, the study stands as an example of an extreme form of quantitative cross-national comparison, which includes many more variables than Gurr (1968), yet the theoretical 'payoff' appears to be considerably less.

In *Agrarian Revolution*, Jeffrey Paige (1975) has a different scholarly goal than either Gurr (1968) or Hibbs (1973), but uses the same comparative method to achieve it. Like Gurr and Hibbs, he seeks to explain the incidence of rebellion and collective violence; however, he focuses only on rural rebellion in the agricultural sector, and he differentiates the dependent variable into reform, revolt, rebellion, and revolution. His empirical sample includes 135 different export sectors in seventy different developing countries for the period 1948–1970 (Paige 1975: 72). In contrast to the psychological and individual theory of Gurr (1968) and the multitude of factors in Hibbs (1973), Paige focuses on the structure of the agricultural sector and its relation to collective violence. For Paige, there are two types of groups in this sector (cultivators and owners) with three sources of income (land, capital, and wages). Owners derive their income from land (plantations) or capital (commercial farms), while cultivators derive their income from land or wages. Different combinations of land, capital, and wages produce the following three different types of conflict between owners and cultivators: revolt, reform, and revolution. His structural theory contends that revolt should be more likely in agricultural sectors where the owners and cultivators earn their income from the land, while revolutionary behaviour is expected in agricultural sectors where owners earn their income from land and cultivators earn their income from wages.

Paige (1975: 73) is keen to point out that studies such as Gurr (1968) posit individual-level motivations for political violence, but use national states as the units of analysis. His study of agrarian organization uses an appropriate unit of analysis, the agrarian sector itself, which is 'defined by the major producing regions for a given export crop within a given country' (Paige 1975: 73). Thus, Paige avoids the problem of ecological fallacy (see Chapter 3 above) and minimizes problems of spuriousness in his statistical analysis. Having defined the unit of analysis, the study operationalizes both agricultural organization and collective behaviour from rural social movements. Each agricultural sector is categorized according to the organization of its labour force and the ownership of its agricultural enterprise (see Table 5.2). Social movements in general are defined as 'collective acts which take place outside the established institutional framework and involve participants who are united by some shared sense of identity' (Paige 1975: 87, see also Chapter 6). Rural movement activities are coded from events reported in newspaper indices and regional press summaries and only if they are collective, non-institutional, involve solidary groups and are 'those actions which involved individuals who perform the physical work of cultivation' (ibid.: 90–91). Each event is coded using different categories, the most important of which is ideology, which allows the relationship between the type of rebellious activity and the structure of agrarian sector to be examined.

Using correlation analysis, Paige (1975: 104–105) finds strong support for a positive relationship between the structure of the agrarian sector and the type of rural social movement. Politically violent activities are carried out primarily by socialist or nationalist revolutionary movements, which are highly correlated with agrarian enterprises based on sharecropping and migratory labour. Thus, revolutionary action is most likely when cultivators derive their income from wages and owners derive their income from the control of land (ibid.: 120; see also Wickham-Crowley 1993: 92). Paige's analysis demonstrates that it is the most vulnerable groups, namely sharecroppers and migratory labourers, that are the most likely to rebel. Like Gurr (1968) and Hibbs (1973), the selection of cases in this study is not dependent on the outcome that is to be explained. The analysis is based on a full consideration of different export sectors in developing countries, which provides sufficient degrees of freedom to test the relationship, and the dependent variable includes revolutionary and non-revolutionary activity from rural

Table 5.2 Types of agricultural organization

Type of organization	*definition*
Commercial manor or hacienda	An individually owned enterprise which lacks power-driven processing machinery and is worked by usufructaries, resident wage labourers, or wage labourers who commute daily from nearby subsistence plots
Sharecropped estate	An individually owned enterprise which lacks power-driven processing machinery and is worked by sharecroppers or share tenants
Migratory labour estate	An individually owned enterprise which lacks power-driven processing machinery and is worked by seasonal migratory labourers
Plantation	An enterprise owned either by a commercial corporation or government body, or by an individual if the enterprise includes power-driven machinery, and worked by wage labourers resident for continuous terms of more than one year
Family smallholding	An individually owned enterprise worked by the owner and his family

Source: Adapted from Paige (1975: 79)

social movements. Like Gurr (1968) and in contrast to Hibbs (1973), the analysis identifies a parsimonious set of factors that account for the patterns of events that are observed.

Despite this strong pattern of correlation between agricultural organization and rural social movement events, Paige (1975: 120) must complete a chain of inference that links the structure of the agrarian sector to collective political dissent. This chain of inference, however, is slightly shorter than the one required by Gurr (1968), since his unit of analysis is closer to the theoretical concepts he develops. In both types of agricultural systems where revolt and revolution are observed, landholders are dependent on the land as a source of income and power, while the cultivators have no strong ties to the land, making them more susceptible to revolutionary behaviour (Paige 1975: 120–121). In addition to the cross-national evidence amassed for his theory, Paige 'triangulates' (Tarrow 1995: 473–474) his study by comparing the three cases of Peru, Angola, and Vietnam – the discussion of which will follow in the next section.

The studies that follow in the footsteps of Gurr (1968), Hibbs (1973), and Paige (1975) tend to focus on one explanatory factor – inequality – in an effort to explain political violence in the world. In general, there have not been a priori arguments for the type of relationship between inequality and political violence, rather this type of comparative work has attempted to provide evidence for four types of relationships, including positive linear, negative linear, U shaped, or inverted-U shaped (see Briefing Box 5.1).[1] Since the collection of cross-national

Briefing box 5.1 Possible relationships between economic inequality and political violence

The relationship between economic inequality and political violence has received much scholarly attention since the seminal work of Ted Robert Gurr (1968; 1970) provided evidence for the link. Over the years, it has been posited that the relationship can assume four basic functional forms: (1) positive, (2) negative, (3) U-shaped, and (4) an inverted U shape (Lichbach 1989: 436–440). Each of these functional forms is depicted below.

Figure 5.3 shows that as levels of economic inequality increase, levels of political dissent also increase while Figure 5.4 shows the opposite relationship. Figure 5.5 shows that the extreme ends of economic inequality are associated with high levels of political dissent, while Figure 5.6 shows the opposite relationship. Over the years, studies that compare many countries have sought to provide evidence in support of one of these basic models.

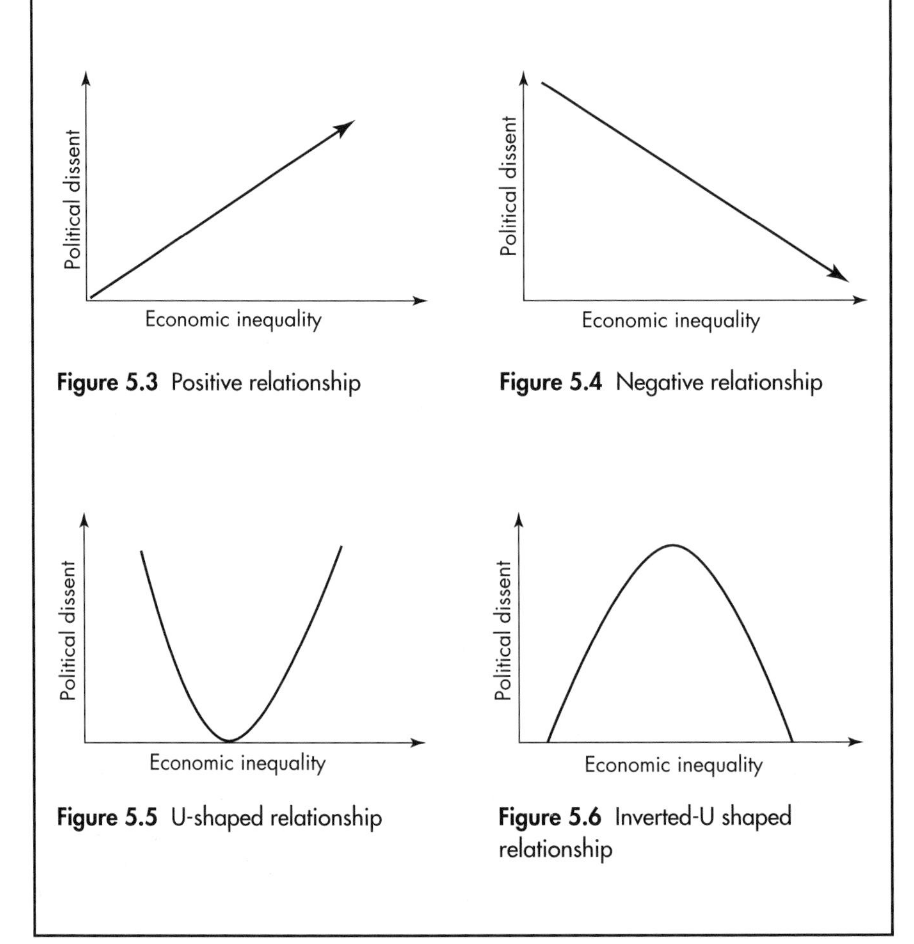

Figure 5.3 Positive relationship

Figure 5.4 Negative relationship

Figure 5.5 U-shaped relationship

Figure 5.6 Inverted-U shaped relationship

studies on inequality and political violence is quite large (Sanders 1981; Lichbach 1989: 435–436), this section will concentrate on two key examples from the comparative literature. The differences between them reside in the different ways in which they conceive inequality (either land or income), the ways in which they measure political violence (internal war or deaths from political violence), and the ways in which they specify their various models.

Sigelman and Simpson (1977) compare indicators of inequality and political violence across forty-nine countries during the mid-1960s, while controlling for the effects of general levels of affluence, patterns of social mobility, degrees of socio-cultural heterogeneity, the rate of social change, and the size of the population. Affluence is measured by the per capita gross national product. The breadth of national educational enrolment represents social mobility. The degree of ethnic division represents socio-cultural heterogeneity. The rate of social change is measured by the change in urban population between 1950 and 1960 (ibid.: 113–114). Inequality is operationalized as the distribution of income as measured by the Gini coefficient (see Briefing Box 5.2). Political violence is measured using the Hibbs (1973) index for internal war (ibid.: 113–114). Thus, the measures of the various concepts are similar to those used by Hibbs (1973), but the study focuses on a smaller topic since it seeks to test only the relationship between income inequality and political violence.

Their comparative analysis tests the linear and non-linear forms of the relationship between income inequality and political violence. Their simple models include only income inequality and population as the independent variables and their results suggest that there is a positive linear relationship between income inequality and political violence. In other words, across the forty-nine countries in their sample, populous countries with high levels of income inequality have high levels of political violence; however, the curvilinear relationship receives no such empirical support. In addition to population and income inequality, their more complex models include the indicators for affluence, social mobility, socio-cultural heterogeneity, and the rate of social change. Again, a positive linear relationship is shown to exist between income inequality and political violence, while social mobility and affluence appear to have a negative effect, and socio-cultural heterogeneity have a positive effect. These results mean that while high levels of income inequality are associated with high levels of political violence, there is less political violence in affluent countries with opportunities for social advancement, and more political violence in countries whose societies are deeply divided.

Ten years after the publication of the study by Sigelman and Simpson (1977), Muller and Seligson (1987) re-examine the relationship between inequality and political violence. In contrast to the earlier study, they compare the effects of land inequality and income inequality on political violence. Both types of inequality are measured using the Gini coefficients for land and income distribution. In a departure from the earlier studies discussed in this section, Muller and Seligson (1987) use 'deaths from political violence' as their measure of political violence, excluding the measures of armed attacks and assassinations found in the Hibbs (1973) index of internal war. Other independent variables in their model include the size of the agricultural labour force, the degree of landlessness, repression, governmental acts of coercion (past and present), political separatism, level of

Briefing box 5.2 The Gini coefficient as a measure of income inequality

Every country has a national income, known as either the gross national product (GNP) or the gross domestic product (GDP), which is the sum of all income earned in any given year. This national income is divided among those individuals who actually earned a share of it. Figure 5.7 illustrates this idea of national income and its distribution. The vertical axis represents the cumulative percentage of total income in a society, while the horizontal axis represents the cumulative percentage of the population that earned some portion of that national income. In a perfectly equal society, each percentage of the population earns precisely the same as the next. In an unequal society, some percentages of the population earn less than others. Thus, at point C in the figure, the lower 50 per cent of the population earn approximately 25 per cent of the national income, while at point F, the top 10 per cent of the population earn 80 per cent of the national income. This depiction of the distribution of income is known as the Lorenz curve (see Todaro 1997: 141–142). In general, the more the Lorenz curve slopes away from the line of perfect equality, the more unequal the distribution of income.

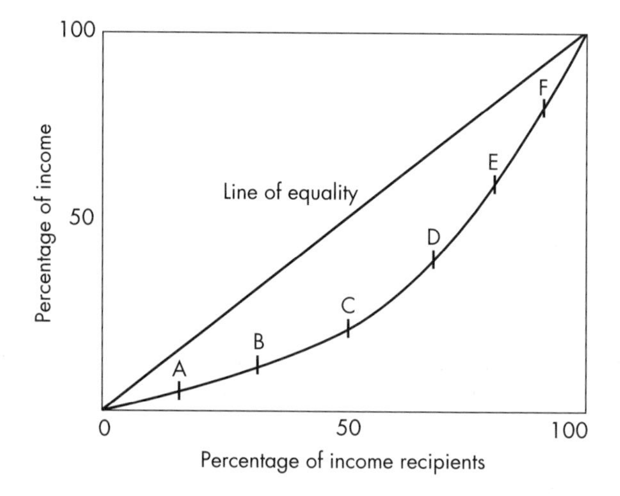

Figure 5.7 The Lorenz curve
Source: Adapted from Todaro (1997: 141)

The way in which to represent this state of inequality in income distribution is called the Gini concentration ratio or Gini coefficient. Figure 5.8 illustrates how this coefficient is calculated. It is the ratio of the area denoted A to the area denoted BCD, which represents the degree to which the Lorenz curve deviates from the line of perfect equality. The Gini coefficient ranges from 0 (no inequality) to 1 (perfect inequality). Thus, the higher the Gini coefficient, the more unequal is the distribution of national income. This measure is a popular measure in studies that compare many countries since it is a common measure that can be applied to all countries in the world.

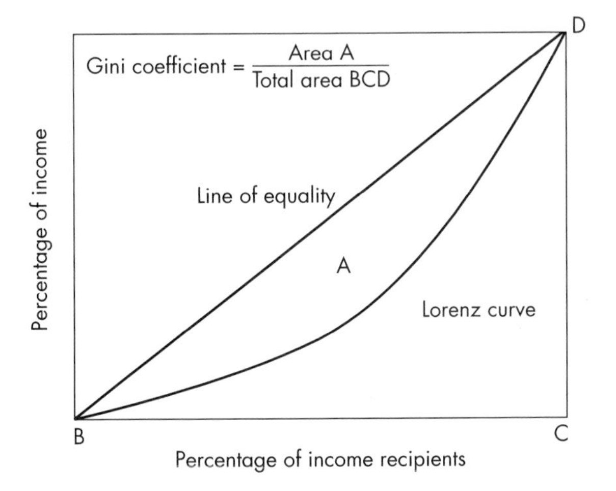

Figure 5.8 The Gini coefficient
Source: Adapted from Todaro (1997: 146)

economic development, and past levels of political violence. The analysis compares sixty-two countries during the 1960s and 1970s using simple and multiple regression techniques to examine the primary relationship between inequality and political violence. The findings are summarized in Figure 5.9, which shows that land and agrarian inequality matter only as they are mediated through general levels of income inequality. In other words, general levels of income inequality have a positive effect on the incidence of political violence. In addition, the authors find that the repressiveness of the regime contributes to political violence, as do government acts of coercion, past levels of political violence (compare Hibbs 1973), and the level of political separatism. It is clear that this study includes many of the independent variables found in Hibbs (1973) and combines them with the income inequality variable in Sigelman and Simpson (1977), while comparing the overall effects of land inequality.

Taken together, these studies represent a field of comparative inquiry dedicated to uncovering the universal factors that best account for political violence. The underlying assumption of all of them is that some form of grievance generated by some type of imbalance in society manifests itself in political violence, while the direct relationship between this imbalance and violence is mediated by other important factors. The strength of this type of comparison lies in the large number of observations and the full variance of the variables in the analysis. With the possible exception of Paige (1975), the main weakness of these studies is the choice of the nation state as the basic unit of analysis. While this choice is in part a

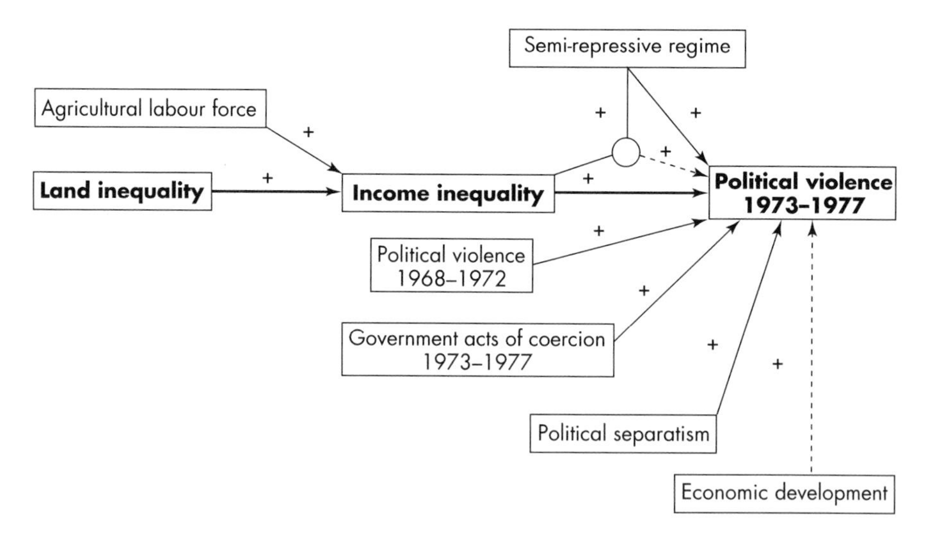

Figure 5.9 Inequality and political violence
Source: Adapted from Muller and Seligson (1987: 442)

function of data availability, the chain of inference required by the studies may lead many to question the overall strength of their conclusions since theoretically, the studies specify a set of relationships at the individual level yet test them with national-level data.

Comparing few countries

The comparison of few countries moves the analysis away from the identification of universal conditions for political violence and seeks to provide more holistic accounts of the groups that form revolutionary movements and the sequence and conjunction of events that lead to successful social revolutions. In stark contrast to the quantitative comparison of many countries, these studies seek to understand how '[t]he relations between army and party, between proletariat, peasantry, and middle class intellectuals are variably conjugated in different situations and not exhausted in simple formulas' (Wolf 1968: 99). This section of the chapter considers Wolf's (1968) *Peasant Wars of the Twentieth Century*; the comparison of Vietnam, Angola, and Peru in Paige (1975); Scott's (1976) *Moral Economy of the Peasant*; Skocpol's (1979) *States and Social Revolutions*; and Wickham-Crowley's (1993) *Guerrillas and Revolutions in Latin America*. In all these studies, a small number of countries are compared to examine the ways in which different groups have become mobilized, how they formed alliances, and how they were able to be successful (or not) in overthrowing the dominant political system under which they lived.

By comparing the history of revolutionary struggles in Mexico, Russia, China, Vietnam, Algeria, and Cuba, Eric Wolf (1968) seeks to identify the common factors that explain the outbreak of peasant wars and their role in fomenting successful revolutions. His 'master variable' is capitalist transformation, which introduced the logic of market mechanisms into agricultural communities historically founded on altogether different systems of production and existence. The commercialization of agriculture challenged the basic risk calculations peasants had been operating for centuries and broke traditional social ties and power relations that provided the basis for the subsistence economy. Wolf argues that all his cases (with the exception of Cuba) had the same starting condition of a large peasantry that was more or less bound to the land. The arrival of capitalism meant that increasingly landholders required more land, which with the growth of the population in each country led to perceptions of scarcity. Other significant variables for Wolf (ibid.: 282–302) include the presence of a central state authority whose power base became rapidly eroded; the presence of middle and 'free' peasants able to be mobilized for revolutionary struggle; and violent peasant rebellion itself, which was carried out to preserve traditional forms of agricultural production.

Table 5.3 summarizes Wolf's (1968) comparison by listing the countries, the main independent variables, the outcome variable, and the main beneficiaries of these revolutions. The table shows that Wolf has adopted the most different systems design (MDSD) of comparison (see Chapter 2 above), where the outcome is always present and the countries all share the main explanatory variables. His study has the problem of selection bias since the dependent variable (social revolution) is not allowed to vary. He does not, for example, compare instances in which peasant wars did not lead to social revolution. Thus, his inferences are less secure and confined to the countries in his study, even though one of his motivations for the study was to guide policymakers in the US to avoid more 'Vietnams' (Wolf 1968: x). Ironically, the main beneficiaries of these peasant wars and revolutions have not been the peasants but rather the middle classes, various revolutionary party organizations, and coalitions of the military and political parties. Nevertheless, like Barrington Moore (1966), his study stands as one of the first examples of comparative history that seek to identify common features across a very different set of countries in an effort to account for a similar set of outcomes.

Paige (1975) shows that the comparison of Peru, Angola, and Vietnam corroborates his findings at the global level. He chooses these three cases because each 'had experienced a particularly well-known and well-described movement and because each promised to provide detailed knowledge of the general principles linking types of agricultural organization and types of rural social movements' (Paige 1975: 123). His Peruvian case study compares the labour movements in the industrial sugar plantations and agrarian movements in the commercial hacienda systems. The Angolan case study examines the revolutionary nationalist movement in the settler-based coffee export sector. The Vietnamese case study considers the war as an example of a revolutionary socialist movement, which occurs in the sharecropping system of a rice export sector (ibid.: 123). Based on significant correlations between rural social movements and the particular structure of the agrarian sector in each of these cases, Paige (ibid.: 210) demonstrates that the 'primary determinant' of political conflict is the distribution of political and economic resources established by new forms of export agricultural organization. In each case, Paige is able to present evidence on the structure of the

Table 5.3 Conditions for peasant wars and revolution in the twentieth century

Variables	*Mexico*	*Russia*	*China*	*Vietnam*	*Algeria*	*Cuba*
Starting conditions	Land-bound peasantry	Land-bound peasantry	Land-bound peasantry	Land-bound peasantry	Land-bound peasantry	Sugar proletariat
Capitalist transformation	Yes	Yes	Yes	Yes	Yes	Yes
Mode of capitalist expansion	Violent expansion of farms	Entrepreneurs	Colonization of new land	Entrepreneurs	Violent expansion of farms	Entrepreneurs
Population growth	Yes	Yes	Yes	Yes	Yes	Yes
Central authority	Porfírio Díaz	Tsarism	Chiang Kai-shek	France	France	Batista
Vanguard supporters	Constitutional army	Russian Army peasant soldiers	Red Army			
Middle and free peasants	Yes	Yes	Yes	Yes	Yes	Yes
Peasant war	Yes	Yes	Yes	Yes	Yes	Yes
Outcome	Revolution	Revolution	Revolution	Revolution	Revolution	Revolution
Beneficiaries	Middle class	Communist Party	Communist Party	Communist Party	Middle class	Army–Communist Party

Source: Adapted from Wolf (1968)

agricultural sector and the incidence of rural rebellion to demonstrate and replicate the relationship established through the global comparison of 135 export sectors.

James Scott (1976) provides a binary comparison of Burma and Vietnam in an effort to demonstrate how his theory of the 'moral economy' accounts for peasant revolutionary behaviour. Drawing on many of the ideas developed in Wolf's (1968) account, Scott develops a model, or portrait, of the peasant community and its basic organization that when transformed by the arrival of market capitalism, contains the seeds for rebellion. The moral economy, as he calls it, develops from the particular nature of the peasant economy, which is organized to meet the basic subsistence of its inhabitants. For him, peasants are both 'risk-averse' and live so close to a basic line of subsistence that they establish community-based networks of support and norms of reciprocity that allow them to survive. His account centres on why peasants rebel rather than the reasons for successful social revolution, yet his analysis rests on similar arguments found in Moore (1966) and Wolf (1968). His master explanatory variable is market capitalism and his dependent variable is peasant rebellion. The intrusion of market capitalism under colonialism in Southeast Asia so transforms the basic 'subsistence ethic' of the moral economy that peasants rebel in an effort to preserve their centuries-old system of organization. Through a qualitative comparison of the history of colonial change and the introduction of market capitalism in Lower Burma and Vietnam, Scott (1976: 157) demonstrates that 'structural change in the colonial period permitted elites and the state . . . to increasingly violate the moral economy of the peasantry and become more exploitative'.

In similar fashion to Wolf (1968), Theda Skocpol (1979) uses the comparative historical method to explain the social revolutions in France, Russia, and China. While her universe of countries is much reduced compared to Wolf (1968), her inclusion of the 'negative' cases of Japan, Prussia, and England is meant to address the problem of selection bias by 'checking' her structural theory of revolution (Skocpol 1979: 37; see also Chapter 3 in this volume). She also draws a distinction between 'social' revolution and 'political' revolution. Social revolution involves a rapid and basic transformation of the state and class structures of a country, while a political revolution reforms the dominant political institutions of the day, but not the social ones (ibid.: 4).

Like Wolf (1968), Paige (1975), and Scott (1976), Skocpol pays close attention to peasants as an important group for social revolution. In contrast to these studies, her master explanatory variable is the absolutist state and its subsequent collapse in the face of mounting international pressure, which provides the necessary political opportunity for revolutionary movements to be successful. In arguing against a purely Marxist account of revolution, Skocpol (1979: 34–35) asserts that

> [c]ausal variables referring to the strength and structure of old-regime states and the relations of state organizations to class structures may discriminate between cases of successful revolution and cases of failure or non-occurrence far better than do variables referring to class relations and patterns of economic development.

Thus, Skocpol (1979) seeks to redress the gap in Marxist explanation with a direct analysis of changes in the patterns of state organization and their relationship to revolutionary movements. Her comparative method explicitly seeks to 'develop, test, and refine causal, explanatory hypotheses about events or structures integral to macro-units such as nation-states' (ibid.: 26). Her inclusion of 'positive' and 'negative' cases of social revolution thus combines the most similar systems design with the most different systems design in an effort to provide a comprehensive theory of social revolution. Table 5.4 summarizes the main evidence marshalled in support of her causal theory of social revolution. The comparison reveals that in addition to a crisis in state authority, relatively autonomous peasant communities and organized peasant protest play a key role in the breakdown of the absolutist states in these three cases. Moreover, the comparisons with Japan, Prussia, and England, reveal that the absence of these conditions led to political revolutions but not to social revolutions.

Having established similar causes of these revolutions, Skocpol (1979) turns her attention to the post-revolutionary period in each case to examine their outcomes. In this phase of her comparison, she compares only the three principal cases while dismissing the negative cases as no longer necessary. The comparison identifies five basic similarities across the post-revolutionary experiences in these countries, all of which Skocpol (1979) attributes to the way in which these revolutions unfolded. First, the so-called 'liberal option' remained closed for these states, while the dominant classes remained vulnerable and the subordinate groups remained susceptible to further mobilization. Her conclusion about France stands in contrast to that reached by Moore (1966), who argued that France is an exemplar of a 'bourgeois revolution' that led to liberal democracy (see Chapter 4 in this volume). Since her analysis extends beyond the revolutionary period (something Moore did not do), she claims that France experienced liberal phases that did not remain stable (Skocpol 1979: 282).

Second, the economies of all three countries continued to be based on agrarian production characterized by a strong presence of peasants. Third, all three continued to be engaged in international competition. Fourth, the process of state-building featured mobilization of popular support against domestic and foreign opponents. Finally, the state itself established a greater presence in all three countries and replaced the landed classes as the pre-eminent and central authority. Overall, Skocpol's comparisons identify the causes and consequences of social revolution. She combines the two methods of comparison – most similar and most different systems design – and reaches some compelling conclusions about the causes, nature, and outcomes of social revolutions.

The final study in this section is Wickham-Crowley's (1993) *Guerrillas and Revolution in Latin America*, which compares the relative fortunes of revolutionary movements in twelve Latin American countries during two successive historical 'waves'. Since all the countries come from the same region of the world, the study adopts a most similar systems design and seeks to identify both the sources of revolutionary behaviour and the conditions that favour successful revolution. While this study draws on the theoretical and operational insights of the many-country and few-country studies, the unit of analysis is the guerrilla movement itself. Wickham-Crowley seeks to strike a balance between the parsimonious

Table 5.4 Conditions for social revolution

	Positive cases			Negative cases		
	France	*Russia*	*China*	*Prussia*	*Japan*	*England*
Crisis conditions:						
Class	Landed commercial class + semi-bureaucratic absolutist monarchy	Weak landed nobility + bureaucratic absolutist state	Landed commercial class + semi-bureaucratic absolutist state	Weak landed nobility + bureaucratic absolutist state	No landed class + bureaucratic state	Strong landed class + no bureaucratic state
Economy	Growing non-capitalist	Extensive growth	No development breakthrough	Capitalist agriculture	Traditional with high productivity	Capitalist agriculture
External pressure	Moderate	Extreme	Strong	Strong/mild	Strong	Mild
Peasants:						
Class structures	Smallholders + opposition to seigniorial system	Peasants own/rent Strong community	Peasants own land, small plots, no community	Smallholders, labourers, no community	Communities dominated by rich peasants	Yeoman farmers + labourers, no community
Local politics	Autonomous villages + royal officials	Sovereign villages + tsarist bureaucracy	Landlords, usurers, literati dominate	Junker dominance	Bureaucratic control over local community	Landlords tied to monarchy
Outcomes	Breakdown of state + peasant revolts	Initial reforms; failed revolution 1905; collapse of state 1917	Breakdown of imperial state; agrarian disorder	Reforms and failed revolution	Political revolution + bureaucratic reforms	Constitutional monarchy
Social revolution?	Yes	Yes	Yes	No	No	No

Source: Adapted from Skocpol (1979: 155–157)

identification of key variables found in the many-country studies with the attention to historical process and contingency found in few-country studies. The first set of comparisons examines the origins and fortunes of guerrilla movements in Cuba, Venezuela, Guatemala, Colombia, Peru, and Bolivia during the period 1956–1970. The second set of comparisons applies the same logic to movements in Nicaragua, El Salvador, Guatemala, Peru, and Colombia after 1970.

The comparison of guerrilla movements and revolutions across countries and historical waves reveals a common set of conditions that account for high levels of peasant support for revolutionary movements and the conditions that must be met for successful social revolution in the region. With regard to the first question, the comparisons reveal four important conditions for high levels of peasant support for revolutionary movements:

- the nature of the agrarian structure;
- disruption of the agrarian structure;
- the presence of rebellious cultures; and
- linkages between revolutionaries and peasants through well-established social networks.

The analysis goes beyond mere identification of these factors and demonstrates that it is the *combination* of these conditions that is important for explaining the proclivity of peasants to support revolutionary movements.

1. Peasant support came when conducive agrarian structures were combined with agrarian disruption in an area with substantial pre-existing linkages joining guerrillas to the peasantry.
2. Peasant support could also be obtained where conducive agrarian structures were joined to a historically rebellious peasantry, or
3. where such a rebellious peasantry was previously linked to the proto-guerrillas before the insurgency (Wickham-Crowley 1993: 308–309).

With regard to the second question, since there were only two successful revolutions in the region after 1956, Cuba in the first wave (1959) and Nicaragua (1979) in the second, the comparisons reveal not only why revolutions succeed, but also why they fail. Table 5.5 summarizes the key variables that emerge in Wickham-Crowley's (1993: 312) analysis, which shows a great frequency of guerrilla attempts to foment revolution (N = 24) that spans the countries and periods outlined above. The table is organized into four basic groups:

1. those cases in which guerrilla movements were successful;
2. those in which guerrilla movements had many of the favourable conditions for revolution but were none the less unsuccessful;
3. those in which guerrilla movements never managed to garner support; and
4. those in which guerrilla movements never got off the ground.

While the fact that the cases of successful revolution contain all five conditions may appear unsurprising, the factors that determine the failure of revolution are an

Table 5.5 Conditions for social revolution in Latin America 1956–1990

	Favourable conditions for revolution					*Revolution*
	Guerrilla attempt	*Peasant worker support*	*Guerrilla military strength*	*Patrimonial praetorian regime*	*Government loses US support*	
Cuba 1956–1959	Yes	Yes	Yes	Yes	Yes	Yes
Nicaragua 1971–1979	Yes	Yes	Yes	Yes	Yes	Yes
Venezuela 1960s	Yes	Yes	Yes			
Colombia 1960s	Yes	Yes	Yes			
Guatemala 1960s	Yes	Yes	Yes			
Colombia 1970–1990	Yes	Yes	Yes			
Peru 1980s	Yes	Yes	Yes			
Guatemala 1975–1990	Yes	Yes	Yes	Yes	Yes	
El Salvador 1975–1990	Yes	Yes	Yes			
Argentina 1974–1978	Yes	Yes		Yes	Yes	
Brazil 1970s	Yes	Yes				
Argentina, *Montoneros*	Yes	Yes	Yes	Yes	Yes	
Mexico 1970s	Yes	Yes				
Uruguay *Tupamaros*	Yes	Yes	Yes			
Argentina 1958–1963	Yes					
Peru 1965	Yes					
Bolivia 1967	Yes					
Nicaragua 1958–1963	Yes			Yes		
Dom. Republic 1963	Yes					
Ecuador 1962	Yes					
Haiti 1960s	Yes			Yes	Yes	
Paraguay 1958–1959	Yes			Yes		
Honduras 1965	Yes					
Brazil 1960s	Yes					
Costa Rica						
Panama 1959–1985						
Panama 1985–1989				Yes	Yes	
Paraguay 1960–1989				Yes		

Source: Adapted from Wickham-Crowley (1993: 312, Table 12–3). Copyright © 1993 by Princeton University Press. Reprinted by permission
Note: N = 28

added dimension to the analysis. Indeed, the two variables that appear to be key for a successful revolution are the presence of a patrimonial praetorian regime and the loss of US support for that regime. In other words, a guerrilla movement in the region may have made an attempt, garnered significant support, maintained sufficient military strength, but did not mobilize against such a patrimonial praetorian regime, the result of which is the failure to overthrow the regime.

Overall, the comparison of few countries allows for closer attention to the role of historical contingency, the examination of class alliances, state strength and structures, and other important factors that are omitted from many-country comparative studies. Moreover, the use of history raises the number of observations and degrees of freedom for more variance in an effort to overcome the 'two many variables' problem (see Chapter 3 of this volume). The comparison of these few-country studies demonstrates the importance of case selection and unit of analysis for drawing inferences. Wolf (1968) looks at positive instances of revolution, Paige (1975) and Scott (1976) examine confirmatory cases, and Skocpol (1979) and Wickham-Crowley (1993) use positive and negative instances of social revolution. For Wolf, Scott, and Skocpol, the unit of analysis is the nation state, for Paige it is the agricultural sector, while for Wickham-Crowley (1993), it is the guerrilla movement itself. It is clear that there are important trade-offs in terms of the types of inferences that can be drawn associated with both case selection and the unit of analysis.

Single-country studies

Rather than compare a series of single-country studies on different politically violent and revolutionary periods in the world, this section of the chapter compares three seminal case studies of violent political dissent and revolution in Mexico. Womack's (1969) *Zapata and the Mexican Revolution*, Nugent's (1993) *Spent Cartridges of Revolution*, and Harvey's (1998) *The Chiapas Rebellion* examine specific groups and events in Mexico. All three authors are insistent on the uniqueness of the 'story' they are recounting, yet use analytical categories developed in more comparative studies to make larger inferences about violent political dissent and the nature of revolutionary activity. Like the many-country and few-country comparisons, they examine the organization of the agricultural sector, the role of peasants in revolutionary processes, underlying economic transformations, as well as the role of the state and its relationship with the various subordinate groups. Womack (1969) focuses on the role of Emiliano Zapata and peasant support in the south central state of Morelos in the struggle for land during the heyday of the Mexican Revolution. Nugent (1993) traces the diachronic and dialectic relationship between state and community in the municipal area of Namiquipa in the northern state of Chihuahua as local cultivators resist repeated attempts to control their land. Harvey (1998) examines the contemporary rebellion led by the Zapatistas in the southern state of Chiapas, a struggle which reflects a larger historical political conflict over land and the cultural understanding of subordination that emerge from the interaction between macro- and micro-political processes. Together, land and who controls it feature prominently in each study as important comparative categories are drawn from the previous studies outlined above.

Where these studies differ from the comparisons outlined above is in their insistence that they seek to provide a deeper and more meaningful *understanding* of political struggle in the Mexican context. Womack insists that his 'social history' is not an explanation or analysis of rebellious behaviour. Rather, it is 'a story because the truth of the revolution in Morelos is in the feeling of it, which I could not convey through defining its factors but only through telling of it' (Womack 1969: x). Similarly, Nugent (1993:28) seeks to examine the 'distinctive historical process in which the community [of Namiquipa] has formed in relation to the state . . . through struggles over land and labor or the production process'. While not ignoring the importance of objective conditions, systemic factors, and influences, he insists that

> [w]hile this specificity does not preclude the possibility of *making comparisons*, an analysis of these struggles in this pueblo [the town of Namiquipa] must focus not only on a series of actions by people on and in the world and relationships between groups and individuals and things, but also on the manner in which actions and relationships are organized by people both practically and conceptually.
>
> (Nugent 1993: 29, emphasis mine)

In similar fashion, Harvey (1998: 12) argues that he uses non-essentialist categories of class, ethnicity, peasant, Indian, state, and citizenship and focuses his analysis on the processes of identity formation, political organization, and engagement with the state. By examining these fluid relationships, Harvey (ibid.: 11) does not seek to 'identify the factors that facilitate or hinder popular mobilization', but to 'grasp the political significance of popular struggle' in the context of Mexico *and other authoritarian states*. Thus, while all three emphasize the historical specificity of their case studies, they also seek to make larger inferences about the process of political struggle under adverse conditions. Further consideration of each study will clarify this observation.

Womack's (1969: ix) study begins with the opening sentence, 'This is a book about country people who did not want to move and therefore got into revolution.' This sentence has a number of assumptions and conceptual categories built into it. It identifies the main group of the analysis as country people, a concept which is later qualified as *campesinos*, or people from the fields (ibid.: x).[2] It implies that some force beyond the power of these country people was changing the nature and possibly the organization of their community. It concludes that this change induced by the outside power resulted in the country people becoming involved in revolutionary activity. From this strong thesis statement, Womack tells an intriguing tale of the revolutionary activities of the common people of Morelos under the leadership of Emiliano Zapata in an effort to protect their land and way of life. The powerful outsiders are the emerging entrepreneurs under the pre-revolutionary period of Porfírio Díaz and then the various governing elites imposed by the revolutionary and post-revolutionary Mexican state. Womack's conclusion after detailing twenty years of complex revolutionary history is worth quoting at length:

> New attitudes, new policies, new laws, new agencies, new authorities – and of the plain country people of 1910, about three-fifths remained. They had won a victory too, simply in holding on as villagers, not in refuge in the state's cities or huddled into the haciendas but out where they felt they belonged, in the little towns and pueblos and ranchos, still reeking at least of 'pacific Zapatismo'. In 1910 the bases of the only life they wanted to live had been breaking down. Although they wore themselves out, dutifully tilling their scattered patches of corn and beans, now and then trading a horse, a cow, for a few pesos marketing eggs, tomatoes, onions, chiles, or charcoal, tending their scrubby orchards, desperately sharecropping on the planters' worst land, they had nevertheless lost the struggle to keep their communities going. In store for them then there had been only a long torment of grief and shame, to labor for a wage in steaming cane fields and rice paddies, to take orders from a boss, eventually to move into huts the boss's boss owned, to watch from a distance while old friends and neighbors and kinfolk moved away too, never to rest, and at the end to die in debt anyway. Now a decade later, two souls having disappeared for every three that stayed, they were still in their bases and back in the struggle. After all, the endurance in the pueblos counted more than the new government, the new champions, the new reforms. Those small communities burdened and threatened for centuries, had just survived the most vigorous, ruthless, and ingenious siege ever mounted against them, spoiling the best if not the last chance that usurpers would have to eradicate them.
>
> (Womack 1969: 370)

It is clear from this passage that Womack (1969) achieves much more than just telling a story. The conclusion is that country people, however defined, will resist change, whether induced through capitalist transformation of agriculture or the imposition of state-led reform projects, a conclusion which has strong resonance in the other studies of rebellion and revolution outlined in this chapter.

Nugent (1993) echoes this conclusion and perception of resistance by examining the dialectical history of community–state relations in Namiquipa. Like Womack (1969), Nugent is uneasy with the term 'peasant' and settles on *serranos*, which literally means 'hill people', who are more generally known as a type of free peasantry. He adopts a non-instrumental view of the state and a relational definition of ideology, which is seen to mediate between the *serrano* people and the state. Using these analytical categories, Nugent travels back and forth through history to unveil common themes in the political struggle for land, which is grounded in resistance to encroachment by 'outsiders'. These outsiders variously include the Apaches in the seventeenth century, the expansion of economic modernization in the nineteenth century, and the imposition of land reforms by the post-revolutionary Mexican state. Overall, his account focuses on questions of land, labour, identity, and revolutionary mobilization in which the key inference is that historically, similar struggles over similar types of grievance have been fought in this region, but the struggles do not follow some linear evolutionary path (ibid.:151). Rather, he concludes that the relationship among land, labour, and politics is embedded in Namiquipa ideology, which responds to the ever-changing challenges from without, but also represents a constant in history that the peasantry, however defined, 'refuse to go away' (ibid.: 165, emphasis in the original).

Finally, Harvey (1998) seeks to examine the Zapatista rebellion, which began officially in January 1994 in the southern state of Chiapas. As its name suggests, the Zapatista rebellion draws on the history of struggle in southern Mexico, but as Harvey contends, adds new dimensions to the older patterns observed. In tracing the history of violent political dissent from peasants, Harvey demonstrates that the Chiapas rebellion drew on the existence of new independent peasant organizations that had developed in the 1960s and 1970s, as well as a variety of networks at the national level. In addition to the demand for land reform in Chiapas, the protagonists of the rebellion demanded the full guarantee and protection of indigenous people's and women's rights, as well as democratization of the Mexican political system (ibid.: 199–200). This newest form of rebellion was brought about by a series of 'dislocations' in the region, including maldistribution of land, economic modernization (hydroelectric dam projects, oil exploration, logging, and ranching), shifts within the Catholic Church, education of bilingual teachers and catechists, post-1968 student activism, and the gradual liberalization of the Mexican political party system (ibid.: 228). For Harvey, the key outcome of the rebellion has been that the rights and culture of indigenous people have become an integral part of the process of democratization in Mexico.

Summary

As in the comparison of studies that examine the relationship between economic development and democracy, it is clear that there are important methodological trade-offs associated with the different types of comparison in this chapter. Table 5.6 summarizes the various studies outlined and compared in this chapter to demonstrate these trade-offs. The selection of studies is by no means exhaustive, but it shows how these different methods allow scholars variously to focus on different factors that help account for violent political activity and full-scale social revolution.

The quantitative comparison of many countries revealed common factors that account for variation in political violence that help guide the comparisons with few countries and the single-country studies. With the exception of the more specific relationship between inequality and political violence, for which there is still little agreement (see Lichbach 1989), the quantitative comparison of many countries revealed the importance of state strength and repression, past patterns of political violence, and the political composition of the current regime. Few-country studies draw on these insights and use macro-causal historical analysis to account for the incidence of rebellious activity and successful revolution, and demonstrate the ways in which key variables interact over time and limited space.

Finally, the three studies of Womack (1969), Nugent (1993), and Harvey (1998) modify the categories and concepts from these other comparative studies to fit the particular context of Mexico, but they continue to provide similar analytical leverage for making inferences that stretch beyond the confines of the Mexican case. They draw on other comparative studies to refine what is meant by the term

Table 5.6 Violent political dissent and revolution in comparative perspective

Method of comparison	*Number of countries*	*Exemplars*	*Result*
Many countries	Between 49 and 114 countries either at one point in time or in different aggregated periods	Gurr 1968; Hibbs 1973; Paige 1975; Sigelman and Simpson 1977; Muller and Seligson 1987	Political violence is variously due to past political violence, patterns of deprivation and inequality, the presence of cleavages and political separatism, degrees of repression, and structural features of the economy, while the functional form of the relationship remains opaque
Few countries (quantitative)	Between 3 and 12 countries, while the number of observations remains large	Paige 1975; Wickham-Crowley 1993†	The structure of the agricultural sector is a key determinant of the type of rural rebellion, while the main conditions for revolution include guerrilla organization and military strength, support for the guerrillas from other sectors of society, and an illegitimate dictatorial regime
Few countries (qualitative)	Between 2 and 6 countries	Wolf 1968; Scott 1976; Skocpol 1979	Key determinants of peasant rebellion are the economic and cultural nature of the peasant community, capitalist transformation of agriculture, and a strong central authority. The conditions for social revolution include peasant rebellion and an absolutist state facing external pressures
Single-country studies	Mexico	Womack 1969; Nugent 1993; Harvey 1998	Peasant rebellion and participation in revolutionary activity are due to their resistance to various historical encroachments on their land and community

Note: †Wickham-Crowley (1993) uses a variety of algebraic reductions to identify the key determinants of successful revolution in Latin America, a method that combines qualitative and quantitative techniques (see Chapter 10)

'peasant'. They are cognisant of the types of relationships between inequality and violence that emerge from the quantitative comparison of many countries, and implicitly test whether these types of relationships are at work in the single country. The focus on a single country allows them to examine in closer detail the interplay between structure and agency and how that interplay shapes the historical process of political struggle. They are concerned with the defensive reaction of a particular social group to the encroachment of various outside forces that seek to disrupt their particular way of life.

Notes

1 A comprehensive review of quantitative cross-national comparisons which examines the relationship between inequality and political conflict concludes that the lack of clear formal modelling and theoretical reflection has led to inclusive results, which are the product of the different operationalization of concepts and different specification of models (see Lichbach 1989).

2 Womack (1969: x) is uncomfortable with the term 'peasant' since it evokes a certain exotic quality he wishes to avoid.

Further reading

Gurr, T. R. (1970) *Why Men Rebel*, Princeton: Princeton University Press.

This is Gurr's full theoretical and comparative statement on the motivation for violent political conflict.

Sanders, D. (1981) *Patterns of Instability*, London: Macmillan.

A comprehensive review of quantitative cross-national studies of political violence.

Lichbach, M. (1989) 'An Evaluation of "Does Economic Inequality Breed Political Conflict" Studies', *World Politics*, 41: 431–470.

A comprehensive review of quantitative cross-national studies on economic inequality and political violence.

Skocpol, T. (1994) *Social Revolutions in the Modern World*, Cambridge: Cambridge University Press.

A collection of Skocpol's essays on social revolution and macro-causal historical comparison.

Chapter 6

Non-violent political dissent and social movements

In addition to periods of violent political dissent and social revolution, history is replete with examples of non-violent political dissent in the form of social movements. Ever since the emergence of the modern state (Tilly *et al.* 1975; Tilly 1978; Tarrow 1994), various forms of direct political action and political protest activities at the national level have challenged dominant political institutions in both the advanced industrial democracies and the lesser-developed countries. Movements led by workers, students, women, peace activists, gays and lesbians, environmentalists and greens, as well as those led by religious fundamentalists, extreme radical right adherents, and ethnic minorities increasingly bring new issues to the political agenda through protests, demonstrations, marches, petitions, and lobbying efforts. Comparative research sees these movements as different from those that espouse violent political dissent in terms of the groups they mobilize, the demands they make, and the goals they seek to achieve. Many of the insights from the literature on violent political dissent, however, continue to inform the study of social movements, including relative deprivation, economic transformation, state power and repression, and identity construction. As in the previous chapter, this chapter assesses key developments in the study of social movements by comparing many, few, and single-country studies in an effort to assess their methodological trade-offs.

The research problem

There are many research questions surrounding the topic of social movements. In general, scholars have sought to explain the emergence, strategies, shape, and success of social movements in different political contexts. Comparative research has focused on *why* social movements arise in the first place, *how* they seek to achieve their ends, and *what* they actually achieve. Studies that examine why social movements arise in the first place focus their attention on the various sources of collective grievance and common identity that lead to popular mobilization and protest. Studies that examine how social movements successfully attract members and followers to participate in their activities focus on the role of social movement organizations and the mobilization of important resources necessary for sustained collective action, such as money, communications, and membership. These studies also examine the different strategies that social movements employ, given the different political systems and political opportunities for mobilization that they confront. Finally, studies that compare the relative success or impact of social movements focus variously on specific movement goals, the legal and institutional levels of impact, and the degree to which values and political behaviour have been altered by prolonged periods of social movement activity.

The study of social movements is often divided between those that examine mobilization from labour and those that examine other social movements. This division is in part a theoretical one. The labour movement is seen as an 'old' movement that articulates demands more closely associated with industrial capitalism, while other social movements (women, gays, greens, and peace) are seen as 'new', since they articulate demands that have more to do with lifestyle choices made possible by post-industrial capitalism. Many have argued that this distinction is overdrawn, since mobilization from such groups as women and greens is nothing new (Fuentes and Frank 1989; Foweraker 1995), and since the focus on new groups tends to neglect those groups located on the right side of the traditional left–right political spectrum. More recently, comparative studies have included the labour movement alongside consideration of other social movements (see Foweraker and Landman 1997), or have included movements from all aspects of the left–right spectrum (see Gamson 1975; Kriesi *et al.* 1995). This chapter compares key examples from the literature and does not make the distinction between old and new movements, but seeks to reveal through the comparison of different studies the key factors that help account for the emergence, shape, and impact of social movements.

Comparing many countries

With the exception of studies that focus on the labour movement and in contrast to the two previous chapters, there are few studies that compare many countries in the field of social movement research. The studies included in this section are Powell's (1982) comparison of non-violent protest in twenty-nine democracies in the 1960s and 1970s; Haas and Stack's (1983) comparison of labour strikes in seventy-one countries; Gurr's (1993) comparison of protest and mobilization from 227 different communal groups in ninety different countries; and Inglehart's (1997) comparison of the proclivity of individuals to support or participate in social movement activity in twenty-one different countries. Together, these studies attempt to provide a parsimonious set of factors that account for either instances of social movement protest or the willingness of individuals to participate in protest activities.

In his comparison of twenty-nine democracies, Powell (1982) provides various indicators for democratic performance across a range of political dimensions, including voting, socio-economic performance, constitutions, party systems, citizen involvement, and democratic stability. His analysis of citizen involvement (Powell 1982: 129–132) includes indicators of 'peaceful protest' taken from the *World Handbook of Political and Social Indicators* (Taylor and Jodice 1983). The indicator measures instances of protest coded from newspaper accounts for two separate decades (1958–1967 and 1967–1976). The author defines peaceful protests as 'organized events in which substantial numbers of citizens participate in an endeavor to win the support of others or of the authorities for a political cause' (Powell 1982: 129). These protests are seen as different from riots since they are non-violent and require larger numbers of participants and greater amounts of organization. The nature of peaceful protests suggests that they will be more prevalent in the democratic countries with large populations and higher levels of economic development.

Across the democracies, Powell (ibid.: 131) finds that the likelihood of peaceful political protest is higher in countries with large populations, greater degrees of social heterogeneity, and higher levels of GNP per capita. More importantly, the analysis shows that democracies with multiparty systems tend to have lower levels of peaceful protest, while systems with strong support for extremist parties tend to have higher levels of peaceful protest. In short, the presence of political parties to absorb and channel the different interests of citizens and groups means that multiparty democracies tend to have lower levels of protest from social movements. This finding leads Powell (ibid.: 130) to make the larger inference that 'protest activity is very frequently an organized mass alternative to the electoral system, when the latter seems unresponsive or inaccessible'. From his sample of democracies, he concludes that protest in the United States is typical of a modernized country with a large population and few effective political parties to channel discontent (ibid.: 131).

For reasons of data availability, Haas and Stack (1983) limit their comparison to seventy-one countries with data on labour strike activity during the period 1976–1978. They are aware that the selection of countries may not constitute a representative sample, but they argue that the selection is still 'fairly large and seemingly representative of the market economies' (ibid.: 49). The selection, however, does cover the globe, including thirteen countries in Africa, sixteen in the Americas, fourteen in Asia, ten in Oceania, and seventeen in Europe. The dependent variable is the strike volume (i.e. the number of person-days lost per total working population) collected by the International Labour Organization (ILO) and is averaged in each country for the three years in order to reduce extreme fluctuation in the measure for some countries. The explanatory variables are similar to many of those used by Hibbs (1973) in his study of political violence (see Chapter 5). They include the level of economic development (per capita GNP), rate of economic growth, the rate of inflation, degree of unionization (union members as a proportion of the labour force), the degree of ethnic fragmentation, rural–urban migration, and the development of the mass media. In addition, the degree of political democracy is measured using Jackman's (1973, 1975) democratic performance index (see Chapter 4).

Initial correlation analysis across all the countries reveals a positive and significant association between the strike volume and the rate of inflation, the degree of unionization, and the development of mass media (Haas and Stack 1983: 53). Further analysis of the comparative data using regression reveals that there is an inverted-U relationship between the level of economic development and the strike volume, suggesting that the 'strike volume increases through low levels of development, peaks out, and then decreases at high levels of development' (ibid.: 54). This curvilinear relationship holds even after controlling for the rate of economic development, the rate of inflation, the degree of unionization, mass media development, ethnic fragmentation, and rural–urban migration. Finally, further analysis demonstrates that the level of political democracy has a negative effect on the strike volume. Overall, the results support a 'liberal' perspective that strike volumes tend to be high in the early stages of economic development, while they tend to taper off in the later stages, owing to a separation between the ownership and control of large firms and general weakening of unionization (ibid.: 44–45).

Following his earlier work on political violence, Gurr (1993: 161) has turned his attention to political protest from groups of individuals whom he labels 'minorities at risk', which comprise 'cultural and religious identity groups that do not have recognized states or institutionalized political status'. His comparison focuses on 227 groups politically salient or active between 1945 and 1989, meeting two defining criteria. First, the group must collectively suffer or benefit from systematic discriminatory treatment. Second, the group is the focus of political mobilization in defence or promotion of its 'self-defined interests' (ibid.: 163). His sample of groups thus includes those that are subordinate plus those that are dominant yet who remain in the minority. Subordinate groups mobilize to attain new advantages and benefits, while dominant groups mobilize to maintain advantages and benefits.

Overall, these groups include ethnic minorities, ethnic nationalists, indigenous groups, inter-communal contenders, and militant sects. Like his work on violent political dissent, Gurr (1993: 166–167) operationalizes notions of relative deprivation and group mobilization in order to uncover the key factors that account for both violent and non-violent political dissent from communal groups. Relative deprivation captures the motivation of political protest as a perceived gap between expected and actual achievement (see Chapter 5 and Gurr 1968, 1970, and 1993: 167). Mobilization, on the other hand, examines the ways in which groups marshal resources in order to sustain collective action (see Gurr 1993: 167; Lichbach 1995; Foweraker 1995). This section will focus on these two perspectives and their relationship with non-violent aspects of communal group protest activity.

The two key dependent variables relevant for the present discussion are Gurr's (1993: 170) measure of 'group protest in the 1980s' and 'mobilization for protest in the 1970s'. High values on both variables denote more protest participation and more organization for protest. As with the findings for violent political dissent outlined in the previous chapter, Gurr's (1993: 179) preliminary analysis of the comparative data suggests that the level of protest is highest for communal groups that face certain economic disadvantages, including scarcity of land, high birth rates, and poor levels of health. In addition, certain political and cultural factors appear to be important determinants of non-violent political protest, including the historical loss of group autonomy and strong group identity (ibid.: 179). The analysis demonstrates that the correlates of political mobilization include: grievances expressed in terms of economic, social, and political demands; the loss of autonomy; group size; and group dispersion (ibid.: 180). His complete models estimate the group and systemic determinants of non-violent political protest, which include the demand for political rights, the demand for political autonomy, previous levels of mobilization, non-democratic forms of rule, and the scope of state power (ibid.: 186).

In contrast to his earlier work on civil strife (see Gurr 1968 and Chapter 5), this study reduces the problem of ecological fallacy since it uses communal groups themselves as the units of analysis. Some problems of aggregation remain for the relative deprivation perspective, but the examination of groups works well for the mobilization perspective. Moreover, his analysis is able to determine in some degree what leads to mobilization in the first place, such as political and economic disadvantages that various groups face, particularly discrimination and poverty, which are in turn associated with group demands for the extension and protection of political rights (Gurr 1993). By including political variables, Gurr (1993: 189) is able to make the more general statement that 'in long-established democracies the utility of non-violent communal activism is high, whereas the process of democratization provides opportunities that spur the mobilization of communal groups for . . . protest'.

The final comparison of many countries examines individual-level data collected for forty-three societies. In *Modernization and Postmodernization* Inglehart (1997) uses data from his larger collection entitled the *World Values Survey* to examine, among other things, the cross-cultural proclivity for individuals to support or join protest movements. While he has data from a total of forty-three countries, he only has data for both his time points (1981 and 1990) for twenty-one countries on four questions that probe non-conventional political activity. His countries are drawn from Europe, North America, Asia, and Southern Africa. His questions include whether the respondent had ever considered or actually joined a boycott, demonstration, unofficial strike, or building occupation (Inglehart 1997: 308–315; Appendix 3, 384–385).

Inglehart's (1997) comparison reveals a monotonic increase in all four forms of unconventional political activity. The percentage of respondents declaring that they had considered or had actually joined a boycott rose in fifteen of the twenty-one countries. The figures for demonstration rose in sixteen countries, for unofficial strikes in fourteen countries, and for building occupations for seventeen countries (ibid.: 313–314). This general increase in the individual proclivity to take part in unconventional political activity is seen to be in large part due to a pattern of economic modernization that has changed the underlying value structure of successive cohorts of individuals. The largest percentages for all four questions appear in the most advanced industrial democracies of the sample, lending support to Inglehart's (1990, 1997) more general theory of the rise of 'post-materialism' in the world (see Briefing Box 6.1). In general, conventional forms of political activity such as voting and party activity have seen a decline in the most advanced countries, while less conventional political activity captured in part by his four questions has seen an increase.

Taken together, these comparisons of many countries represent various attempts to uncover the determinants of non-violent political dissent and social movement activity. The studies used different samples of countries, including democracies (Powell 1982), a selection of democracies and non-democracies (Inglehart 1997), and two global samples (Haas and Stack 1983; Gurr 1993). The studies also used different units of analysis, including nation states (Powell 1982; Haas and Stack 1983), communal groups (Gurr 1993), and individuals (Inglehart 1997). Despite these choices of countries and units of analysis, the studies reveal common determinants of non-violent political dissent. Powell (1982) Haas and Stack (1983), Inglehart (1997), and by implication, Gurr (1993) all demonstrate that economic change accounts for some variation in protest activity, whether in the form of growth, level of development, or structural imbalances in the economy. Powell (1982), Haas and Stack (1983), and Gurr (1993) all show that social heterogeneity in the form of ethnic fragmentation or communal group mobilization are important factors that account for political protest. Haas and Stack (1982) and Gurr (1993) demonstrate that group organization is important for non-violent political protest. The key difference in these studies lies in their results for the effects of democratic forms of rule on political protest. For Haas and Stack (1983), democracy tends to inhibit labour strike volume, whereas for Gurr (1993), it tends to provide the necessary political opportunity for communal group mobilization. These and other differences surrounding the labour movement and other social

Briefing box 6.1 Ronald Inglehart and post-materialism

Drawing on years of research based on mass surveys carried out first in advanced industrial democracies and then moving to countries from all regions of the world, Ronald Inglehart (1977, 1990, 1997, 1998), has consistently argued that there is a relationship between individual values and the level of economic development in a country. Inglehart has argued that as countries develop, there will be an overall shift in the value orientations of individuals and that these will be less concerned with the provision of immediate goods and resources (jobs, money, cars, mass consumption) and more concerned with lifestyle issues (clean environment, social justice, peace, and human rights). The former set of values he calls 'materialist' and the latter set of values he calls 'post-materialist'. Using a battery of questions to probe the value orientations of mass publics, he has been able to derive a scale that measures the degree to which individuals exhibit these 'post-material' values and, most recently (Inglehart 1997), use the scale across a selection of forty-three different countries (see Table 6.1). To derive the scale, individuals are ranked according to the priority they assign to each indicator.

Table 6.1 The materialist/post-materialist scale

Materialist indicators	*Post-materialist indicators*
Maintain law and order	More say on the job
Fight against crime	Less impersonal society
Economic growth	Ideas count
Stable economy	More say in government
Strong defence	Freedom of speech
Fight rising prices	More beautiful cities

Source: Adapted from Inglehart (1998: 65)

Theoretically, post-materialism can be seen as either a dependent variable or an independent variable. As a dependent variable, post-materialism is seen to be a symptom of economic modernization. For example, all modern and developed countries ought to exhibit a high percentage of individuals that adhere more closely to the core set of post-materialist values. As an independent variable, it is used to explain differences in the individual proclivity to carry out different forms of political action. For example, so-called post-materialists ought to be more likely to support the political activities of those social movements that issue demands for peace, equality, justice, and the protection of the environment than for those movements that make demands concerning job security and law and order.

movements form much of the basis of the comparative work on social movements in few countries to which the discussion now turns.

Comparing few countries

Controlled comparison of few countries yields important insights into the origins, shape, and impact of social movements since it allows a more detailed look at the dynamics of social mobilization and the features of the political contexts in which social movements seek to bring about change. This section considers five such studies: Kitschelt's (1986) comparison of anti-nuclear movements in France, Sweden, the United States and West Germany; Dalton's (1988) comparison of individual-level protest data in the US, Britain, West Germany, and France; Kriesi *et al.*'s (1995) comparison of social movement dynamics in The Netherlands, Germany, France, and Switzerland; Foweraker and Landman's (1997) examination of citizenship rights and social movements in Brazil, Chile, Mexico, and Spain; and Bashevkin's (1998) comparison of the women's movement in Britain, the United States, and Canada.

Kitschelt (1986) argues that the anti-nuclear movement is suitable for comparison since it appeared in Europe and North America at roughly the same time, yet it experienced different fortunes in the four cases of his study (France, Sweden, the United States, and West Germany). He points out that single case studies of the movement provide a 'wealth of descriptive detail, [but] individually they are not suited to the task of arriving at a generalized understanding of the factors that determine the dynamics of social movements' (ibid.: 57). Thus, his comparison of these four cases is meant to make larger inferences about the factors that shape the dynamics and impact of social movements. His key explanatory factor is the political opportunity structure, which is a configuration of resources, institutional arrangements, and historical precedents for social mobilization, where the difference in this structure across the cases either facilitates or constrains the development of protest movements (ibid.: 58). He argues that adopting this comparative framework can 'explain a good deal about the variations among social movements with *similar demands in different settings if other determinants are held constant* (ibid.: 58, emphasis mine).

Kitschelt (ibid.: 60–61) carefully lays out his selection criteria and explains why his comparison is well suited to discovering the effects of institutional constraints on social mobilization. The four movements made similar demands for the end of nuclear power in terms of existing power stations, ongoing plant construction, and new projects. All four movements emerged from the local level to the national level at about the same time (1973–1974). All four movements shared the same 'subjective sense of deprivation and grievance' in terms of the social bases of the activists, which comprised three groups: professionals and public sector employees; affected farmers and property owners; and students and young radicals (ibid.: 61). Moreover, the governments in all four countries were similarly committed to developing the nuclear power industry.

The concept of the political opportunity structure is operationalized using a simple set of dichotomous categories that define a country's political input structures and its output structures. Input structures represent the relative openness and responsiveness of a country's institutions to groups making demands and are seen to be either 'open' or 'closed'. Output structures, on the other hand, represent the capacity of a country's institutions to satisfy group demands and redress their grievances through an appropriate policy response, and are seen to be either 'strong' or 'weak'. The combination of these two dimensions produces a 2 x 2 matrix, where the four cases of this study fit into each of the resulting boxes (see Figure 6.1). This fourfold *classification* (see Chapter 2) of countries is then used to explain both the strategies and impacts of the anti-nuclear movement.

In terms of social movement strategies, Kitschelt (ibid.: 67–72) finds that movements in more open and responsive political opportunity structures (Sweden and the United States), adopted more 'assimilative' strategies, such as lobbying, petitioning, and political party activity. In contrast, movements operating in closed and less responsive political opportunity structures (France and West Germany) adopted more confrontational strategies, including public demonstrations and acts of civil disobedience. In terms of impact, movements achieved more procedural gains in the open and responsive political opportunity structures of Sweden and the United States, where greater access to formal decision-making had been made (ibid.: 74). Substantive movement impact such as the decommissioning of existing nuclear power plants, the slowing down of construction, and the cessation of funding for new plants, was much higher in the open and responsive political opportunity structures (ibid.: 77–82). The strength of green parties, which represent a structural impact of movements, is much higher in the least responsive political opportunity structures. In short, movement strategies, the degree to which they achieved their aims, and the legacies they leave behind are in large part determined by the types of political contexts in which they mobilize.

In *Citizen Politics in Western Democracies* Dalton (1988) compares individual-level data on social movement activity in the United States, Britain, West Germany, and France. The data are from a series of surveys that establish a scale of social movement activity ranging from the least confrontational and orthodox to the most confrontational and unorthodox (ibid.: 63–64). Using regression techniques, Dalton compares the effects of six important explanatory variables on the scale of social movement activity and finds consistent patterns across all four countries. For these

		Political input structures	
		Open	Closed
Political output structures	Strong	Sweden	France
	Weak	United States	West Germamy

Figure 6.1 Political opportunity structure
Source: Kitschelt (1986: 64)

countries, well-educated young men with strong political party identification, a personal sense of political efficacy, and overall dissatisfaction with government policies tend to engage in more confrontational social movement activity, including demonstrations, boycotts, and unofficial strikes (ibid.: 69–70). The patterns in these four democracies led Dalton to conclude that political protest is less likely among deprived and alienated individuals than among those that possess political and social resources.

Kriesi *et al.* (1995) use protest event data in their comparative analysis of four countries in Western Europe in order to examine the origins, nature, and to a limited degree the impact of the 'new' social movements in the context of larger patterns of mobilization from other social groups. They thus focus on the women's, student, peace, green, and gay movements in The Netherlands, Germany, France, and Switzerland, while comparing protest from right-wing groups. The protest event data are coded from a reading of the Monday issues of major newspapers in the four countries. This selection of events is not random, but the authors argue that it is representative and the most likely way to capture the majority of protest events while not requiring the vast time and resources to code everyday news coverage (Kriesi *et al.* 1995: Appendix). Their analysis concentrates on the political opportunity structure these movements face in order to explain the observed differences across the four cases in their level of protest, magnitude of events, and types of strategies they employ.

The four key contextual factors important for explaining new social movement activity include the degree to which traditional cleavages have become pacified (see Briefing Box 6.2), formal institutional structures, the left–right configuration of power, and the different policy areas addressed by movements. In an almost zero-sum fashion, new social movements appear to have more space to be politically active in those countries where traditional cleavages have been pacified such as Germany and The Netherlands (Kriesi *et al.* 1995: 25). Like Kitschelt (1986), the authors find a direct relationship between social movement activity and the institutional strength and responsiveness of the state in each country. On the one hand, countries with weak and inclusive states (such as Switzerland) exhibit high aggregate levels of social mobilization which are characterized by more conventional forms of political action. On the other hand, countries with a strong exclusive state (such as France) tend to have lower levels of social mobilization that is concentrated into more confrontational forms of action (Kriesi *et al.* 1995: 51–52). In countries where the 'old left' (i.e. socialist and labour-based parties) has been pacified, new social movements strengthen the new left within and outside established political parties (ibid.: 81). The different policy orientations of the various new social movements determine in part the type of response they receive from government. Movements that challenge high-profile policy issues (e.g. national defence, energy, immigration, and nuclear weapons) confront a more closed system while those that challenge low-profile policy issues (e.g. transportation, environment, and international solidarity) face a more open system (ibid.: 105–110).

Finally, their comparison of the dynamics of protest waves across the four countries reveals the importance of several factors for comparative social movement research. Descriptively, Germany and The Netherlands experienced

Briefing box 6.2 Traditional societal cleavages

In examining the origins of group interests and the formation of political parties, Lipset and Rokkan (1967: 1–64) identified four possible characteristics of countries which become key areas of difference in the process of economic modernization and nation state formation. These differences are labelled 'cleavages', since they can divide societies over national policy priorities. These cleavages include centre–periphery, state–church, land–industry, and worker–owner.

The centre–periphery cleavage developed in Europe during the sixteenth and seventeenth centuries and involves questions of national versus supranational religion (e.g. Church of England vs. Catholic Church), and national languages versus Latin. The state–church cleavage involves questions of secular versus religious authority over social policy such as mass education, marriage laws, baptism, abortion, etc. The land–industry cleavage involves questions of the proper economic balance between the agricultural sector and the industrial sector with the regard to taxes, quotas, and tariffs. Finally, the owner–worker cleavage involves questions of labour exploitation and control over the means of production. After the Russian Revolution, it also involved questions of national versus supranational levels of worker identification and whether workers were committed to the international revolutionary movement (ibid.: 47).

While these four cleavages were born of historical developments that span from the sixteenth to the early twentieth century, they have a tremendous impact on the formation of political parties and their presence is still felt in the contemporary period. Religiously based political parties claim differences over the centre–periphery cleavage as well as the state–church cleavage. Liberal and conservative political parties claim differences over the state–church cleavage. Communist, socialist, and labour parties claim that more should be done for the plight of the worker under the throes of industrial capitalism and in certain countries, post-industrial capitalism. Over time, it is argued, these traditional cleavages become less stark and more pacified so that new issues begin to create new cleavages. Thus, Kriesi *et al.*'s (1995: 81) comparison of social movements in Western Europe shows that pacification of the owner–worker cleavage across the four countries has a direct impact on the degree to which social movements have supported the development of the new left. Indeed, the rise of post-materialism and the 'new' social movements (see Briefing Box 6.1), is seen as the creation of a new cleavage in some countries.

well-developed protest waves which lasted more than half a decade and which exhibited large increases in the number and magnitude of protest events, increased involvement of social movement organizations, and the extension of protest nationally (Kriesi *et al.* 1995: 116). In terms of protest activities, the waves in Germany and The Netherlands saw early periods with less violent protest give way to more violent tactics towards the end of the period (see discussion of Tarrow below). The role of organizations is also similar across the countries. Initial phases of protest are not led or accompanied by formal, professional social movement organizations owing to their difficulty in mobilizing quickly and their reluctance to get involved in activities that may not achieve desirable outcomes. Finally, a wave of protest ends with an increased level of institutionalization of movement organizations and patterns of political reform (ibid.: 136–137).

In shifting the focus away from the confines of welfare capitalist countries, Foweraker and Landman (1997, 1999) compare the mutual relationship between citizenship rights and social movements in Brazil, Chile, Mexico, and Spain. Their analysis traces the political origins and impact of social movement activity in terms of the protection of individual rights of citizenship. In order to raise the number of observations, the cases are compared over periods of political liberalization and democratic transition, comprising the period from 1964–1990 in Brazil, 1973–1990 in Chile, 1963–1990 in Mexico, and 1958–1983 in Spain (N = 99). The authors argue that all four countries are 'instances of authoritarian regimes that have experienced a fluctuation in the guarantee of citizenship rights' and which 'exhibit a rise and fall of social mobilization over time' (Foweraker and Landman 1997: 49), placing them in the 'mirror-image' of the most similar systems design (see Faure 1994 and Chapter 2 in this volume).

Like the quantitative comparative work on economic development and democracy (see Chapter 4 in this volume), the authors use various measures of political and civil rights protection to illustrate the contours of citizenship rights in the four cases. Rights 'in principle' are coded from a reading of the regimes' constitutions, decree laws, and institutional acts (Foweraker and Landman 1997: 51–52). Rights 'in practice' are measured by combining a series of published abstract scales on rights protection (ibid.: 52–62). Both these rights measures are then used to derive a third measure that represents the difference between principle and practice (ibid.: 62–65). Social movement protest events from labour are gathered from the International Labour Organization, and events data from other social movements are coded using primary and secondary sources on activity from grass-roots groups, self-help groups, women's and peasant organizations, among others. Both measures of social mobilization are used to demonstrate the contours of social movement activity in the four cases. Both the rights and movements measures are then used to examine the direct relationship between rights and movements while controlling for underlying economic factors, including the growth rate, level of development, and inflation (ibid.: 172).

The initial comparisons reveal that the four cases show large fluctuations over time in their protection of the political and civil rights of citizenship, a general pattern that demonstrates their collective move away from authoritarianism towards democracy. These general similarities are contrasted to the differences in the nature of their democratic transition. Chile and Spain have 'rapid' transitions to democratic rule, and Brazil and Mexico experience 'protracted and incomplete' transitions (ibid.: xxiv). Moreover, the comparison shows the different ways in which the regimes in these countries protected rights in principle and rights in practice. The authors see this difference between principle and practice as critical to an understanding of the origins and impact of social movement activity (ibid.: 117–118), as well as a reflection of one aspect of the political opportunity structure (Foweraker and Landman 1999).

Using the protest event data, the authors show that similar waves of mobilization from labour and other social movements appeared in the four countries. Each wave has a distinct beginning, peak, and end where mobilization from the labour movement tends to precede mobilization from other social movements. This temporal primacy of labour mobilization suggests that it is the working class which leads a more general wave of mobilization under authoritarian conditions and is then complemented by mobilization from other social movements (Foweraker and Landman 1997: 133–138). In all cases, the pattern of demands issued by social movements suggests that as a wave of mobilization builds, demands shift from material and economic concerns to the protection of basic political and civil rights (ibid.: 143–150).

Having described the contours of both citizenship rights and social movements, the comparison of the four cases uses correlation, regression, and a form of Boolean analysis to examine the ways in which rights and movements are related. The authors posit unidirectional and mutually constitutive relationships between rights and movements (see Briefing Box 6.3). The correlations are strongest between labour mobilization and rights protection, suggesting either that increased rights protection motivates movements or that movements achieve the extension of rights. The regression analysis confirms that there is indeed a strong, mutually constitutive relationship between rights protection and social mobilization in Brazil, a mutually conditioning but partial relationship in Chile, a relatively weak relationship in Mexico, and a highly concentrated relationship in Spain. In addition, the Boolean techniques show how the relationships differ across shorter moments within the overall time periods that are compared. Taken together, these various relationships suggest that the process of democratic transformation in these cases is characterized by the 'halting and contradictory' struggle for rights by social movements (ibid.: 232).

The final study in this section compares the fortunes of the women's movement in three countries with conservative governments: the Reagan and Bush administrations in the United States (1981–1992); the Mulroney premiership in Canada (1984–1993); and the Thatcher and Major years in Britain (1979–1997). Silvia Bashevkin (1998: 3) begins *Women on the Defensive* with the following three important questions for comparative social movement research:

> Whatever happened to the vibrant social movements of the 1960s and 1970s? Were they swallowed up in the greedy good times of the 1980s? Did the lean, mean 1990s spell final disaster, as more and more people adopted a 'me first' approach to life?

Her comparison of the same movement under similar governmental conditions seeks to answer these questions by focusing on the 'valley' of the women's movement after its 'peak' of the 1970s marked by the 1975 UN International Year of the Woman. In all three countries, the women's movement entered a period of retrenchment while their respective governments pursued social policies based on an extreme form of neo-liberal individualism, which paradoxically sought to limit women's freedom of choice with respect to their reproductive and other rights. The scope of her comparison includes an assessment of gains and losses before, during,

Briefing box 6.3 Citizenship rights and social movements

Studies in history, sociology, and political economy variously specify the relationship between citizenship rights and social movements from three different perspectives: (1) the rights perspective, (2) the movement perspective, and the (3) dual perspective. The rights perspective suggests that the language of individual rights acts as a banner for social movements and as a common currency of social protest whereby individual rights elicit social movements. The movement perspective suggests that social struggles by poor, downtrodden, and excluded groups achieve the extension of individual rights in an incremental fashion over long periods of time whereby social movements disseminate a knowledge of rights as well as secure them for themselves. As its name suggests, the dual perspective argues that rights and movements actually encourage each other, acting as mutual catalysts. These three perspectives are pictured in Figure 6.2 and the comparative data analysis carried out by Foweraker and Landman (1997) on the cases of Brazil, Chile, Mexico, and Spain demonstrates empirical support for the dual perspective.

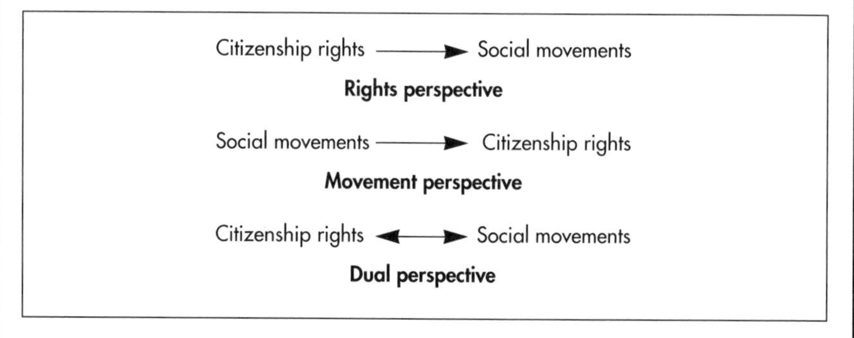

Figure 6.2 Three perspectives on the relationships between citizenship rights and social movements

Source: Adapted from Foweraker and Landman (1997: 226–231)

and after these periods of conservative rule through an examination of the legislative-juridical record and over one hundred interviews with women activists. The study thus stands as an example of a most similar systems design that seeks to examine the particular case of the women's movement, while making larger inferences about social movement success in general.

The comparative assessment of legislative and juridical decisions concerning issues raised by the women's movement (see Figure 6.3) demonstrates that in Britain and the United States it suffered setbacks in formal terms, where the percentage of positive decisions declined for the periods of conservative governance. Only the Canadian movement saw gains during the Mulroney years, where the percentage of positive decisions increased dramatically. Of the three countries, the movement in the United States suffered the most setbacks,

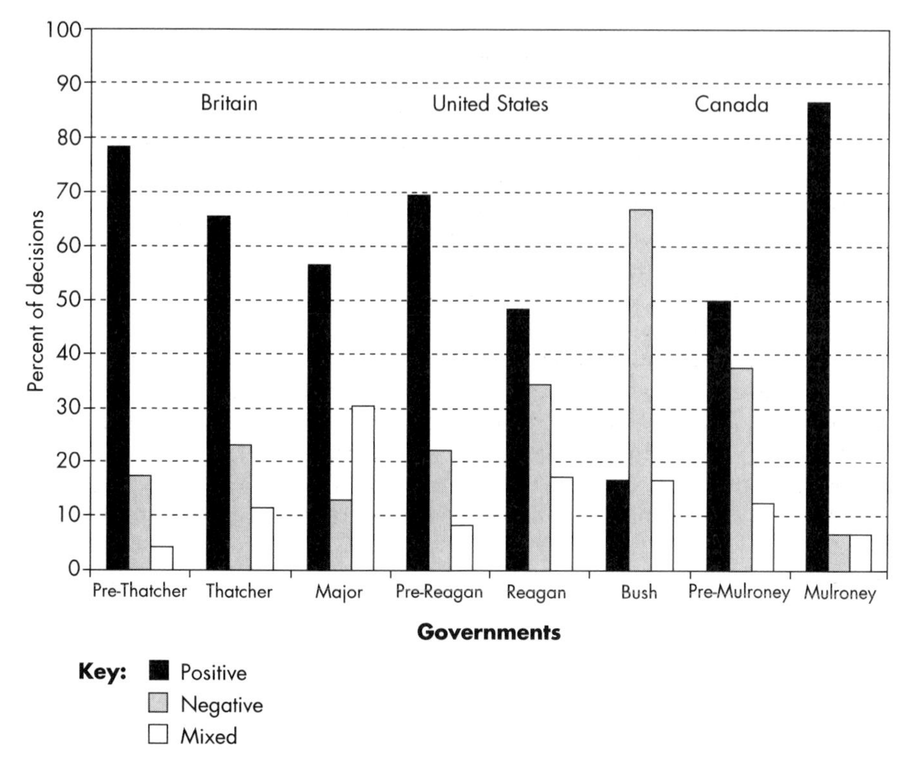

Figure 6.3 A comparison of women's legislation and juridical decisions in Britain, the US, and Canada
Source: Adapted from Bashevkin (1998: 249–256)

particularly during the Bush years where the percentage of negative decisions was higher than the percentage of positive decisions. Bashevkin (1998: 47) explains these cross-national differences in part by the presence of the European Court of Justice in the case of Britain, and the passage of the Charter of Rights and Freedoms in the case of Canada, both of which limited conservative politicians' ability to roll back pro-feminist legislation.

The qualitative comparison of activist women's discourse concerning the challenges they faced during conservative rule equally reveals the variety of experiences across these three political contexts. Activists in all three countries describe the difficulties they faced and the more defensive stance their various campaigns had to take while confronting the new conservative agenda. The movements in all three cases faced a concerted effort to divide them politically by exploiting lines of cleavage in the movements (Bashevkin 1998: 165–166). Despite these similarities, activists in Britain framed their struggle in light of the dominant role of Margaret Thatcher as the leader of the Conservative party and as an ex-prime minister with continued influence in the Major government (ibid.: 161). In the United States, activists dealt with more decentralized political institutions that spanned the executive, legislative, and judicial branches of the federal government, as well as the organs of the state governments. They also benefited from a more highly developed set of interest groups, which led them to pursue pragmatic strategies involving coalitions, lobbying efforts, and non-confrontational campaigns (ibid.: 163). Finally, in Canada, activists were cognisant of a 'spillover of social and economic conservatism from the United States', while they saw that their overall 'progress during the Mulroney years was more in spite than because of the government' (ibid.: 163–164).

In contrast to the comparisons of many countries, the studies outlined here show that the number of observations can remain quite high while the analysis includes more complexity about the various aspects of social mobilization. Kitschelt's (1986) comparison illustrates how similar movements pursue different strategies and achieve different types of impact precisely because they faced a different set of political opportunities. Not only does his study refine the notion of the 'political opportunity structure', but his analysis invites extension to other political contexts and other social movements (see Tarrow 1994; McAdam *et al.* 1996). Kriesi *et al.* (1995) confirm Kitschelt's (1986) finding concerning the importance of the political opportunity structure for movement dynamics. Foweraker and Landman (1997) operationalize the theoretical and analytical concepts necessary to examine the connections made between citizenship rights and social movements in contemporary authoritarian contexts. Finally, Bashevkin (1998) has advanced an important method for measuring social movement success and examined it by comparing similar movements confronting similar regimes while accounting for the remaining differences she observes.

Single-country studies

The three single-country studies in this section represent important examples of work that has advanced the comparative study of social movements by providing particularly useful analytical concepts and ways of measuring them despite only focusing on one country. Gamson's (1975) *The Strategy of Social Protest* compares fifty-three challenging groups in the United States to examine the strategy and success of social movements between 1800 and 1945. In *Democracy and Disorder*, Tarrow (1989) examines protest events from a variety of social movements to gauge their effects on Italian democracy between 1965 and 1975. Anne Costain's (1992) *Inviting Women's Rebellion* provides a comprehensive study of the women's movement in the United States that examines the relationship between protest events, legislation introduced and passed in the Congress, and patterns of public opinion. A comparison of these studies illustrates clearly their various contributions to the study social movements.

Between 1800 and 1945, Gamson (1975: 19) identifies between 500 and 600 different 'challenging groups' (or social movement organizations) in the United States, of which he argues his sample of fifty-three is representative. His analysis 'explores the strategies they used and the organizational characteristics that influenced the success of their challenges' (ibid.: ix). A challenging group is a formal organization that is the 'carrier of a challenge to the political system' and that has the capacity to carry actions necessary for realizing the challenge: 'holding meetings, planning events, issuing statements, calling demonstrations, and raising money' (ibid.: 14). His random sample includes ten socialist groups (19%), six right-wing groups (11%), seventeen reform groups (32%), and twenty occupational groups (38%). These various groups were most active in the 1830s, 1860s, 1880s, 1900, and 1930s, which suggests a certain recurring and cyclical nature to their mobilization (ibid.: 21).

His notion of group success includes two dimensions. The first dimension concerns the degree to which the group gained acceptance by its main antagonists, which means that the group has experienced a change from 'hostility or indifference to a more positive relationship' (ibid.: 31), and it is coded as 'full' or 'none' (ibid.: 28–29). The second dimension concerns the degree to which the group achieved new advantages for its members, which he divides into the categories 'many' and 'none' (ibid.: 29). The combination of these two dimensions produces a fourfold set of outcomes including full response, pre-emption, co-optation, and collapse. Figure 6.4 shows this fourfold classification and the number of groups that fall into each of the categories.

The figure shows that the largest portions of his sample either collapsed or achieved full response, 42 per cent and 38 per cent respectively. The remainder of the study seeks to explain these differences by examining the various group characteristics, strategies, and important historical factors.

Through a series of simple bivariate comparisons, Gamson identifies the key factors that account for high levels of success. In terms of group characteristics, large, bureaucratic, centralized groups with very little internal factionalism and high levels of outside sponsorship are more successful in achieving their aims. In terms of strategy, single-issue groups that do not seek to displace their antagonists and that offer selective incentives to their members are more successful. In addition, these same groups are more successful if they are willing to use violence and are able to avoid arrest by the authorities. Finally, in light of the time period for

New advantages		**Acceptance**	
		Full	None
	Many	Full Response 20 (38%)	Pre-emption 6 (11%)
	None	Co-optation 5 (9%)	Collapse 22 (42%)

Figure 6.4 Outcomes of fifty-three 'challenging groups' in the US, 1800–1945
Source: Adapted from Gamson (1975: figs 3.1 and 3.2)

his sample of groups, those that made challenges before the outbreak of the two World Wars and the Great Depression were more successful than were those that made challenges during these periods of international and national crisis.

These findings challenge much of the popular wisdom on social movements in the United States as well as other advanced societies in many important ways. First, they suggest that social movements are not an irrational response to an underlying failure of the political system, but organized, bureaucratic, and rational instances of group challenge. Second, collective action is most effective when groups offer 'selective incentives' to their members (see Briefing Box 6.4). Third, the use of violence and the level of repression have a direct bearing on movement outcomes. In addition to these three developments, his findings have provided a fruitful number of paths of scholarly inquiry for subsequent studies of social

Briefing box 6.4 Mancur Olson and selective incentives

In *The Logic of Collective Action*, Mancur Olson (1965) develops a theory that raises a paradox concerning the propensity of individuals to join groups. First, he assumed that individual political behaviour is similar to individual economic behaviour, where it is rational for people to weigh the costs and benefits of choosing to follow some course of action. Second, he assumed that groups that mobilize around some common interest are providing a collective good, or a good that extends beyond the members of the group, such as environmental protection. Third, Olson argues that the provision of the collective good is not enough to make people join groups, since an individual does not have to join the group in order enjoy the benefits of its actions. Such an individual is known as a 'free rider', since he or she can enjoy the benefits of the group without enduring the cost of taking part in its activities. Fourth, if it is rational for individuals to be free riders, then Olson argues groups must provide certain goods only for those who participate. These goods are known as 'selective incentives' (ibid.: 51). Selective incentives can either be punishment for not participating or reward for participating. These are known respectively as negative and positive selective incentives (ibid.: 51). Only by offering such incentives can a group begin to mobilize supporters.

The idea of selective incentives is important for the study of social movements since it is not at all obvious that grievance alone is enough to bring people to action (see Foweraker 1995: 15–16). Involvement in social movement activity is costly in terms of time, money, and other resources. In extreme cases, social movement activity can turn violent and thus threaten the physical well-being of movement participants. Formal social movement organizations such as environmental groups, or labour unions, women's groups, gay liberation groups, etc. must in some way provide a set of selective incentives in order to mobilize supporters. These incentives can come in many different forms, such as monthly newsletters, discounts on health or car insurance, reduced interest rates on credit cards, or more simple ephemera like bumper stickers, mugs, and shirts that send a signal to outsiders that members of the organization are in some way special.

movements in different time periods and in other countries. For example, the study of social movement organizations has continued to be important (see Zald and Ash 1966; Dalton 1994; Kriesi 1996) and there is a line of new comparative inquiry into the policing of social movement protest activity (see Della Porta 1996; Della Porta and Reiter 1998).

Sidney Tarrow (1989) examines how the boundaries of mass politics have been extended using the case of protest in Italy during the turbulent decade 1965–1975. During this period the country saw a wave of protest that started with organized strikes and university protests and spread to workers and high school students, doctors and patients, railroad men and commuters, bishops and priests, and rival regions and cities (ibid.: 5). His choice of Italy is defended on several grounds. First, its wave of protest started earlier, lasted longer, and affected its society more than other patterns in Western Europe. Second, the Italian case has long been ignored by other work on social movements and serves as a *least likely* case study (see Chapter 2 in this volume) since Italy, of all the systems in Europe, still managed to survive the disorders of this decade of mass protest (ibid.: 5–6). Third, according to Tarrow (ibid.: 7), the Italian case demonstrates that not only was it capable of surviving the crisis, but it emerged as a 'mature capitalist democracy'. Drawing heavily on previous work on social movements such as Gamson (1975), Tarrow (1989: 7–8) focuses on forms of action, their evolution over time, the structure of their demands, and their interaction with antagonists in an attempt to understand the magnitude and dynamics of change in politics and society. Like Gamson and others, he sees collective protest as an 'outcome of a calculus of risk, cost, and incentive' (ibid.: 8).

One of the key contributions of this study for other comparative work on social movements is the notion of a 'cycle of protest' (see discussion of Kreisi *et al.* 1995 above), which has the following identifiable features and trajectory:

> a cycle of protest begins with conventional patterns of conflict within existing organizations and institutions. As it gathers strength, new actors use expressive and confrontational forms of action, demonstrating to others less daring than themselves that the system is vulnerable to disruption and that they have grievances in common. This expands the range of contention to new sectors and institutions, but without the confrontation or the excitement of the 'early risers'. Confrontation gives way to deliberate violence only towards the end of the cycle, as mobilization declines, repression increases, people defect to interest groups and institutions, and extremists are left to compete for support from a shrinking social base.
>
> (Tarrow 1989: 8)

He combines this notion of the cycle of protest with that of the political opportunity structure (see Kitschelt 1986) to account for the patterns of protest and decline that he observes in the Italian case.

Drawing on earlier studies of political violence and the comparison of social movement activity in many countries, the study uses the protest event as the unit of analysis. Like Tilly (1978) and Kriesi *et al.* (1995), the study gathers protest data using a detailed event-coding protocol that includes the type of event, its main actors, its target and direction, the type of organizations involved in the event, the direct outcomes of the event, and the various responses of government (Tarrow 1989: 349–356). These data are collected primarily from newspaper coverage of events (*Corriere della Sera*) and corroborated with other primary and secondary materials (movement documents, statistical records, and interviews) – a process which yields nearly 5,000 protest events for the Italian case (ibid.: 30–31; 360). The time-series analysis of the data is complemented with a qualitative focus on archetypal social movement organizations from the student, worker, and religious movements. Overall, the quantitative and qualitative evidence is used to provide descriptive accounts of this particular Italian cycle of protest, analytical statements about the origins, shape, and outcomes of social movements in Italy, as well as larger inferences about social movements and democracy.

Tarrow (ibid.: 58) argues that by the mid-1960s the post-war settlement that characterized the Italian political system began to show certain cracks due to 'the conflicts of a maturing capitalist society and the divisions in its political class'. These cracks created the political opportunity for mobilization by organized labour, newly emerging immigrant workers, and new middle-strata groups. Their demands and grievances centred on distributional claims that expanded to more general claims for new rights (ibid.: 138). The cycle of protest that Tarrow (ibid.: 62) describes reached its first peak in the spring of 1968, levelled off through 1969–1970 and then peaked again in 1971, and again in the middle of 1972, after which it declined until the end of period. While the cycle of protest was largely characterized by 'classical forms of democratic public expression', the protests during the 1972 peak and decline saw a rise in more confrontational and violent forms of action, which were still in a distinct minority (ibid.: 81).

For the Italian case, Tarrow (ibid.: 323–324) concludes that the cycle of protest came to an end with the rise of violent protest and repression on the one hand, and political institutionalization on the other. These experiences with violence and institutionalization changed Italian political culture and gave ordinary people a new sense of autonomy and efficacy in contrast to earlier forms of paternalism (ibid.: 329). The cycle of protest introduced new actors into the political sphere who asserted new collective identities that erode traditional patterns of support for existing political parties (ibid.: 331). Finally, the cycle of protest led to real policy reforms across a range of new issues, such as abortion (ibid.: 335–336).

In addition to these conclusions about the Italian case, Tarrow draws larger inferences about the relationship between disorder and democracy. He argues that protest produces instability and even violence, but in the long run it does not undermine democracy. Rather, 'democracy expands, not because elites concede reform or repress dissent, but because of the insistent expansion of participation that occurs within cycles of protest' (ibid.: 347–348). The limits of making inferences from a single-country study appear to be reached when Tarrow switches his focus to non-democratic systems. For him, cycles of protest under authoritarian and totalitarian systems are 'parenthetical' periods 'in a long dreary saga of repression and demobilization' (ibid.: 346). But this conclusion stands in stark contrast to the one reached by Foweraker and Landman (1997), whose comparison demonstrates that social mobilization is a critical component to regime liberalization and democratic transition, as well as a catalyst for greater participation.

The final study in this chapter is on the women's movement in the United States from 1950 to 1985 (Costain 1992). Like Tarrow (1989) it is a single-country study of social movement activity in a mature capitalist democracy that uses the same protest-coding techniques and posits a relationship between changing political opportunities and patterns of protest. Like Gamson (1975), the study gauges the impact of the women's movement, and like Bashevkin (1998), it uses legislative decisions as a measure of movement success. Costain (1992) codes protest data from the *New York Times Index* and legislative events from the *Congressional Quarterly*. These data are supplemented with newspaper coverage of women's issues, individual-level data on support for the movement, interviews with lobbyists from major social movement organizations (e.g. the National Organization for Women, Women's Equity Action League, and the National Women's Political Caucus), and documents from these organizations.

For the latter half of the twentieth century, women's mobilization saw a decline through the late 1950s, a slight rise in the late 1960s, a peak in 1975, a decline and peak again in 1980, after which it saw a decline through the end of the period (Costain 1992: 9–10). For the twentieth century, the number of women's bills introduced and laws passed in the Congress rose sharply and peaked between 1919 and 1921. It peaked again between 1943 and 1944, while the highest peak in history was reached in 1973 and 1974 during the 93rd Congress (ibid.: 10–11). Through the remainder of the study, Costain (ibid.: 25) examines the relationship between the patterns of protest and lawmaking by focusing on the movement's mobilization of resources, the empowerment of supporters through consciousness-raising, and the ways in which government facilitates movement activities.

She argues that the structure of political opportunities changed significantly as the New Deal coalition began to break down in the late 1960s and early 1970s, which in part explains the patterns in protest and legislation that she observes in the 1970s and 1980s (ibid.: xiv–xv). In addition, the changing opportunities for women with the advent of more effective birth control and the impact of them entering the workforce raised new issues and a new constituency for the women's movement that had not previously existed. To this coincidence of events was added the direct facilitation of the movement by the government initially signalled by John F. Kennedy's creation of the Presidential Commission on the Status of Women (ibid.: 23). By this time, the women's movement had the organizational capacity and an increasing willingness to seek collective solutions to women's problems (ibid.: 26).

With the aid of her time-series data, Costain chronicles the highs and lows of the movement as it struggled to bring about reform of America's dominant political institutions and culture. Rather than seeing a one-way flow of politics from movement to government, however, Costain paints a more nuanced picture of the mutually constitutive relationship among the movement, Congress, and public opinion. This relationship is neatly summarized in a statistical model in her Appendix and has been developed further in later work (see Costain and Majstorovic 1994). Beyond her immediate conclusions about the women's movement in the United States, Costain (1992) makes important inferences about the relationship between movements and governments. This relationship is not always an antagonistic one, and as Bashevkin (1998) also shows, many gains can be made within a political context that may be perceived initially as hostile to movement interests. Moreover, her study adds to the growing literature on social movements a series of effective methods for measuring and analysing the political nexus between movements and governments.

Summary

The comparison of comparisons in this chapter has pointed to a development in the social movement literature in terms of useful analytical concepts and the corroboration of important findings. The comparison of movements has refined the idea of a 'wave' or 'cycle' of protest that exhibits certain identifiable features and components, including the shape of mobilization, the participants, and the shifting pattern of strategies and demand-making. The political opportunity structure has proved a useful explanatory variable for movement strategy, shape, and impact. Finally, the idea of social movement organization (or SMO) is a useful category that appears to 'travel' quite well across different political contexts.

The comparisons variously demonstrated the explanatory importance of economic transformation, the social bases of protest groups and activity, collective identity, levels of organization, and political context. In terms of movement impact and outcomes, the studies have shown that the most likely result of protest is institutionalization, reform, the extension and protection of rights, and in many ways the public acceptance of political protest as a legitimate and alternative means for changing the dominant political institutions and culture. The comparisons have also revealed much about the relationship between protest and democracy, which may be further differentiated across movement sectors. Protest is more likely in democracies with less than three effective political parties. Political protest is likely to strengthen the ideal of democracy through increased political participation, which in turn may have important historical and cultural legacies. Finally, political protest is a critical component to political liberalization and democratic transition (see Table 6.2).

Further reading

Della Porta, D. and Diani, M. (1999) *Social Movements: An Introduction*, Oxford: Blackwell.

A thorough review of social movement theory and research in advanced industrial democracies.

Foweraker, J. (1995) *Theorizing Social Movements*, London: Pluto Press.

A comprehensive review of social movement theory and its ability to be used in contexts outside North America and Europe.

McAdam, D., McCarthy, J., and Zald, M. N. (1996) *Comparative Perspectives on Social Movements*, Cambridge: Cambridge University Press.

This presents further developments in social movement theory and research.

Tarrow, S. (1994) *Power in Movement*, Cambridge: Cambridge University Press.

This work traces the development of social movement theory and research.

Table 6.2 Summary of comparative work on non-violent political dissent and social movements

Method	Number of countries	Exemplars	Origins	Results: Shape/Strategy	Results: Impact
Comparing many countries	Between 29 democracies and 90 countries	Powell (1982); Haas and Stack (1983); Gurr (1993); Inglehart (1997)	Underlying economic change (growth, development, structural change), social heterogeneity, and group organization are important determinants of protest. Mixed results for the effects of political democracy		
Comparing few countries	Between 3 and 10 countries from North America, Europe, and Latin America	Kitschelt (1986); Dalton (1988); Dalton (1994); Kriesi et al. (1995); Foweraker & Landman (1997); Bashevkin (1998)	Movement supporters in Europe comprise well-educated, middle income, and professional people Changing protection of political and civil rights can lead to increased mobilization	Different political opportunities can determine different movement strategies Movements exhibit 'waves' of mobilization with a distinct rise, peak, and decline Early periods of protest are less violent than late periods Labour mobilization tends to precede mobilization from other social movements	Political opportunities affect the type of movement impact Mobilization can change public opinion about movement issues Movements can make gains in 'lean' years Social movements are a key component to the process of democratization
Single-country	Italy and the United States	Gamson (1975); Tarrow (1989); Costain (1992)	Government action can facilitate movement activity	Cycles of protest comprise early risers who are then joined by other sectors in a general peak of mass mobilization Movement tactics change from more conventional to less conventional during a cycle of protest	Positive association between movements and legislative decisions Cycles of protest enrich and strengthen democracy

Chapter 7

Transitions to democracy

As the previous chapters have demonstrated, both the establishment and maintenance of democracy have long been a focus of comparative politics. Chapter 4 assessed the many comparisons of the relationship between economic development and democracy. Chapters 5 and 6 compared the ways in which scholars have analysed violent and non-violent challenges to political rule, as well as how those challenges are related to democracy. In addition to these research topics, the comparative study of democracy has also included a focus on critical historical moments of democratic transition. Democratic transitions increasingly became the object of comparative inquiry after the end of the Portuguese dictatorship in 1974, an event which ushered in the so-called 'third wave' of democracy in world history (Huntington 1991). The process of democratic transition that started in Portugal would spread to other authoritarian countries in Southern Europe, Latin America, Africa, Asia, and Eastern Europe so that by 1996, there were over 120 'formal' democracies comprising approximately 60 per cent of the total independent countries in the world (Diamond 1999: 24–29).

This global spread, pace, and process of democratization have become important topics for comparative politics and have led to the development of a sub-field in the discipline known as 'democratization studies' (Whitehead 1996a). While the bulk of democratization studies focus on the post-1974 transitions, some studies have sought to draw on the insights gained from researching earlier processes of democratization (Moore 1966; Therborn 1977; Rueschemeyer *et al.* 1992; Fischer 1996). This chapter assesses key studies in this sub-field of comparative politics in an effort to demonstrate the different methods that have been used to answer a core set of common research questions surrounding the global proliferation of democratic rule.

The research problem

The comparisons outlined in this chapter variously seek to describe the global spread of democracy, to explain why, when, and where it happens, and to assess the future prospects for democracy in the world. Despite their different temporal and geographical foci, several defining research questions have remained the same. First, are there certain objective 'preconditions' for the establishment and maintenance of democracy (see Chapter 4 and Karl 1990)? Second, who are the 'agents' of democratization? Third, in reference to third-wave democracies, why have some countries that were initially thought to be 'doomed to endless authoritarianism', experienced democratic transitions (Levine 1989: 377; Przeworski 1991: 1)?[1] Fourth, what external factors help to promote democratic transitions? The studies included in this chapter have all sought to answer these questions; however, as in the previous chapters, the answers they provide are often a reflection of the comparative method they adopt.

Comparing many countries

As Chapter 4 demonstrated, the comparative literature is replete with examples of many-country studies that seek to explain democracy, but very few have focused on the process of democratic transition itself. The comparisons of democratic transition in this section include Huntington's (1991) qualitative global comparison of democratization; Jaggers and Gurr's (1995) description and classification of regimes during the third wave; and Vanhanen's (1997) global comparison of democracy since the 1850s. In each comparison the authors offer definitions of democracy and outline its different measures, while two of the studies examine a parsimonious set of explanatory factors for its appearance in time and geographical space.

In *The Third Wave*, Huntington (1991: 15) defines a *wave of democratic transition* as a group of transitions from non-democratic to democratic regimes that occur within a specified period of time and that significantly outnumber transitions in the opposite direction during that period. He identifies three such waves in world history: the first was 1828–1926; the second 1943–1962; and the third 1974–1989. Each wave was punctuated by a period of democratic 'reversals' in which previously democratic regimes break down and authoritarian regimes are established. Since the first wave, both the number of countries and the number of democracies have increased to the extent that by 1990, Huntington (1991: 26) considers 58 of the total 129 countries in the world to be democratic.

Figure 7.1 shows that inter-war and war years saw a great reversal in democratization, while the immediate post-war years saw a dramatic increase in the number of democracies. More importantly, however, Huntington (1991) stresses that during the third wave the growth of democracy, expressed as a percentage increase, has been unprecedented in world history. His global qualitative comparison thus seeks to explain *why* and *how* countries became democratic during this period. The value of his study lies in his description of the third wave and less so in his explanation of it, which appears more as a series of possible factors that merit further comparative study. For the methodological purposes of this book, this section examines his use of evidence in supporting his five propositions about why countries have become democratic during the third wave.

The five explanatory factors for the democratic transitions between 1974 and 1990 are:

1. a developing crises of legitimacy in the previous authoritarian regime;
2. the high levels of economic growth in the 1960s;
3. changes in doctrine and practice within the Catholic Church;
4. a change in policies of important external actors; and
5. a general demonstration, or 'snowballing' effect across the globe (Huntington 1991: 45–46).

He argues that there is no single cause of democratization and thus sees these five explanations as interdependent and cumulative (ibid.: 38). His study amasses various types of evidence in support of these five propositions, including aggregate statistics, anecdotal evidence, and informed personal impressions.

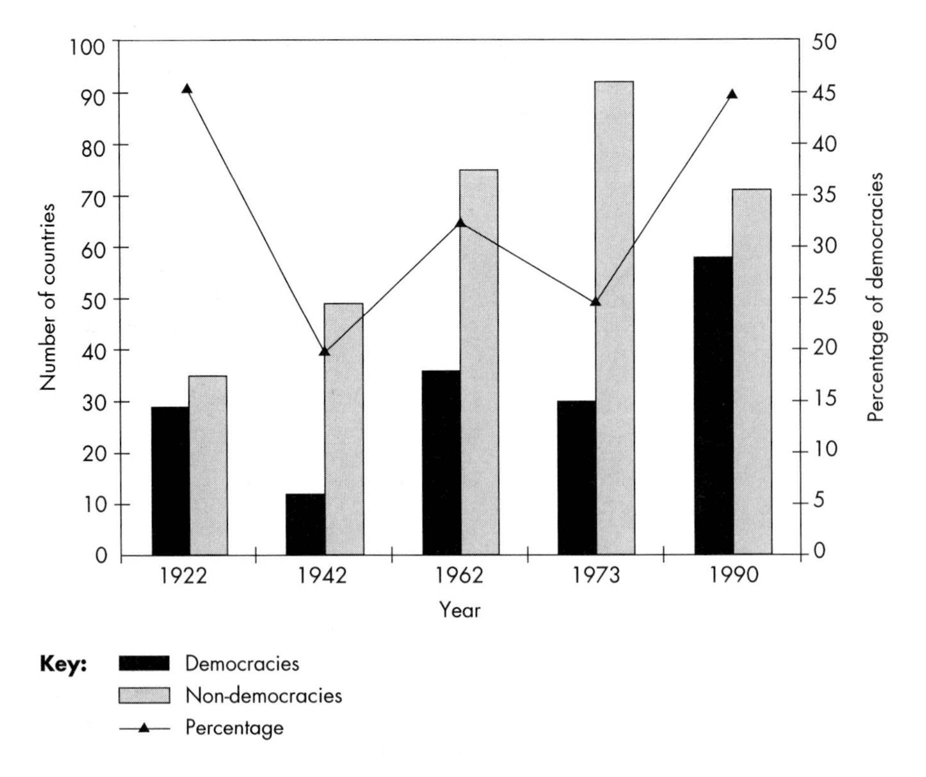

Figure 7.1 The growth and decay of democracy in the world
Source: Adapted from Huntington (1991: table 1.1)

Despite the comprehensive scope of the study, evidence is used to make qualitative comparisons that do not demonstrate the statistical significance of the patterns in democratization that are observed. Moreover, Huntington argues that a detailed comparison of the explanatory factors is beyond the scope of his study, particularly in reference to the role of legitimacy crisis, external actors, and demonstration effects. For example, he sees legitimacy as a 'mushy concept that political analysts do well to avoid' (ibid.: 46). In reference to external actors, he argues that the direct effects of President Carter and President Reagan's foreign policy on the process of democratization 'varied greatly from country to country and it would require extraordinary effort to evaluate the impact even in a single country' (ibid.: 95), where '[n]o definitive evaluation of the US role in third wave democratizations is possible here' (ibid.: 98). Finally, he suggests that '[to show] demonstration effects in individual cases is difficult and would require more intensive study than is possible here' (ibid.: 100).

In short, two of the five explanations for the third wave of democratization receive more than impressionistic and anecdotal support, which perhaps is a good demonstration of the possible limitations of qualitative global comparisons, while pointing to future areas of research. For the two remaining factors (economic growth and the impact of the Catholic Church), Huntington provides more robust evidence. For the post-1960 level of economic growth, virtually 90 per cent of the countries that experienced political liberalization or democratic transition reside in the 'middle range' of world per capita GDP, while half of the third-wave countries have incomes between US$1,000 and US$3,000 (ibid.: 63). While conceding that there is not a necessary relationship between economic development and democracy, he none the less implies that there is a positive association between the two such that economic development 'provided the basis for democracy; crises produced by either rapid growth or economic recession weakened authoritarianism' (ibid.: 59). He argues further that economic development involving significant industrialization unleashed a complex set of social forces which authoritarian regimes were unable to control, such as new values, education, better resources, trade liberalization, and the expansion of the middle class (ibid.: 65–66; compare Rueschemeyer *et al.* 1992).

For the role of the Catholic Church in fostering democracy, Huntington (1991: 76) argues that nearly 75 per cent of the third-wave countries were Catholic. The wave started in Portugal and Spain, moved to Central and South America, the Philippines, back to Chile and Mexico (?), and then to Poland and Hungary. Huntington claims there are several reasons for this 'Catholic effect'. First, traditionally poor Catholic countries experienced rates of growth that facilitated transitions to democracy (ibid.: 77). Second, the progressive turn of the Catholic Church at both the global and regional level led to increased grass-roots organizing and the mobilization of lay people in an effort to express grievances about conditions of poverty and repression. Third, a series of Papal visits to authoritarian countries encouraged regime liberalization. In sum, authoritarian regimes were pressured by the Catholic Church from above and below to initiate transitions to democracy (ibid.: 79–85).

In contrast to Huntington's (1991) qualitative comparison of the third wave, Jaggers and Gurr (1995) have employed the global and time-series Polity III data set[2] to 'track' the third wave descriptively across the globe and by region. The data set includes two measures of regime type – autocracy and democracy – which, when combined, give an overall measure of democracy in a given country at a specific time. The combined measure expresses the difference between the level of autocracy and democracy in a country across five main indicators, including the competitiveness of political participation, regulation of participation, competitiveness of executive recruitment, openness of executive recruitment, and constraints on the chief executive (ibid.: 472). Countries are awarded points on the democracy scale for high competitiveness of participation and executive recruitment, the absence of regulation, openness of recruitment, and restrictions on executive authority. Alternatively, countries are awarded points on the autocracy scale for having little or no competitiveness, high degrees of regulation, closed recruitment, and few constraints on executive authority (ibid.: 472).

Overall, the democracy minus autocracy measure ranges from positive ten for states that are purely democratic and negative ten for those that are purely autocratic (ibid.: 473). The score itself is highly correlated with other measures of democracy previously used in comparative studies of democratic performance (see Chapter 4 above), leading the authors to conclude that the measure of democracy is empirically valid (Jaggers and Gurr 1995: 476). Beyond the quantitative aspects of the measure, it seeks to capture the idea that a country may have democratic and autocratic elements that coexist. Descriptively, a time-series plot of the measure since 1960 shows that 'until the late 1970s, the post-1960 global trend was one of increasing autocracy in the international state system and a concomitant decline in the degree of democracy' (ibid.: 476). Only with the democratic transitions in Spain and Portugal, followed by those in Latin America, Eastern Europe, and parts of Asia and Africa, does this downward trend become reversed. Thus, by 1990, the 'degree of democracy in the international system surpassed the degree of autocracy' (ibid.: 476). These quantitative trends thus corroborate Huntington's (1991) description of the third wave.

These descriptive trends are analysed further in two ways. First, the authors examine the differences in the degree of democracy among five regions in the world: the Americas, Eurasia, Africa, the Middle East, and Asia and the Pacific. For the 1990s, only countries in sub-Saharan Africa and the Middle East have higher levels of autocracy than democracy. Second, they classify the globe into coherent and incoherent polities, which can be either democracies or autocracies. On the one hand, coherent democracies and coherent autocracies are located at the extreme ends of the combined measure (coherent democracies ≥ 7 and coherent autocracies ≤ –7). On the other hand, incoherent democracies and incoherent autocracies occupy the middle range of values (–6 ≤ incoherent autocracies ≤ 0 and 0 ≤ incoherent democracies ≤ 6) (Jaggers and Gurr 1995: 478–479). Conceptually, incoherent polities are most vulnerable to regime change either in a positive direction towards democracy or a negative direction towards autocracy. By 1994 the world (151 countries) is comprised of 18 per cent coherent autocracies, 50 per cent coherent democracies, 19 per cent incoherent autocracies, and 13 per cent incoherent democracies. These results suggest that 32 per cent of the world's countries may either move towards democracy or experience a reversal towards autocracy while a further 18 per cent await an initial impulse towards democracy (ibid.: 479).

This global comparison of regime type based on the difference between the level of autocracy and democracy in a country is useful for the descriptive patterns of the third wave, even though the authors have yet to identify the 'causes of these different patterns of regime change' (ibid.: 479). The global comparisons outlined in Chapter 4 that examined the relationship between economic development and democracy demonstrated one way in which these causes may be identified; however, these studies were not concerned with democratic transition *per se*. In contrast, the work of Tatu Vanhanen (1984, 1990, 1997) does seek to identify a causal explanation for democratization that holds across the globe (between 119 and 172 countries) and for all time (1850 to the present). This section of the chapter considers Vanhanen's latest comparative effort entitled *The Prospects of Democracy* (Vanhanen 1997).

Rather than rely on subjective measures of the degree of democracy in a country using a series of ranked indicators, Vanhanen establishes an objective measure of democracy using two electoral indicators thought to capture the democratic principles of *competition* and *participation*. Competition is measured using the percentage votes cast in either presidential or parliamentary elections (or both) for the smaller political parties (i.e. 100 minus the share of the largest party). Participation is measured by the percentage of the population who actually voted in the election (Vanhanen 1997: 34). Assuming that both these principles are essential for democracy and that both are of equal value, an Index of Democratization (ID) is created by multiplying the measures of competition and participation together. Thus, high values denote a greater degree of democracy, while a zero on either component reduces the index to zero (ibid.: 35). This index of democratization serves as the dependent variable for the global comparisons, which Vanhanen carries out for the periods 1850–1979 (119 countries), 1980–1988 (147 countries), and 1991–1993 (172 countries).

The independent variable is a combination of six separate indicators that represent the distribution of power resources in a country. The six indicators include the number of university students per 100,000 inhabitants, the area of family farms as a percentage of the total area of holdings, the degree of centralization of non-agricultural economic resources, as well as the urban population, the non-agricultural population, and the literate population, all expressed as a percentage of the total population (ibid.: 42). In contrast to the studies outlined in Chapter 4 above, the index of power resources includes indicators of economic development as well as measures that capture the distribution of resources in a society. Thus, it leaves room for poor countries with well-distributed resources and rich countries with concentrated resource distributions. Vanhanen (ibid.: 155) argues that the distribution of power resources is the most important single causal factor to account for democratization in the world since 1850.

The remainder of his analysis uses correlation and regression to examine the relationship between the distribution of power resources and democratization for his three global samples of countries. The results of the statistical analysis show that the distribution of power resources explains 66 per cent of the variance in the degree of democracy for the total sample for 1850–1993, while it explains between 59 and 65 per cent of the variance for the sample from 1991–1993 (ibid.: 155). Using these findings over time and space, Vanhanen seeks to predict on a regional and country-specific level, the likelihood that democratization will take place. Table 7.1 summarizes his predictions for the regions of the world, which appear to be upheld in three: (1) Latin America and the Caribbean (democracy), (2) Sub-Saharan Africa (non-democracy), (3) East and Southeast Asia (non-democracy). His model is unable to account for the collapse of the Soviet Union and the democratic transitions in Eastern Europe. It failed to predict the maintenance of authoritarianism in North Africa, the Middle East, and East Asia, and did not foresee the process of democratization in South Asia and Oceania.

These contradictions in Vanhanen's results highlight the trade-offs associated with different methods of comparison. Like the comparisons in Chapter 4 above, a simple set of variables may account for regularities observed at the global level, yet the examination of the findings at the regional level become problematic, leading scholars to search for additional explanatory variables. To be fair, Vanhanen does not rule out other explanations for democracy such as political culture, external influences, and political institutions, but his comparative aspirations prevent him from operationalizing more context-specific variables. The comparative studies in the next section consciously examine a smaller number of

Table 7.1 Prospects for democracy in the world

Regions	*Number of countries Total = 172*	*Prediction*
Europe & North America	40	Prospects for democracy in North America are very high despite the serious problem of low electoral participation in the US Democracy likely to survive in Western Europe Collapse of socialist systems in Eastern Europe not predicted, yet the level of resource distribution is high enough to maintain democracy Democracy will survive in the new states of the former Soviet Union
Latin America and the Caribbean	29	The victory of democracy in Latin America in the 1980s was not unexpected from the perspective of resource distribution, and democracy will be more or less permanent in the region
North Africa, Middle East, and Central Asia	29	Democratization in the region has been much lower than expected, and the region shows the highest number of deviant cases for which alternative explanations are necessary
Sub-saharan Africa	44	The region has the lowest level of democratization in the world, which is consistent with its equally low degree of resource distribution Despite the desire for democratization, the chances for establishing long-lasting democratic institutions are still very poor
South Asia	7	The degree of democracy was higher than expected Region demonstrates that democracy is possible in poor countries with a sufficient distribution of power resources
East Asia and Southeast Asia	16	The degree of democracy deviates very little from what was expected Popular pressures for democratization will be resisted by socialist and former socialist countries in the region
Oceania	7	The degree of democracy is higher than expected

Source: Adapted from Vanhanen (1997: 106–154)

countries in an effort to be sensitive to such context-specific factors while still attempting to draw larger inferences about the process of democratic transition.

Comparing few countries

In general, the sub-field of democratization studies emerged from the comparison of few countries as scholars responded to the first democratic transitions in Southern Europe and Latin America. Studies using this method of comparison tend to suffer from selection bias, since their focus is usually on countries that had experienced or were experiencing democratic transitions (compare the discussion of Wolf 1969 in Chapter 5 above). This chapter examines three such studies, including O'Donnell *et al.*'s (1986a, 1986b, 1986c) *Transitions from Authoritarian Rule*, Peeler's (1992) comparison of elite settlements in Venezuela, Colombia, and Costa Rica, and Linz and Stepan's (1996) *Problems of Democratic Transition and Consolidation*. The O'Donnell *et al.* (1986) volume is a collection of essays written by various scholars on fifteen countries of Southern Europe and Latin America and stands as the origin of the current sub-field of democratization studies in comparative politics. Peeler's (1992) piece follows in the same tradition yet looks back in history to earlier transitions in Latin America, while Linz and Stepan's (1996) volume seeks to move beyond the study of democratic transition and makes larger inferences about the process of democratic consolidation in Southern Europe, Latin America, and post-communist Europe.

The scholars that comprise the four-volume set of studies of *Transitions from Authoritarian Rule* (O'Donnell, Schmitter, and Whitehead 1986) spent time together at the Wilson Center for International Scholars in Washington DC in an effort to explain and understand the democratic transitions in Southern Europe and Latin America. Volumes I and II contain thirteen single-country studies of democratization, and volumes III and IV draw together the comparative findings across the cases. While conceding that transitions from authoritarian rule can lead to the 'instauration of political democracy, or the restoration of a new, and possibly more severe form of authoritarian rule', the thirteen studies focus primarily on processes of political liberalization and democratization (O'Donnell and Schmitter 1986: 3–14).[3] The countries that comprise the studies in the volume include Italy, Greece, Portugal, Spain, Turkey, Argentina, Bolivia, Brazil, Chile, Mexico, Peru, Uruguay, and Venezuela. The authors accept the diversity of these contexts, yet their comparison searches for points of convergence across all the cases to help explain the process of democratization, while avoiding a 'test' of a specific theory of democratic transition (ibid.: 3).

To begin an assessment of this collection of studies, Table 7.2 summarizes the main explanatory factors and outcomes of each of the thirteen case studies in order to demonstrate the areas of convergence and divergence in the process of democratization across the countries. To some degree, the studies avoid selection bias since some of the countries have not experienced democratic transitions. Since the studies were written during the third wave, many of the political outcomes in the table are cases of no transition, yet the authors tried to anticipate the political changes that were to come in the future.

Table 7.2 Transitions from authoritarian rule

Author	*Country*	*Main explanatory factors*	*Outcome*
Pasquino	Italy 1943–1948	Overthrow of dictator Allied liberation & Cold War Domestic forces (parties and resistance) Process of constitution drafting	Democratic transition
Maravall and Santamaría	Spain 1975	Pacts and negotiations between elites	Democratic transition
Maxwell	Portugal 1974	Decolonization Progressive military coup followed by popular mobilization Failure to liberalize	Democratic transition
Diamandouros	Greece 1974	Elite calculations Cyprus crisis General mobilization	Democratic transition
Sunar and Sayari	Turkey	Military dominated process Legacy of centralized state power	Liberalization
Cavarozzi	Argentina 1955–1983	Cycles of civilian–military regimes Failure of neo-liberal economic model Defeat in Malvinas/Falklands Radical Party leadership of Alfonsín	Democratic transition
Whitehead	Bolivia 1977–1980	General Banzer initiates transition Crisis in military-peasant pact Warring factions split authoritarian regime Inconclusive electoral results (3 elections) Absence of minimum alliance conditions	No, but weak democracy established in 1982

Table 7.2 continued

Author	*Country*	*Main explanatory factors*	*Outcome*
Martins	Brazil 1974–1985	Political liberalization initiated in 1974 End of economic miracle Military controls prolonged liberalization Increased social mobilization	Liberalization
Garretón	Chile 1980–1986	1980 referendum and constitution Regime crisis in early 1980s No opposition with alternative vision to military regime	No transition
Middlebrook	Mexico 1977–1986	Popular protest and repression in 1968 Alternative party formation Raise legitimacy of governing party	Liberalization
Cotler	Peru 1963 and 1977–1980	Intense social and political struggle Economic crisis in 1977 Elite bargain and 'transfer of office'	Democratic transition
Gillespie	Uruguay 1973–1984	Elite negotiation between dominant parties Public approval of liberalization pacts	Redemocratization
Karl	Venezuela 1958	Presence of petroleum Political pacts between two dominant political parties	Democratic transition

Source: Summary of O'Donnell *et al.* (1986a, 1986b)

Overall, the studies establish the conceptual differences between liberalization, democratic transition, and redemocratization (O'Donnell and Schmitter 1986: 2–14), while their comparisons reveal a common set of factors that help account for these different types of regime.

In the final volume to the series, O'Donnell and Schmitter (1986) draw tentative conclusions about the thirteen cases. They accept the inherent uncertainty of the outcomes, and this highlights a more general problem with the comparativist's 'preoccupation with the immediate, leading to a certain trendiness – a penchant for wanting to follow the events of the day' (Valenzuela 1988: 78). Indeed, some of the non-democratic countries listed in Table 7.2 are now recognized as having undergone democratic transitions (Chile, Brazil, and Bolivia), while others have seen a reversal of their transitions (e.g. Peru). In most cases, the impulse for liberalization comes from within the authoritarian regime itself; from a conflict between 'hard-liners' who seek to maintain the authoritarian regime and 'soft-liners' who seek to initiate a process of liberalization in an effort to legitimize the regime (O'Donnell and Schmitter 1986: 15–21). These two different groups of elites within the regime effectively weigh the costs of further authoritarianism (domestic and foreign opposition and loss of legitimacy) against the costs of liberalization (increased social and political instability).

In most cases, liberalization of the authoritarian regime is accompanied by the 'resurrection of civil society' (ibid.: 26–27, 48–56) in which increased social mobilization creates pressure for democracy (see also Foweraker and Landman 1997). Despite this 'bottom-up' impulse for democratization, the authors in this series tend to emphasize the important role played by elites in the democratic transition as they form 'negotiated pacts', which set out the 'rules governing the exercise of power' (O'Donnell and Schmitter 1986: 37; see also Howarth 1998b). Finally, the moment of transition in most of the countries is accompanied by the announcement of elections either for a constituent assembly (as in the case of Peru) or for the first elections for some set of representatives (as in the case of Brazilian governors), or for both purposes. These elections serve to motivate both the political parties from before the authoritarian period and newly formed political parties to assume a more prominent role in the democratic transition, while the election itself is seen to be a founding event (O'Donnell and Schmitter 1986: 57).

Adopting a similar focus to the previous set of studies, Peeler (1992) compares the historical experiences of Colombia, Costa Rica, and Venezuela, all of which have shown reasonable stability in their democratic institutions since the 1950s and serve as possible models for countries undergoing democratic transition during the third wave. While recognizing the differences between these cases, the comparative analysis examines how 'elite settlement' helps found the democratic regimes and how 'elite convergence' contributed to their survival (ibid.: 83; see also Briefing Box 7.1). In addition, Peeler's study looks at the relationship between elite and mass behaviour at the moment of transition. He argues that democratic consolidation is more likely in countries where participation has been extended to all elites while some form of vertical control is established for channelling popular demands (ibid.: 83).

Table 7.3 summarizes the comparison with separate rows for prior conditions, crises, the moment of transition, and the period of consolidation. Colombia

Briefing box 7.1 Elite settlement and elite convergence

The twin concepts of *elite settlement* and *elite convergence* have been used to explain the process of democratic transition and prospects for democratic consolidation from a perspective in which elites stop fighting with one another and essentially 'agree to disagree' within a peaceful framework of governance. An elite settlement is a political situation in which two warring factions of elites 'suddenly and deliberately reorganize their relations by negotiating compromises on their most basic disagreements' (Burton *et al.* 1992: 13). Once the basic differences have ceased to cause violence between factions, they pave the way for open and peaceful competition and they may eventually lead to democratic consolidiation. In general, elite settlements stem from long periods of conflict and crises that threaten to rekindle widespread violence. Examples of elite settlements from history include England (1688–89), Sweden (1809), Mexico (1929), Costa Rica (1948), Colombia (1957–1958), Venezuela (1958), and Spain and the Dominican Republic (1970s) (Burton *et al.* 1992: 14).

Elite convergence occurs after an elite settlement and is isolated to unconsolidated democracies. It is characterized by a coalition of opposing factions within a disunified set of elites who are able to mobilize significant electoral majorities to dominant government executive power (ibid.: 24). Elite convergence progresses until the subordinate group of elites learns to beat the dominant group through the electoral process. This acceptance of the democratic rules of the game and the eventual sharing of electoral victories leads to democratic consolidation. In addition, competition over the middle set of voters necessarily means that the political spectrum becomes less polarized (ibid.: 25). Examples of elite convergence from history include: France from 1958 to the period of co-habitation in the 1980s; Norway and Denmark (1900–1933); and Italy, Japan, and Greece (1970s–1990s) (ibid.: 25).

and Venezuela were important political and economic centres for the Spanish empire whereas Costa Rica was isolated and offered nothing of interest to Spain. All three cases developed strong political classes and a coffee export economy. The years of crisis had similar origins that led to political conflict and violence between rival elites, and both Colombia and Venezuela experienced periods of dictatorship. In all three cases, the transition to democracy 'involved explicit pact making on the part of competing elites', which established 'competition within an agreed-upon framework of rules' (Peeler 1992: 94). Finally, all three cases have withstood serious challenges to democratic rule from domestic and foreign sources where Costa Rica and Venezuela have fared the best in terms of democratic stability.

The final study in this section is Linz and Stepan's (1996) comparison of few countries in Southern Europe, Latin America, and post-communist Europe. Conducting their research after the third wave and during what some have called the fourth wave (post-1989), the authors are able to expand the scope of the comparison to the post-communist world and to extend their substantive focus to

Table 7.3 Elite settlements and democratic transition

	Colombia	*Costa Rica*	*Venezuela*
Prior conditions	Colonial centre and strong creole upper class Strong Liberal and Conservative Parties Elections seen as a device for legitimation Coffee export economy (late)	Isolated, weak, and poor Individual politics no development of parties Elections seen as a device for legitimation Coffee export economy (early) Development of public schooling	Colonial centre and strong planter class Liberal and Conservative parties, local boss rule Elections seen as a device for legitimation Coffee export economy (early)
Years of crisis	Great Depression and WWII Communist and populist parties Violence and dictatorship until 1958	Great Depression and WWII Communist and populist parties Personalist regime	Great Depression and WWII Communist and populist parties Dictatorship 1948–1958
Democratic transition	Explicit pact between competing elites National Front agreement and rotation of power	Explicit pact between competing elites Figueres–Ulate pact	Explicit pact between competing elites Three-way pact called Punto Fijo
Democratic consolidation	Deconsolidation and breakdown since 1974	Unbroken series of elections since 1953	Unbroken series of elections since 1958†

Source: Adapted from Peeler (1992: 84–108)

Note: †Venezuela experienced a series of coup attempts in 1992 followed by the impeachment of Carlos Andres Perez (see Landman 1995)

questions of democratic consolidation. The post-communist countries possess different 'starting conditions' and therefore face different constraints in the process of democratic transition and consolidation. For the countries from Southern Europe, there has been some time since their transitions, so the authors can make larger inferences about the key factors for successful democratic consolidation. They compare fifteen countries in total: three from Southern Europe, four from South America, and eight from post-communist Europe. The authors consider the first set to be 'completed consolidations' and the second set 'constrained transitions', while they argue the third set faces 'most complex paths and tasks' in order to consolidate democracy.

Their comparison seeks to develop a set of master variables that help account for different types of democratic transition and different modes of democratic consolidation. The set includes a total of seven variables: two macro-variables, two middle-range variables, and three contextual variables. The first macro-variable is 'stateness', which captures the degree to which a country is sovereign and has established a national identity and national cohesion (Linz and Stepan 1996: 16–37). The second macro-variable is the type of regime that preceded the democratic transition, including authoritarian, totalitarian, post-totalitarian, and sultanistic (ibid.: 38–54; see also Briefing Box 7.2). The middle-range variables include the leadership base of the previous regime (hierarchical military, non-hierarchical military, civilian, or sultanistic) and who initiates the democratic transition (civil society, regime collapse, armed revolution, non-hierarchical military coup, or hierarchical state) (ibid.: 66–71). The three contextual variables are international influences, the political economy of regime legitimacy, and the environment in which the new democratic constitution is promulgated (ibid.: 72–83).

Briefing box 7.2 Linz and Stepan's (1996) classification of prior regime type

A critical variable for Linz and Stepan's (1996) comparative project is the type of regime that precedes the democratic transition. They argue that the type of regime establishes constraints and determines in large part the paths to democracy. Like Aristotle and Finer (see Briefing Box 1.1), they use classification to define four basic types of modern non-democratic regimes, ranging from least to most authoritarian. These four types are *authoritarianism*, *totalitarianism*, *post-totalitarianism*, and *sultanism* (Linz and Stepan 1996: 40–54). In addition, they specify three sub-types of post-totalitarianism, including early post-totalitarianism, frozen post-totalitarianism, and mature post-totalitarianism. Each of these prior regime types is categorized according to differences among their degrees of pluralism, their establishment and use of ideology, their capacity for popular mobilization, and their composition and style of leadership (ibid.: 44–45).

Following early work by Linz (1964) and O'Donnell (1973), Linz and Stepan argue that authoritarian regimes have limited forms of pluralism (particularly in the economic sphere), no overarching ideology, low levels of regime-led popular mobilization, and a small group of leaders who seek to incorporate sympathetic dominant elites. Totalitarian regimes have no pluralism, a hegemonic political party with a totalizing ideology and vision for social transformation, a strong capacity and tendency for popular mobilization, and often charismatic and arbitrary leaders with a committed, lower-level staff. Post-totalitarian regimes evolve from totalitarian regimes and have limited pluralism and possible parallel forms of opposition, a dominant party with a totalizing ideology and vision for social transformation that has begun to wane, less of a capacity and interest in popular mobilization, and less charismatic and more bureaucratic leaders. Sultanistic regimes have a low degree of pluralism that is subject to the arbitrary whims of the leader, a personalistic ideology that is not justified or strongly supported outside the inner circle of the leader, periodic regime-led popular mobilization, and a personalized, charismatic, and arbitrary leader. In addition to these four basic regime types, the authors specify a further three regime sub-types that lie on the continuum of post-totalitarianism. Early post-totalitarianism is the closest to totalitarianism, frozen post-totalitarianism is in the middle of the continuum, and mature post-totalitarianism is closest to marking a transition to either authoritarianism or democracy (Linz and Stepan 1996: 294). These regime types and sub-types are summarized with modern examples in Table 7.4.

Table 7.4 Modern non-democratic regimes

Regime type	*Examples*
Authoritarian	Argentina, Brazil, Chile, Spain, Portugal, Poland
Totalitarian	Soviet Union until Brezhnev period
Post-totalitarian	Soviet Union under Gorbachev; Russia, Estonia, Latvia after collapse of Soviet Union
Early post-totalitarian	Bulgaria
Frozen post-totalitarian	Czechoslovakia
Mature post-totalitarian	Hungary

Source: Adapted from Linz and Stepan (1996)

These seven variables are then examined across the fifteen countries in an effort to differentiate the experiences of democratic transition and to specify the degree to which democracy has been consolidated in each country. Table 7.5 summarizes the comparison by listing all fifteen countries in the first column followed by columns for the seven variables and a column for the outcome, *viz.* democratic consolidation. Immediately apparent from the table is the problem of 'too many variables not enough countries' (see Chapter 3 above), since seven variables each with several categories cannot fully vary across the fifteen countries. None the less, their comparison does yield tentative inferences that can be extended to those areas of the world that have not experienced democratic transitions or those that have yet to consolidate democracy. The two variables that have the most impact on successful democratic consolidation are *prior regime type* and the *initiator of the transition*. Previous civilian authoritarian regimes that had some form of 'pacted' transition appear to face fewer obstacles to democratic consolidation than any other combination of variables. Previous sultanistic and near totalitarian regimes with some form of regime-led transition appear to face the most obstacles to democratic consolidation. In addition, problems with stateness continue to hinder efforts at democratic consolidation in Hungary, Romania, Russia, Estonia, and Latvia.

For the authors, a consolidated democracy must have no problems with stateness, a 'free and lively civil society', a 'relatively autonomous and valued political society', the rule of law, and an 'institutionalized economic society' (Linz and Stepan 1996: 7). In addition to historical evidence, they provide individual-level data on the degree to which citizens of these countries support the idea of democratic rule. Table 7.5 shows that of the fifteen countries, only four have consolidated their democratic regimes, and of those four, two are considered to be of 'low quality' (Greece) and 'risk prone' (Uruguay). Thus, the remaining countries all have significant problems in one or more of the 'five arenas' of consolidated democracy (ibid.: 7), a finding that suggests students of democracy must tone down their 'third wave' enthusiasm for global democracy (ibid.: 457).

Despite these somewhat pessimistic conclusions, the study represents an advance on earlier studies in this field of inquiry. The expansion of the scope of countries in the comparison beyond Southern Europe and Latin America introduces new and important explanatory variables that have not been specified in previous studies. The notion of stateness is rarely specified (with the exception possibly of Spain) and serves as an important variable in the countries of post-communist Europe. In the past, little attention has been paid to the type of the prior regime, while more emphasis has been placed on the initiator and type of the democratic transition. In line with their earlier work on democratic breakdowns (Linz and Stepan 1978), they examine the interaction between the macro and micro levels of politics (see Chapter 1 above). In contrast to O'Donnell *et al.* (1986a, b and c), Linz and Stepan (1996) stress the importance of international influences. Finally, apart from the problems of research design, their study offers an example of the *contextual description*, *classification* and *hypothesis-testing* functions of comparative politics (see Chapter 1 above).

Single-country studies

The final section in this chapter examines three studies on democratic transition in Spain (Foweraker 1989), Poland (Colomer and Pascual 1994), and Portugal (Maxwell 1995), which show the various strengths and weaknesses of making inferences from a single country. In *Making Democracy in Spain*, Foweraker (1989) presents an in-depth analysis of the role played by the working class in Spain during the two decades that preceded the death of Franco in preparing the terrain for democratic transition. Colomer and Pascual (1994) examine the democratic transition in Poland using formal game theory techniques. In *The Making of Portuguese Democracy*, Maxwell (1995) offers an exhaustive account of the Portuguese transition which extends from the period of decolonization in Africa and the overthrow of the dictatorship by the Movement of the Armed Forces (MFA) to the final consolidation of democratic rule. In each study, contextual description is used in an effort to make larger inferences about the process of democratic transition.

In similar fashion to Womack (1969), Nugent (1993), and Harvey (1998), Foweraker (1989) examines the personal historical trajectories of key activists from the Southern region of El Marco de Jerez and their struggle against the Franco regime in Spain. This 'case-study within a case-study' seeks to understand

Table 7.5 Democratic transition and consolidation in Southern Europe, South America, and post-communist Europe

Country	*Explanatory variables*							*Outcome*
	Stateness	*Prior regime type*	*Base of leadership*	*Initiator of transition*	*International influences*	*Political economy*	*Constitutional environment*	
Spain	Problematic	Civilian authoritarian	Civilian	Elites	European Community	Economic decline	Consensus not majoritarian	Democratic consolidation
Portugal	Not problematic	Civilian authoritarian + weak party	Civilian	Non-hierachical military	US, EC, and European socialist parties	Strong economic growth	Military dominated process	Democratic consolidation
Greece	Problematic	Non-hierarchical authoritarian	Fragmented military	Hierarchical military	European Community	Weak economy	Military trials, contested constitution	Low quality democratic consolidation
Uruguay	Not problematic	Authoritarian	Hierarchical military	Military		Weak economy		Risk-prone consolidation
Brazil	Not problematic	Authoritarian	Hierarchical military	Military		Weak economy, inequality	Military constrained	Unconsolidated
Argentina	Not problematic	Authoritarian	Hierarchical military	External defeat, military	Malvinas/ Falklands	Weak economy		Unconsolidated
Chile	Not problematic	Authoritarian	Hierarchical military	Military		Strong economy	Military constrained	Unconsolidated
Poland	Important factor	Authoritarian	Military, Com. Party	Regime	*Perestroika, glasnost*	Economic reform, debt		Unconsolidated
Hungary	Problematic	Mature post-totalitarian	Communist Party	Communist Party internally	*Perestroika, glasnost*	Economic reform, debt	Post-election amendment	Unconsolidated

Table 7.5 continued

Country				*Explanatory variables*				*Outcome*
	Stateness	*Prior regime type*	*Base of leadership*	*Initiator of transition*	*International influences*	*Political economy*	*Constitutional environment*	
Czechoslovakia	Not problematic[†]	Frozen post-totalitarian	Communist Party	Civil society, regime collapse	*Perestroika, glasnost*	Economic reform, debt	Used old federal design	Unconsolidated
Bulgaria	Not problematic	Early post-totalitarian	Communist Party	Regime	*Perestroika, glasnost*	Economic reform, debt	Tightly constrained	Unconsolidated
Romania	Problematic	Sultanistic-totalitarian	Ceauşescu	Civil society, internal purge	*Perestroika, glasnost*	Economic reform, debt	Tightly controlled	Unconsolidated
USSR/Russia	Very problematic	Post-totalitarian	Communist Party	Regime	Disintegration of USSR	Economic restructuring	No democratic procedures	Unconsolidated
Estonia	Problematic	Post-totalitarian	Communist party	Regime	Russia and EU	Economic restructuring	Dominated by nationalism	Unconsolidated
Latvia	Problematic	Post-totalitarian	Communist Party	Regime	Russia and EU	Economic restructuring	Dominated by nationalism	Unconsolidated

Source: Adapted from Linz and Stepan (1996: 87–458)
Note: [†]The 1992 breakup of Czechoslovakia into two independent republics is not seen as a problem either for the democratic transition or for democratic consolidation.

the ways in which grass-roots organizing and personal networks constructed the spaces necessary in a nascent and constrained civil society for the *democratic transformation* that took place over twenty years before the transition itself (Foweraker 1989: 9). In addition to 'telling the story' of these activists and their role in forging the terrain upon which the democratic transition would unfold, Foweraker (ibid.: 2) argues that 'the story of the struggle . . . has a political interest and potential application far beyond the boundaries of Spain itself'. The study thus has well-defined empirical (the activists), analytical (personal networks), and methodological (case study) components, all of which help make a larger statement about democratic struggle under authoritarian conditions.

The activists that feature in this study are drawn from the proletarianized rural working class with little initial political consciousness but with a history and personal experience with the Spanish Civil War, the terror that followed it, and the strong arm of the Francoist state. Without unnecessarily privileging the working class, Foweraker (ibid.: 6) argues that it was a crucial group that both 'spearheaded' and represented the 'standard bearer' of the democratic struggle. In terms of their organization, these activists were variously involved in the clandestine workers' commissions, the illegal Communist Party, or worked from within the official corporatist structure of Franco's Vertical Syndicate (ibid.: 5). From these different organizational bases, the activists pursued legal and extra-legal strategies to address their basic grievances, which over time, evolved from purely economic demands to more political ones.

The setting of El Marco de Jerez has several important features for the study of democratic struggle. It had both an urban and rural working class, a strong commercial sector, a successful and unified bourgeois oligarchy, and it was the site of 'consistent and strategically sophisticated struggles' (ibid.: 3), all of which combined to make the region a 'microcosm of Spanish civil society' (ibid.: 60). The first part of the study examines the early lives and political memories of the activists, their clandestine activities of organizing the workers, as well as the political economy of the region and of the nation under Franco. The second part discusses the nature of corporatist labour relations under the Vertical Syndicate, and the ways in which the workers' commissions sought to serve the interests of the workers independently from the rule of the Vertical Syndicate. The Vertical Syndicate was designed to promote a total vision and ideology which eliminated the need for class struggle while providing organizational authority and control at the national, regional, and local levels (ibid.: 81). In contrast, the workers' commissions, whose birthplace Foweraker (ibid.: 91) traces to El Marco de Jerez, were a collective response to the lack of appropriate representation of worker grievances (i.e. wages and conditions of work) through the formal channels of the Vertical Syndicate. Far from providing a unified challenge to the Vertical Syndicate, however, the growth of workers' commissions at the regional and national levels proceeded in heterogeneous fashion (ibid.: 92–93). This part of the study concludes with a narrative account of the expansion of challenges grounded in the workers' commissions that culminated in a peak of protest in 1969 (ibid.: 125–129).

The third part of the study examines the three-way relationship between the workers' commissions, the Communist Party, and the regime over the twenty-year period. While both the commissions and the Communist Party sought an end to the

Franco regime, they represented competing organizations in the struggle. While the Communist Party, by its own assertions and as the main target of the regime, has been seen as the key protagonist for the democratic struggle in Spain, its leadership was divided between those in exile and those in Spain, and its political practices were criticized for being heavy-handed and dogmatic (ibid.: 133–136). The study seeks to redress the elite bias to previous studies that privileged the role of party leaders and look to the everyday struggles of the workers. Foweraker (ibid.: 185) contends that the struggle for democracy during this period is best understood by the relationship that developed between the workers' commissions and the Communist Party. The study thus examines the evolving and contingent relationship between these two organizations in El Marco de Jerez in order to gain some insight into the overall development of the democratic movement at the national level. Far from being a unified and unidirectional movement pursuing a singular idea of democracy, Foweraker (ibid.: 198) is keen to stress that the 'democratic project contained and expressed the contingent outcomes of a specific political process' where the democratic consciousness of the individuals in the struggle 'was formed through the complex choices they confronted within this *process*'.

Through induction (see Chapter 1 above), the final part of the study seeks to bring the empirical and the theoretical together in an effort to make a larger statement about the democratic transformation of civil society and its role in transitions from authoritarian rule. Figure 7.2 summarizes in graphical fashion the main steps of the argument drawn from the intensive study of El Marco de Jerez and its overall relation to both the level of the Spanish national political landscape and the conceptual level of democratic transformation. The arrows in the figure do not represent causality, but the connections made between the various steps in the narrative discussion. The economic oppression in El Marco de Jerez and the political repression of the Franco regime did evoke the 'unquiet hearts' of the workers (ibid.: 13–28), which as mediated through their personal networks, found representation in the workers' commissions, the Communist Party, and in some degree through activities within the Vertical Syndicate. The relationship between the workers' commissions and the Communist Party was not altogether harmonic, yet collectively, these two organizations stood in opposition to the Vertical Syndicate. Finally, the study concludes that over twenty years of incremental and piecemeal struggle, those involved in the political contestation expanded their sense of individual citizenship and so transformed Spanish civil society.

The second study in this section identifies the key political actors in the Polish democratic transition and seeks to model the strategic interaction between them during the 1980s using a popular analytical technique in political science called 'game theory' (see Briefing Box 7.3). Colomer and Pascual (1994) argue that the Polish transition featured two important political actors: on the one hand, the Polish government, controlled entirely by the Communist Party, and on the other, the democratic opposition to the government, represented by the Solidarity movement. The authors argue that each of these two actors faced two choices concerning the political situation during the 1980s. The government either wanted to continue with the status quo (i.e. the maintenance of post-totalitarian rule) or reform the political system (i.e. legalize the opposition and implement political

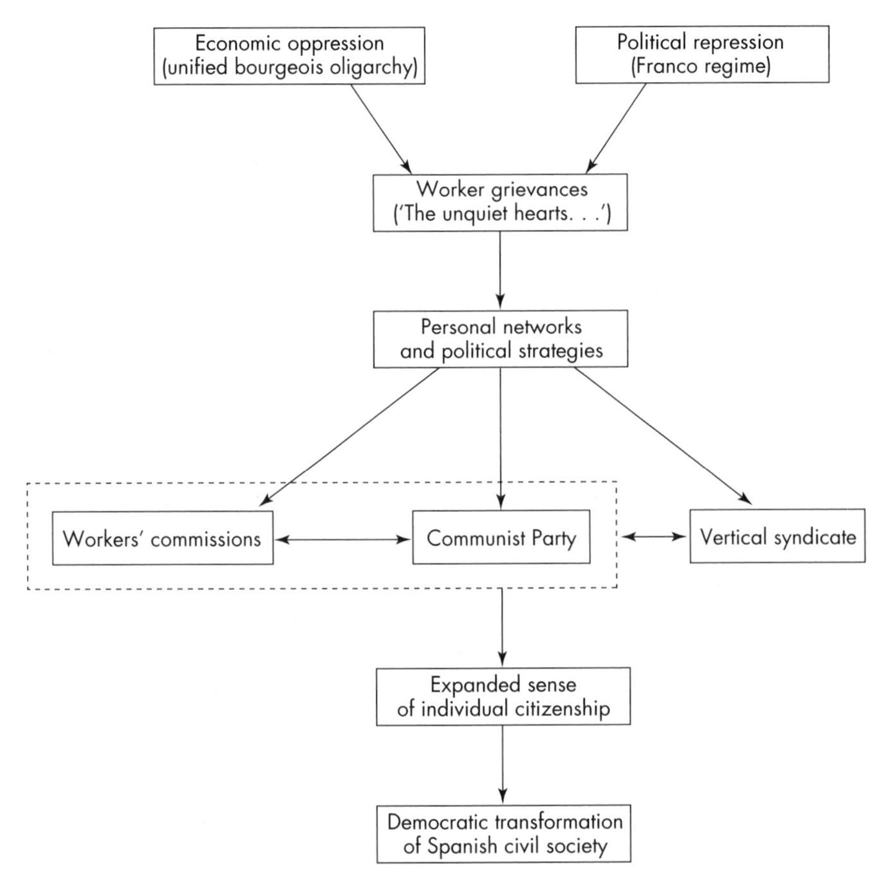

Figure 7.2 Democratic transformation in Spain: summary of Foweraker (1989)

Briefing box 7.3 Game theory and political science

As Chapter 1 made clear, some political scientists prefer to analyse the political world from a micro-perspective by focusing on individuals. This perspective evolved from an examination of the psycho-sociological aspects of political behaviour to the specification of a rational model of political behaviour (see Cohen and Arato 1992; Lichbach 1995). The rational approach borrows a certain conception from economic theory that holds that individuals have a set of 'preferences' they pursue through the application of reason and instrumental action. Preferences in politics can include anything from higher wages, a cleaner environment, world peace, or the realization of democracy. In addition, individuals rank these preferences in a consistent and transitive manner. For example, someone who prefers Pepsi Max to Diet Pepsi and Diet Pepsi to regular Pepsi, also prefers Pepsi Max to regular Pepsi. The application of reason and instrumental action means that individuals intentionally choose the best strategy for achieving their ends (Cohen 1994: 39).

Scholars using this approach examine the different ways in which such rational individuals interact with one another as they pursue their various political preferences. One such way to examine this interaction is to use 'game theory', which specifies a simple set of choices available to the individuals (players) and then models their interaction given their preferences. This game can involve many players with many choices; however, in order to reduce the complexity associated with a game with many players, it is common in political science to specify a two-player game, each with two choices, yielding a 2 x 2 matrix of possible outcomes. Given the ranking of these outcomes by the two players, certain 'pay-offs' or rewards can be assigned to the players. By knowing the preferences and pay-off structures, the political scientist can examine all possible combinations of choices by the two players. In addition, the players can engage in a single interaction with one another, or multiple interactions with one another.

A popular game in game theory is that of the 'Prisoner's Dilemma', which formalizes an interaction of two players made popular in police and crime programmes. In this common scenario, two thieves have been arrested by the police for the same crime, are locked away in two separate cells in the county jail, and are unable to communicate with each other. Each thief has two choices, either to confess to the crime or not to confess to the crime. The police use the fact that the two thieves are separated to their advantage by giving the thieves a range of options. If one thief confesses to the crime and the other does not, the thief that confesses gets a sentence of two years while the thief that did not confess gets twelve years. If both thieves confess to the crime, they get a sentence of six years. If both thieves do not confess to the crime, they both get a sentence of three years. This simple situation is depicted in Figure 7.3. For each thief, the dilemma rests with the expectation of what the other thief will choose while both know that it is rational to minimize their prison sentences. Since neither can trust the other, the rational solution to the dilemma is for both to confess, which gives them both a six-year sentence. While the sentence is not the least or the greatest number of years, it is the best outcome given the nature of the game.

The task of the political scientist using game theory is to identify the actors in the game and specify their choices as well as their preferences so as to model their strategic interaction. The most important aspect of game theory is that none of the

		Thief 2	
		Confess	Do not confess
Thief 1	Confess	Both get 6 years	Thief 1 gets 2 years Thief 2 gets 12 years
	Do not confess	Thief 1 gets 12 years Thief 2 gets 2 years	Both get 3 years

Figure 7.3 The Prisoner's Dilemma

outcomes is certain, but *contingent* upon the actions of both (or many) players. The basic form of the 'Prisoner's Dilemma' (and many other types of games) has been used throughout political science, including the modelling of trench warfare (Axelrod 1984), the basis for a liberal theory of society (Gautier 1986), the reform of bureaucracies in Latin America (Geddes 1991), the breakdown of democracy in Chile and Brazil (Cohen 1994), transitions to democracy (Colomer 1991; Przeworski 1991; Colomer and Pascual 1994), and research problems in comparative politics more generally (Tsebelis 1990).

liberalization). In contrast, Solidarity either wanted to foment a radical break from the past (i.e. overthrow the government) or implement similar reforms envisaged by the government. The resulting combination of these two actors with two choices is depicted in Figure 7.4.

The Communist Party (government) is at the top of the figure and the Solidarity movement (opposition) is on the left-hand side of the figure. The four cells represent the strategic interaction, or 'game' between these two actors. Each cell represents a particular outcome, which either actor ranks from least-preferred to most-preferred. Cell I illustrates the situation where the government chooses continued hard-line rule and the opposition openly confronts the government. Cell II shows the situation where the government chooses reform and the opposition a radical break. This outcome is considered worst for the government since it means that it has 'caved in' to the opposition. Cell III shows the situation where the government chooses to continue with the status quo while the opposition seeks reform. This outcome is considered worse for the opposition since it means that it has 'caved in' to the government. Finally, Cell IV demonstrates the situation where both the government and the opposition choose reform. These four outcomes are

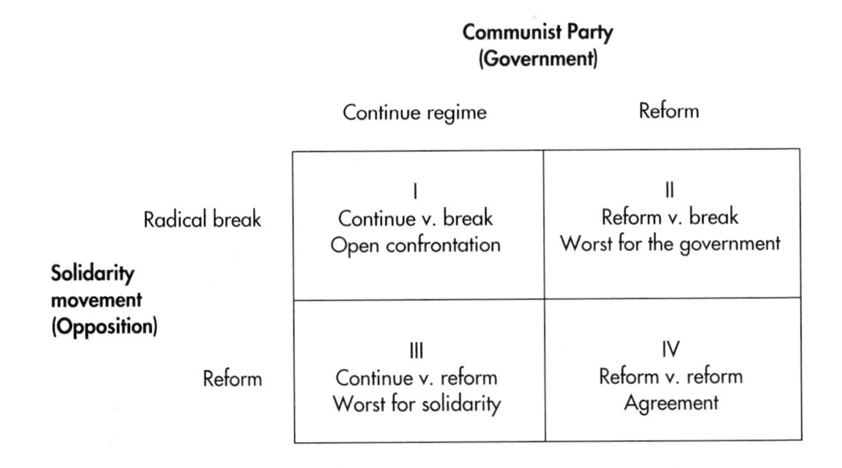

Figure 7.4 Game theory and the Polish democratic transition
Source: Adapted from Colomer and Pascual (1994: 279–280)

not predetermined but are logical combinations resulting from the different choices available to the two actors.

With this basic framework in place, the authors examine the historical sequences surrounding the Polish democratic transition, including the open confrontation, initial agreement, and declaration of martial law in 1981, as well as the Round Table and final agreement in 1989. For the early 1980s, the authors argue that Solidarity most preferred the outcome where the government caves in to its open challenge (Cell II). These preferences are followed in decreasing order by the outcomes in Cells IV, I, and III, respectively. In other words, if Solidarity could not get the government to cave in, it then preferred a mutual agreement, followed by open confrontation, and lastly giving in to the government. The first preference for the government during this period was to continue with its post-totalitarian rule while Solidarity caves in (Cell III). This preference was followed by the outcomes in Cells IV, I, and II.

By formalizing the choices and preferences of the two actors, Colomer and Pascual (1994) are able to model the sequence of historical events. In 1980, the initial state of play is represented in Cell III in which the post-totalitarian government dominates the opposition (compare Linz and Stepan 1996 in Table 7.5). The 1980 strikes led by Solidarity represent the first move in the game in which the opposition confronts the government openly and shifts the interaction to Cell I. In the second move, the government and the opposition reach an initial agreement (Cell IV); however, claims of betrayal on both sides led to a shift back to open confrontation and the declaration of martial law in 1981. Since the opposition continues to confront the regime during the period of martial law, Colomer and Pascual (1994) argue that the outcome is represented by Cell I. Thus, the sequence of historical events in the early 1980s modelled as a game shows how the two actors made a series of choices that ultimately yielded a stable but confrontational outcome.[4]

During the period of martial law, a number of important events occurred, such as Gorbachev's implementation of *glasnost* and *perestroika*, which made the government change its order of preferences while the opposition maintained the same order of preferences as in the early 1980s (ibid.: 284). Given this new state of affairs, the government in 1989 had a strong preference to implement reforms that would legalize Solidarity, allow nominal representation in the Polish parliament (the Sejm), while maintaining its overall political control. In this case, the government preferred the outcome in Cell IV, followed by the outcomes in Cells I, III, and II (ibid.: 286). Thus, the start of play is Cell I, the condition that was sustained for the balance of the 1980s. The first move occurred when the Minister of the Interior, General Kiszczak, began negotiations with Lech Walesa, the leader of Solidarity. As the Round Table negotiations developed, the order of play shifted from Cell I to Cell IV, where ultimately Solidarity was legalized and participated in the first elections for the Sejm (ibid.: 284–291).

The final single-country study in this section seeks to link together the historical and international influences surrounding the Portuguese democratic transition in 1974. In developing a fuller argument about the Portuguese case than in the O'Donnell, Schmitter, and Whitehead series (see Table 7.2), Maxwell (1995) presents an exhaustive account of the Movement of the Armed Forces (MFA) that overthrew the dictatorship, the immediate problems of post-dictatorial rule that confronted the new regime, and the subsequent consolidation of democracy. Maxwell (ibid.: 1–2) stresses the need to take a longer view on the democratic transition and emphasize the unique features of the Portuguese case so as not to homogenize it into a larger comparative framework. The account begins with the rise of the Portuguese empire in the fifteenth century and ends with democratic consolidation and membership of the EU in the 1980s. The uniqueness of the Portuguese case centres on the non-hierarchical and radicalized military officers who put an end to the Salazar dictatorship (compare Linz and Stepan 1996 in Table 7.5), a historical process that was couched in an international environment dominated by the United States, the Soviet Union, and the European Community (later European Union).

The challenge for Portugal during the transition period was to come to terms with the end of its empire in Africa and to tame the radicalized lower echelons of the military, whose initial period of rule sought to revolutionalize and transform the political system. While the military revolt overthrew a right-wing authoritarian regime, throughout the late 1970s and early 1980s, it threatened to replace it with a left-wing one (Maxwell 1995: 160). Indeed, the success of the period was the marginalization of the radical military and the appropriation of the 'gains of the revolution' (land expropriations, socializing clauses in the 1976 constitution) by the Socialists (ibid.: 2). Like Foweraker (1989), Maxwell (1995: 3, 182) argues that Portuguese democracy was born of struggle, but it was a struggle that was ultimately won by the civilian politicians whose moderate position led them to oppose the radical military. This moderate solution was supported financially and encouraged diplomatically by foreign powers.

In concluding this section, it is important to compare the chain of inferences each of these single-country studies is constructing in terms of the distance between the unit of analysis and the final conclusion. Foweraker (1989) begins with the detailed account of the individuals in El Marco de Jerez in the 1950s, who through personal struggle experienced the expansion of their own sense of citizenship. The experiences in this one region are extrapolated to all of Spain, and the political process that he describes is then applied to the general case of democratic struggle under authoritarian conditions. Colomer and Pascual (1994) focus on two (collective) actors over ten years of history and use their interaction to develop an abstract model of democratic transition, where the Polish case serves to confirm their general theory. Maxwell (1995) begins with the Portuguese empire, proceeds to the period of decolonization, the radicalization of the MFA and its role in the democratic transition, and ends with the period of democratic consolidation. He links this long historical process, however, to the beginning of the third wave, the end of the Cold War, and the collapse of the Soviet Union (ibid.: 180). For the Spanish and Polish studies, the final inference is limited to democratic transitions *in similar cases*, while the Portuguese study extends its inferences to a series of events well beyond the scope of the original study. None the less, in following Eckstein (1975), each succeeds in generating hypotheses, confirming theories, and providing fruitful areas for further research.

Summary

In contrast to the research topics of the three preceding chapters, the study of democratic transitions was initially carried out through the comparison of few countries and then as the universe of democratic countries increased, comparative efforts sought to become more comprehensive. Thus, the study of transitions followed the history of the third wave while trying to make larger inferences about the process of democratization by comparing within the current experiences as well as comparing between the current and older experiences. Broadly speaking, the literature has either focused on the role of elites and the nature of pacts that are formed between them (see Howarth 1998b), or has focused on the role of members of civil society and the ways in which they struggle for democracy. As in the comparisons in the previous chapters, the few-country and single-country studies include a deeper focus on the specific events, factors, and contingencies associated with democratic transition, while the many-country studies seek to identify common features that help account for democratization.

Table 7.6 summarizes the main findings of the studies that have been outlined in this chapter, where it appears that there is not a broad consensus on the main factors that help explain democratic transitions. These differences are due to several important factors concerning the study of democratic transition. First, apart from the studies that use some form of rational choice and game theory (e.g. Colomer and Pascual 1994), the comparative study of democratic transitions has been and continues to be largely an inductive process through the examination of an increasing number of countries that have made transitions. While Linz and Stepan's (1996) comparison advances the study of democratic transition by classifying prior regime type and linking the classification to challenges of transition and consolidation, the multiple paths to democracy they identify threaten to be filled by only single countries. Second, and perhaps more importantly, there has not been a clear definition of the dependent variable in the field of democratization studies (see Whitehead 1996a: 354). For some, the outcome is democracy while for others it is the *process* of democratization, which includes liberalization, democratic transition, and democratic consolidation. Defining a ***dependent variable*** as a process and then seeking to identify a range of important explanatory variables is difficult (ibid.: 361–366). Linz and Stepan (1996) establish thresholds for determining in which phase of democratization a country resides (liberalization, transition, or consolidation), but since their study has too few countries for the number of variables, the strength of the inferences about them is necessarily limited.

In sum, the challenge for democratization studies in comparative politics lies in better classification and definition of the object of inquiry, and better research design (Przeworski 1991: 3; Whitehead 1996a). There are still problems with the definition of democratic consolidation. If a consolidated democracy is a political situation in which democracy has become the only game in town (Przeworski 1991; Linz and Stepan 1996: 5), then it is plausible to argue that no country has a consolidated democracy. Indeed, as the previous two chapters have demonstrated, democracies continue to be threatened by a range of challenges and challengers who may not see democracy as the only game in town. Moreover, many countries

Table 7.6 Transitions to democracy in comparative perspective

Method of comparison	*Number of countries*	*Exemplars*	*Result*
Many countries (qualitative)	30 countries over time	Huntington 1991	Transitions due to legitimacy crisis, economic growth, Catholic Church, international influences, and democratic diffusion
Many countries (quantitative)	151 to 172 countries over time	Jaggers and Gurr 1995; Vanhanen 1997	For Jaggers and Gurr, a measure of democracy maps the contours of the third wave and show that the world is constituted by 50% coherent democracies For Vanhanen, democracy is a function of the distribution of power resources, although certain regions contradict expectations about the level of democratization
Few countries	Between 3 and 13 countries over time	O'Donnell *et al.* 1986; Peeler 1992; Linz and Stepan 1996	For O'Donnell *et al.*, democracy is an uncertain outcome, largely due to impulses from within the authoritarian regime, and a negotiated pact between elites For Peeler, democracy is the outcome of elite pacts For Linz and Stepan, the likelihood of democratic consolidation depends on the prior regime type, the initiator of the transition, and problems with stateness
Single-country studies	One country over time	Foweraker 1989; Colomer and Pascual 1994; Maxwell 1995	For Foweraker, Spanish democracy is made from the long struggle for individual citizenship For Colomer and Pascual, Polish democracy is the product of a strategic game between the government and opposition For Maxwell, Portuguese democracy is the result of the collapse of empire, the radicalized military, and the triumph of civilian moderate politicians

that would fall into the category of a consolidated democracy (e.g. Chile before 1970) experienced military coups and long periods of authoritarian rule. In this sense, it may be that democratic consolidation is merely a political situation in which democracy has not broken down. In terms of research design, the study of democratization ought to adhere to the methodological principles outlined in Chapters 2 and 3: namely, if the number of explanatory variables increases, the number of countries in the study must also increase so as to avoid an indeterminate research design.

Notes

1 This third question applies equally to the military authoritarian regimes of Latin America as well as to the communist 'totalitarian' regimes in Eastern Europe. Indeed, one line of inquiry concluded that the location of some dependent capitalist countries of Latin America necessarily meant that they would undergo prolonged and necessary periods of authoritarianism (O'Donnell 1973), while another line of inquiry suggested that totalitarian regimes were the *least likely* to experience democratic transitions (Kirkpatrick 1979).

2 The polity project seeks to measure and document regime types in the world from 1800 to the present and has produced three editions (Polity I, Polity II, Polity III), the most recent of which is used to describe the global contours of the third wave. In addition, the data set has been used to account for the causes and consequences of democratic rule (see Gleditsch and Ward 1997).

3 The fourth volume, *Tentative Conclusions about Uncertain Democracies*, was written by Guillermo O'Donnell and Philippe Schmitter, while the other three volumes were edited by O'Donnell, Schmitter, and Whitehead.

4 It is stable since neither actor would shift from the choices that constitute this particular outcome. It is confrontational since the choice of each actor is the furthest from mutual agreement.

Further reading

Hadenius, A. (1997) *Democracy's Victory and Crisis*, Cambridge: Cambridge University Press.

A collection of essays on the political, economic, and cultural aspects of democratization.

Rustow, D. A. (1970) 'Transitions to Democracy: Toward A Dynamic Model', *Comparative Politics* 2: 337–363.

A definitive and concise statement on democratic transition and consolidation with contemporary relevance and applicability.

Shin, D. C. (1994) 'On the Third Wave of Democratization: A Synthesis and Evaluation of Recent Theory and Research', *World Politics*, 47 (October): 135–170.

A review of the main studies of the third wave, including theory, method, and research design.

Whitehead, L. (1996) *The International Dimensions of Democratization: Europe and the Americas*, Oxford: Oxford University Press.

A collection of essays on various international aspects of democratization.

Chapter 8

Institutional design and democratic performance

This final chapter in Part II examines the comparative study of institutional design and democratic performance. Institutional design involves the actual choice and set of institutions within a country that both link the citizens to the government and shape the relationship among its various branches. Institutions are related to democratic performance since they embody the representative and accountability functions of democracy and structure the ways in which political conflicts under democratic rule are mediated, and the ways in which distributional questions are settled. In this sense, they are linked to both the intrinsic (representation, accountability, and rights) and extrinsic (resource allocation and distribution) dimensions of democracy. Different combinations of institutional arrangements and their relationship to democratic performance are particularly relevant for scholars and politicians alike who have an interest in the stability and survivability of the third-wave democracies (Mainwaring 1993; Jones 1995).

The comparative study of institutions is not new in political science. Indeed, the early 'public law phase' of political science (Valenzuela 1988: 65–66) involved the largely descriptive cross-national comparison of constitutions, which examined the similarities and differences in the powers of governmental branches. While the 'behavioural revolution' in political science in the 1950s (Eulau 1996: 95–106; Goodin and Klingemann 1996a: 10–11) led scholars away from such static comparisons of constitutions, the renewed interest in institutions in the 1980s and 1990s produced an increasing number of studies that not only compare the similarities and differences in institutions, but gauge the effects of these differences (March and Olsen 1984; Mair 1996: 311). Both the comparison of institutions and the linking of institutional design to democratic performance thus bring comparative politics back in a full circle to its origins, but with the added insights and additional analytical techniques that have been developed in the interim (see Chapter 10 of present volume).

As in the previous chapters, this chapter reviews key comparative studies that examine the nature and effects of institutional design on democratic performance. The main aim of these studies moves beyond the search for objective preconditions of democracy to a focus on the best institutional arrangements for the maintenance of democracy and in some cases, the realization of its normative aspirations. Again, the different comparisons and the selection of cases that constitute them often has a direct bearing on the types of inferences that these studies are able to draw about the relationship between institutional design and democratic performance. In addition to the selection of countries, the differences in results are also due to the types of institutional questions each study examines and the ways in which they operationalize the notion of democratic performance.

The research problem

For the purposes of this chapter, the comparative study of institutional design involves three types of institutions that are of greatest importance for democracy, including *executive–legislative arrangements*, the *electoral system*, and as a consequence, the *political party system*. Executive-legislative arrangements concern the relative power given to the executive and legislative branches of government both in terms of the way each is constituted and the powers that each possesses with respect to the other. Typically, the comparative work in this area specifies three basic types of executive–legislative arrangements, including pure presidentialism, pure parliamentarism, and some hybrid between the two (see Briefing Box 8.1). The electoral system provides the rules and formulas through which the votes of the electorate are converted into support for popularly elected executives and members of the representative assemblies. Like executive–legislative arrangements, the electoral system assumes three forms, including majoritarian (also known as plurality, first-past-the-post, or single-member district), proportional, and some hybrid between the two (see Briefing Box 8.2). The party system is seen to be closely related to the electoral system and includes those parties that are successful in achieving enough electoral support in the electoral arena to hold power in government. In all democracies, the party system consists of two or more parties.

It is clear from the specification of these different elements of institutional design that countries comprising comparative analysis in this research area must meet some minimal procedural definition of democracy. For example, 'a political system where multiple political parties compete for control of the government through relatively free and fair elections' (Foweraker 1998: 651). Without such a political system, the key components of institutional design would not be in place or have any particular meaning, nor could the question of democratic performance be examined. Beyond this minimal definition, however, modern democracies vary a great deal in terms of their capacity to deliver both intrinsic democratic goods (e.g. political and civil liberties, minority rights, due process, representation, political equality) and extrinsic public goods (political stability, economic growth and stability, social welfare, national security, physical quality of life) to their citizens. Thus, the comparative study of institutional design seeks to uncover the ways in which different combinations of the main components of institutional design affect the intrinsic and extrinsic aspects of democratic performance.

Briefing box 8.1 Executive–legislative relations

A key aspect of any institutional design for new or old democracies is the formal relationship established between the executive and the legislature. This set of arrangements not only guides the formation, passage, and implementation of public policy but also influences the day-to-day functioning of modern democratic government. In general, there are three types of formal executive–legislative relations: (1) pure presidentialism, (2) pure parliamentarism, and (3) some mixed system. The key distinction between pure presidentialism and pure parliamentarism lies in the degree of dependence or independence between the executive and the legislature. Pure presidential systems have independent sources of democratic legitimacy for the executive and the legislature since both branches of government are elected separately, while prime ministers in pure parliamentary systems are dependent on the confidence of the majority in the legislature, which is elected in a single election. Presidents can be dismissed by a lengthy impeachment procedure, while prime ministers can be dismissed with a vote of no confidence from the legislature. Presidents cannot dissolve legislatures, while prime ministers (usually in conjunction with the head of state) can dissolve the legislature and hold new elections. Table 8.1 summarizes these different types of executive–legislative relations, the key features that make them distinct, and provides examples of each type.

Table 8.1 Types of executive–legislative relations

Type	*Main features*	*Examples*
Pure presidentialism	Mutual independence of executive and legislature Executive is elected by the people for a fixed term and has its own source of democratic legitimacy Legislature is elected by the people for a fixed term and has its own source of democratic legitimacy.	United States Colombia Venezuela Costa Rica
Pure parliamentarism	Mutual dependence between executive and legislature Executive depends on confidence of the majority (or coalition) in the legislature The executive can dissolve the legislature (usually in conjunction with the head of state) There are not separate elections for each executive and legislature	United Kingdom The Netherlands Belgium Norway Sweden Italy Iceland Denmark
Mixed system	Generally combines key features of both systems Executive is elected by the people for a fixed term and has its own source of democratic legitimacy Prime minister requires confidence of a majority in the legislature	France (president and prime minister) Germany (president and chancellor) Portugal (president and prime minister)

Source: Stepan and Skach (1993); Sartori (1994)

Briefing box 8.2 Electoral systems

In addition to the various types of executive–legislative relations (see Briefing Box 8.1), the electoral system itself is an important dimension of institutional design. In general, countries have proportional systems, majoritarian systems, or some mixture of these two systems. Proportional systems (called PR for proportional representation) award seats in the legislature according to the proportion (or percentage) of the popular vote that parties receive in elections. Examples of countries with proportional systems include Austria, Italy, Greece, Iceland, and Belgium, and all of Latin America (Jones 1995; Foweraker 1998). Majoritarian systems (called SM for single-member districts) award seats in the legislature to the single party that wins the highest percentage (majority or plurality) of the popular vote. Examples of majoritarian systems include the United States, Britain, India, and Canada (Lijphart 1994). For any given electoral district, proportional systems can have many seats in the legislature, while districts in majoritarian systems by definition have only one seat. Mixed systems combine some features from both the proportional and majoritarian systems. Typically, a mixed system may elect some representatives through majoritarian means and then add a 'top-up' list of parties (as in Germany and Scotland). Studies of the relationship between votes and seats demonstrate that on balance, proportional systems tend to have a larger number of parties in the legislature than majoritarian systems and mixed systems (e.g. Lijphart 1994; Sartori 1994).

In addition to these main differences between the systems, there are variations among proportional systems that award the seats differently. In the purest proportional systems, voters number candidates in order of preference and the seats are distributed accordingly, taking into account the redistribution of votes for the least-preferred candidates. This system is known as the single-transferable vote (or STV). Other variants include the 'largest remainder' method, the 'highest average method' (also known as D'Hondt), and the Saint Laguë method, all of which use different mathematical formulae to convert the vote share into the seat share in the legislature (Sartori 1994: 8). Overall, these various proportional systems achieve a greater or lesser degree of proportionality in representation.

These different combinations and comparisons raise a series of important research questions for political science. For example, are presidential systems more or less stable than parliamentary regimes? Does the combination of a presidential regime with a proportional electoral system signal the worst prospects for democratic longevity? Are the protection of rights and the maintenance of political stability better under presidential two-party systems or parliamentary multiparty systems? Do presidential multiparty systems have more problems with legislative impasse than do parliamentary multiparty systems? Do majoritarian or consensus democracies provide greater economic and political stability? In each case, the research question seeks to link the configuration of the different components of the institutional design to some key aspect of democratic performance. As in the previous chapters comprising this part of the volume, this chapter compares how many-country, few-country, and single-country studies have sought to answer these important questions.

Comparing many countries

The recent spread of democratization across the world has provided a new opportunity to investigate the relationship between institutional design and democratic performance since the increase in the number of democratic countries allows both institutional design and democratic performance to vary considerably over time and space. As Part I made clear, the increase in the number of observations enhances the strength of the comparative inferences that can be drawn about this research area. In response to the proliferation of democratic transitions in the world, scholars have endeavoured to compare many countries in an effort to examine the various questions surrounding institutional design and democratic performance. Far from there being a dearth of empirical evidence on questions of institutional design (Przeworski 1991), comparative work in this area has blossomed since the early 1990s. This section considers Shugart and Carey's (1992) *Presidents and Assemblies*, Stepan and Skach's (1993) global comparison of democratic stability, and Lijphart's (1994a) *Electoral Systems and Party Systems*. Each study examines the effects of a specific configuration of some or all of the components of institutional design on democratic performance.

In *Presidents and Assemblies*, Shugart and Carey compare up to forty-six different countries at different time periods in order to examine a range of important questions surrounding presidential forms of government and democratic performance. They are interested in key aspects of presidential democracies, including the election of the president and assemblies, the formation of cabinets, the legislative power of the president, and the ways in which electoral systems produce different party systems (Shugart and Carey 1992: 272). Each of these concerns is linked to two key aspects of democratic performance. First, they examine the extent to which different presidential systems are likely to experience democratic breakdown. Second, they demonstrate how different presidential systems produce a trade-off between the principles of democratic *efficiency* and democratic *representation*. Efficiency is the principle that voters ought to be able to assess the responsibility of and exercise control over the incumbent government. Democratic representation is the principle that voters ought to have a large 'menu of partisan choices' so as to maximize the articulation of different interests across the executive and legislative branches (ibid.: 273).

The question of democratic survivability is first examined through a comparison of democratic countries grouped into three categories – parliamentary, presidential, and other – and then compared across those that experienced democratic breakdown and those that did not. For the whole sample, the comparison reveals that presidential democracies are more likely to break down than parliamentary democracies. Isolating the comparison to Third World countries shows that parliamentary regimes are more likely to break down than presidential regimes (ibid.: 40–41). These simple comparisons obscure important differences among the presidential democracies that may have a bearing on democratic survival. Using a list of ten legislative and non-legislative powers of the president (see Table 8.2), the authors examine whether the differences in presidential power are related to democratic survival. A comparison across a sample of forty-four presidential democracies reveals that those systems with a vast number of presidential legislative and non-legislative powers are more likely to have problems with democratic breakdown (ibid.: 154–157). Thus, it is not presidentialism per se that is the problem for democratic survival, but strong presidentialism, since countries with these systems are more likely to have more extreme conflicts between presidents and assemblies. In contrast, systems with strong assemblies are better for resolving conflicts and reaching compromises (ibid.: 165).

Using the four indicators from the list of non-legislative powers outlined in Table 8.2, Shugart and Carey (1992: 158–165) draw a further distinction between presidential regimes based on the president's control over the cabinet and the relative independence of the assembly. The resulting typology reveals four 'ideal' types. Pure presidential systems have strong presidential power over the formation of cabinets and separation of powers between the president and assembly. On the other extreme, premier-presidential regimes require assembly oversight in the formation of cabinets while the president has authority to dissolve the assembly. In between the two extremes are hybrid regimes – president parliamentary and assembly-independent – in which either the president has increased authority over cabinets or restricted ability to dissolve the assembly (ibid.: 158–160). While the countries in their sample variously cluster into each of these four ideal types, the authors point out that these differences have a direct effect on democratic performance. Their analysis suggests that instability is most likely in systems where the authority for cabinet formation is shared between the president and the assembly, since it is not clear who 'owns' the ministers in the cabinet (ibid.: 165).

Their next set of comparisons assesses the relationship among presidential systems, electoral systems, and party systems. For party systems, the authors devise a scale that measures whether the party leadership controls its rank and file

Table 8.2 Legislative and non-legislative powers of popularly elected presidents

Legislative powers	*Non-legislative powers*
Package veto/override	Cabinet formation (exclusive or controlled)
Partial veto/override	Autonomy from legislative censure
Decree laws	Cabinet dismissal
Exclusive introduction of legislation	Dissolution of assembly
Proposal of referenda	
Budgetary powers	

Source: Shugart and Carey (1992: 150)

members, where a higher score represents stronger party leadership (ibid.: 176). Through a comparison of seventeen countries from their sample of presidential democracies, the authors examine the relationship between the strength of party leadership and the strength of presidential legislative power. The comparison reveals that countries with strong presidential powers tend to have weak party leadership while those with weak presidential powers tend to have strong party leadership. Moreover, those systems with strong presidents and weak parties have experienced more problems with breakdown than those systems at the other extreme, a finding that adds a further dimension to the relationship between strong presidentialism and democratic failure.

The electoral system, on the other hand, is seen to be the key factor that links the presidential system to the party system. Following Duverger (1951, 1954, and Chapter 1 this volume), the authors demonstrate that systems with plurality electoral systems tend to have fewer 'effective parties' than those systems with proportional electoral systems (see Briefing Box 8.3). The different electoral systems also affect the selection of the president. Plurality electoral systems tend to produce two identifiable blocs while majority run-off elections tend to produce more fragmented support. In addition, the timing of elections can also affect the structure of power within presidential democracies. Systems in which both the president and the assembly are elected at the same time (concurrently) tend to have fewer problems with 'divided government' or 'co-habitation' than those systems in which both offices are elected at different times (not concurrently). Divided government occurs in pure presidential systems when a different party than the party of the president controls the assembly (e.g. the United States from 1994–2000). Co-habitation occurs in premier-presidential systems when the president is from a different party than the prime minister (e.g. France in 1986).

Taken together, different combinations of presidential, electoral, and party systems can have profound effects on democratic performance. The comparison of presidential regimes demonstrates that more difficulties arise in systems with strong presidential powers, a large number of weak parties, and non-concurrent elections for the president and assembly. These difficulties are due to the conflicts that arise between both institutions that lay claim to democratic legitimacy. Since the president and the assembly are elected separately, and depending on the strength of party support that a president may enjoy, the resolution of political conflicts becomes problematic, which in extreme cases may threaten the stability of the democratic regime. Overall, Shugart and Carey (1992: 287) do not seek to prescribe a particular institutional design to ensure better democratic governance. Their comparisons do reveal, however, that presidentialism is far from a monolithic regime type; it can vary in terms of the president's overall powers as well as the degree of support in the assembly, given differences in both the electoral and party systems. Thus, the lesson for new democracies is that the choice of institutions is directly linked to the challenges of democratic consolidation.

Stepan and Skach (1994) focus on how key differences between pure presidentialism and pure parliamentarism affect democratic performance, which is operationalized using a variety of measures. In addition to democratic survival, the authors compare the relationship between institutional design and the following variables: the number of effective parties; Vanhanen's democracy prediction

Briefing box 8.3 Counting the effective number of parties

Political parties are a central element of modern representative democracies. For comparative political scientists, the number of political parties in a given political system has been an important variable for research. Counting the number of parties, however, has not been a straightforward exercise, since there are more parties in the political system than actually succeed in gaining seats in the national legislature. Thus, political scientists have devised different ways of counting the number of political parties. Drawing on the pioneering work of Douglas Rae (1967), a consensus has emerged within the discipline that counting the number of 'effective parties' (i.e. those that actually have seats in the legislature) is the best way to represent a particular party system. Laakso and Taagepera (1979) have developed the most popular and widely accepted formula (see below) for calculating the effective number of parties, expressed either as the vote share or seat share that a party receives. Either measure is derived by squaring each party's share of seats (or votes), summing these squares, and taking the reciprocal of the resulting number. The final number expresses the effective number of parties in the political system, weighted according to their size (see Lijphart 1994: 68–69; Mainwaring and Skully 1995: 28–29). The effective number of parties has become a standardised measure that 'travels' well to new democracies and features prominently in comparative studies of institutional design and democratic performance.

Vote share	Seat share
$\frac{1}{\Sigma\,(\mathit{Vote}\ \%)^2}$	$\frac{1}{\Sigma\,(\mathit{Seat\ number})^2}$

Figure 8.1 Counting the effective number of parties
Source: Laakso and Taagepera (1979)

residuals (see Chapter 7 and Briefing Box 1.3); a scale of political rights; the susceptibility to military coups; the likelihood of legislative majorities; and cabinet stability. Across all these measures, pure parliamentary regimes perform better than pure presidential regimes. A brief discussion of each measure and the results of the comparisons illustrate how these findings were achieved.

First, for the forty-three countries that had continuous democracy between 1979 and 1989, pure parliamentary regimes are associated with a large number of parties in their legislatures, while pure presidential regimes are not associated with a large number of political parties. From this difference in the number of effective parties, the authors infer that presidential democracies are unable to draw on the conflict-reducing function of multiparty systems (Stepan and Skach 1994: 121). In contrast, using the logic of the arguments found in Shugart and Carey (1992), it is possible to suggest that those presidential regimes with multiparty systems were unable to maintain continuous democracy over the period. Second, using Vanhanen's residuals, whose positive and negative values capture democratic 'over-achievers' and 'under-achievers', the comparison of fifty-nine deviant countries in Vanhanen's analysis reveals that presidential regimes are over three times as likely to be democratic under-achievers. In other words, countries with presidential systems tend to have lower than expected scores on Vanhanen's index of democratization, given the distribution of their power resources (Stepan and Skach 1994: 123). Thus, institutional design appears to be an important intervening variable between socio-economic variables and democratic performance.

Third, using a sample of fifty-three non-OECD countries to control for the effects of development, the authors demonstrate that pure presidential regimes were less likely to maintain continuous democracy during the period 1973–1989, and were twice as susceptible to military coups over the same period (ibid.: 124–125). Fourth, using the same sample of non-OECD countries, presidential systems were almost half as likely to have legislative majorities that support the executive. Fifth, of the ninety-three countries that became independent between 1945 and 1979, none with presidential regimes experienced continuous democracy for the period 1980–1989. Finally, using data on the duration and reappointment of cabinet ministers, their comparisons of countries in Europe, the United States, and Latin America show that presidential regimes experience less frequent reappointment of cabinet ministers with a shorter duration in office (ibid.: 127).

Taken together, these comparisons across different samples of countries using different measures of democratic performance seek to demonstrate what Linz (1990) has called the 'perils of presidentialism'. At their most extreme, the perils produced by the mutual independence of the president and the assembly include the tendency for minority governments, executive violation of the constitution, and support for military intervention in political affairs (Stepan and Skach 1994: 128). Since their comparisons are isolated to either new countries or new democracies (or both), the authors are concerned with the tendency of countries to adopt presidential regimes, an observation and concern equally raised by Shugart and Carey (1992). While Stepan and Skach (1994) are pessimistic about the prospects of democratic performance under pure presidentialism, Shugart and Carey argue that all presidential regimes are not alike and that certain types of electoral and party systems may exacerbate the problems of presidentialism.

In *Electoral Systems and Party Systems*, Lijphart (1994a: 1) examines the 'operation and political consequences of electoral systems' with respect to the ways in which individual votes are converted into seats in the assembly and the structure of the party system. To that end, his study compares twenty-seven democracies from 1945 to 1990 using basic properties of electoral systems, including the electoral formula, the district magnitude, the electoral threshold, and the size of the assembly. The electoral formula refers to plurality, proportional, or hybrid systems (see Briefing Box 8.2). The district magnitude is the number of representatives that are elected per district or constituency. The electoral threshold concerns the minimum amount of electoral support that a party needs in order to obtain seats in the assembly (see Briefing Box 8.4). The size of the assembly simply refers to the

Briefing box 8.4 Electoral threshold

In all political systems there are minimum and maximum percentages of the vote that parties need in order to gain representation in the legislature. A lower threshold is the minimum percentage needed to make it possible for a party to win a seat, while the upper threshold is the maximum percentage where a party is guaranteed to win a seat. Imagine a majoritarian electoral system (see Briefing Box 8.2) with ten candidates competing. The winning candidate need only win slightly over 10% of the vote if all the other candidates evenly split the remaining 90% of the vote (i.e. all other candidates receive less than 10%). This 10% is the lower threshold. The upper threshold is 50%, since in a race with two strong candidates, the winning candidate must garner more than 50% of the votes (i.e. 50% plus one vote). Thus, both the lower and upper thresholds for parties are a function of the size of the electoral district (number of representatives elected per district), the electoral formula (proportional, majoritarian, or mixed), and the number of political parties that compete with each other. Lijphart (1994: 27) has devised a way to calculate the effective threshold for political parties in any given electoral system, which is expressed as the sum of the average of the lower and upper thresholds. Formally, the effective threshold (T_{eff}) is as follows:

$$T_{eff} = \frac{50\%}{(Magnitude + 1)} + \frac{50\%}{2 * (Magnitude)}$$

For political science research, the effective threshold is a measure of the relative difficulty for parties to get represented in the legislature, and by extension, the 'representativeness' of the political system.

number of seats in the lower chamber of the representative body in a bicameral system or the representative body in a unicameral system. The selected countries in the comparison are all examples of long-standing democracies (i.e. continuous democracy for more than twelve years) from Western Europe, Southern Europe, Scandinavia, North America, Latin America, Asia and the Pacific, and the Middle East.

The *electoral system* serves as the unit of analysis instead of the individual countries, while elections under the same electoral system are the repeated observations (Lijphart 1994a: 7). Electoral systems are defined as 'sets of essentially unchanged election rules under which one or more successive elections are conducted' (ibid.: 7). The use of the electoral system gives the comparison enough degrees of freedom (in this case seventy) for quantitative analysis. Moreover, using the most similar systems design, Lijphart can compare different electoral systems within one country to examine the effects of change in the electoral system while all other factors are held constant. The fact that some electoral systems in certain countries have changed means that the cases are not independent, but Lijphart (ibid.: 7–8) seeks to control these changes by using a reduced sample of fifty-three electoral systems. This section will concentrate on Lijphart's (ibid.: 95–117) comparisons that use the full data set of seventy electoral systems across twenty-seven democracies over forty-five years in an effort to show the relationship between a key aspect of institutional design on democratic performance.

The first three comparisons gauge the effects of the electoral system variables, including the degree to which the system is proportionally representative, the number of effective parties, and the generation of majorities in the assembly. The first comparison reveals that plurality systems have a higher degree of disproportionality, a lower number of effective parties, and more frequent majorities in the assembly than proportional systems. In terms of democratic performance, this means that plurality systems aggregate the interests of citizens into larger, more inclusive blocs, which may obscure differences and lead to the under-representation of certain groups, but they produce the majorities in the assembly necessary for governance. Comparing across the systems using the effective threshold does not change the main difference in these effects between plurality and proportional systems, but does allow Lijphart (ibid.: 100) to discriminate among the proportional systems. For the most part, proportional systems with a lower effective threshold for parties to obtain seats in the assembly tend to have lower disproportionality, a higher number of effective parties, and less frequent majorities. In this way, representation is improved but governance is made more problematic. Finally, comparing only those countries with proportional systems reveals that the size of the assembly is associated with lower degrees of disproportionality, but has only a weak relation to the number of effective parties and the generation of majorities (ibid.: 100–102).

Using regression analysis and a combined model, Lijphart (ibid.: 107–114) is able to compare the independent effects of the various aspects of the electoral systems on his main indicators of disproportionality, the effective number of parties, and the frequency of majorities. Disproportionality is most often explained by the difference in electoral systems and the most important explanatory factor is the effective threshold, which when combined with effects of the assembly size, explains 63 per cent of the variance in disproportionality. The effective threshold explains between 8 and 42 per cent of the variance in the effective number of parties and the frequency of majorities in the assembly. These findings hold across a smaller sub-set of countries to eliminate the problem of influential cases. Overall, Lijphart's cross-sectional and within-case comparisons (not reported here) demonstrate that the effective threshold is the single most important factor which helps determine the disproportionality of the electoral system. In other words, for new democracies and those democracies seeking to alter their electoral systems, manipulation of the effective threshold is a useful method to change the degree to which citizen votes are accurately converted into representative seats in the assembly.

This section of the chapter has demonstrated that the global proliferation of democracy has provided a robust set of countries and periods of time with which to examine the relationship between institutional design and democratic performance. The studies that were considered show great variation across all components of institutional design and each has shown various ways in which to operationalize key elements of democratic performance. The large number of countries available for comparative analysis has made this research question, like those in the previous chapters, susceptible to quantitative analysis in an effort to uncover generalizations that hold across a large part of the sample. The next section will illustrate how the results of these studies can be examined using a smaller sample of countries.

Comparing few countries

This section considers three examples of studies that investigate the relationship between key aspects of institutional design and democratic performance using a smaller sample of countries, all of which fit within the most similar systems design of comparative method. Lijphart (1994b) compares the intrinsic and extrinsic democratic performance of eighteen established democracies across a range of indicators. Jones (1995) compares the performance of sixteen Latin American presidential democracies. Finally, Mainwaring and Scully (1995) compare the party systems of Latin American democracies. In each study it is assumed that the comparison controls for similarities such as the level of economic development, culture, and history, while the remaining differences expressed in the various independent variables account for the variation in the dependent variables used to operationalize democratic performance.

In contrast to his comparison of electoral systems, Lijphart (1994b) examines the democratic performance of countries across one primary difference: whether they have a majoritarian or proportional electoral system. He operationalizes both intrinsic and extrinsic aspects of democratic performance using several indicators. For intrinsic performance, he uses women's representation, voter turnout, and Dahl's democracy score (see Chapter 4). For extrinsic performance, he uses measures of innovative family policy, income distribution, riots, deaths from political violence, economic growth, inflation, and unemployment. He divides his sample of eighteen countries into parliamentary plurality systems, parliamentary proportional systems, and other systems (e.g. presidential and hybrids). His comparisons reveal that those countries with proportional systems do better across all indicators of intrinsic democratic performance and *no worse* across the indicators of extrinsic performance. For example, women's representation, which is a proxy measure for minority rights, is higher among the proportional systems, while there are no statistical differences between the systems for levels of political violence and macro-economic performance. These findings are corroborated by a further comparison using a refined index that differentiates between majoritarian and proportional systems. Overall, the comparisons of eighteen democracies suggest that proportional systems are 'to be preferred over plurality since [they offer] both better representation and at least as effective public policy-making' (Lijphart 1994b: 8).

Lijphart (1994b: 12–15) makes some important methodological points concerning his study which necessarily limit the types of inferences that can be drawn from it. The most similar systems design shows that for the eighteen countries, proportional systems outperform the others, but his analysis invites replication using a different sample of countries. The original sample contains long-standing and well-established parliamentary democracies, such as Austria, Belgium, Denmark, Finland, Germany, Italy, The Netherlands, Norway, and Sweden; it therefore ignores the important intervening variables of economic development and political culture. In other words, most of the countries with proportional systems have well-established welfare states which tend to promote equality of representation and have developed a certain democratic civic culture. Thus, the superior performance of these countries may have less to do with their electoral systems than with the development of the welfare state and an egalitarian political culture. While Lijphart (1994b: 11) excludes the Nordic countries from the analysis to control for these effects, a comparative study using a different sample of countries that lie outside the confines of the old democracies may add new insights to his findings. As outlined in Chapter 3 of the present volume, however, the addition of new and more dissimilar countries to the analysis may lead to the problem of conceptual stretching, and having noted these problems, Lijphart (ibid.: 12–13) remains cautious in his recommendation that proportional systems offer the greatest benefits for new and emerging democracies.

In *Electoral Laws and the Survival of Presidential Democracies*, Jones (1995) draws on the comparative analysis found in Shugart and Carey (1992) but limits his comparisons to sixteen Latin American countries, placing his study squarely within the most similar systems design. All of these countries have presidential systems and by limiting the comparisons to Latin America, Jones (1995: 65) is able to control for such intervening factors as religion, colonial history, and culture. He argues that '[b]y restricting the analysis to a relatively small set of nations, there is a greater opportunity to conduct an informed contextual analysis which is enhanced by a developed understanding of the culture and history of the region' (ibid.: 65). Moreover, to triangulate his study, he compares the performance of twenty-eight different provincial systems in the single case of Argentina. His study seeks to demonstrate that successful performance among presidential democracies relies on the degree to which the electoral system produces legislative support for the president. Through a series of comparisons across the region, Jones links the problems of governance to the absence of legislative support for the president, which is a function of the difference in electoral laws.

His analysis begins by demonstrating the problems of democratic governance at the global level. A comparison of stable democratic countries from 1945 to 1994 shows that with the exception of Chile (1932–1973), countries that have not produced a legislative majority or near-majority for the president have experienced democratic failure (ibid.: 35–39). Such a global comparison, however, may contain a possible spurious relationship between this aspect of institutional design and democratic performance, a problem which can be minimized by his 'intra-presidential system comparison' (ibid.: 38). In light of these considerations, Jones limits the scope of his comparison to Latin America and refines a measure of democratic performance, which he relates to the degree of legislative support for the president.

His refined measure of democratic performance is the percentage coverage of executive–legislative conflict in the *Latin American Weekly Report* over the period 1984–1993 (ibid.: 41–43). Presidential support is operationalized with two different measures. The first represents the percentage of seats the president's party controls in the lower chamber of the legislature. The second is a dichotomous variable indicating whether the president has a majority or near majority of seats in the lower chamber (ibid.: 44). In addition to examining legislative support for the president, his comparison includes four additional explanatory variables, including the percentage of the president's term that has been completed, the power the president has over the legislature, the capacity the legislature has to censure the cabinet, and the amount of presidential control over the presidential party legislators (ibid.: 44–48). His analysis uses presidential years as the unit of analysis to compare across fourteen countries spanning the terms of thirty-one presidents over the period, which yields a total of ninety-nine presidential years.

The comparison uses regression analysis to determine the independent effects of each of these explanatory variables on the level of executive–legislative conflict. The results demonstrate that both measures of presidential legislative strength have a significant effect on the level of conflict, which means that the less legislative support a president enjoys, the more conflict there is between the two branches. In addition to this key finding, his analysis shows that the level of conflict decreases with the amount of time the president has been in office, and tends to be lower in systems where the legislature does not have the power to censure the cabinet. Taken together, his initial comparisons across Latin American democracies show that countries with low levels of legislative support for the president are more prone to conflict and, by extension, to democratic failure.

But what are the sources of low legislative support for the president? The answer lies in the level of multipartism in the legislature, which is a function of the electoral system. Systems with a large number of parties in the legislature necessarily create problems in generating legislative support for the president (Jones 1995: 75–86), and certain key features of the electoral system tend to produce a large number of parties. Thus, in the remainder of his study, Jones (ibid.: 76–154) seeks to examine the relationship between elements of the electoral system and the number of political parties in the legislature. These elements include the formula to elect the president (plurality or majority run-off), the timing of executive and legislative elections (concurrent or non-concurrent), the effective magnitude of electoral districts, the system for converting votes into seats, and whether the legislature contains a single chamber (unicameral) or two chambers (bicameral).

The comparative analysis reveals that of all these aspects of the electoral system, the timing of elections and the formula for electing the president have the most effect on the number of parties in the legislature. Both concurrent elections for the president and the legislature and plurality electoral formulas for selecting the president tend to reduce the number of parties and therefore increase the likelihood of presidential support. The path of the comparative evidence and the substantive argument is summarized in Figure 8.2. First, the regression analysis established positive relationships among the various aspects of the electoral system and multipartism, the strongest of which are the majority run-off formula for electing presidents and the non-concurrent timing of elections for both branches. Second, multipartism leads to problems of support for the president. Third, low presidential legislative support, expressed in terms of seats and majorities, and controlling for legislative censure, has a negative effect on democratic performance

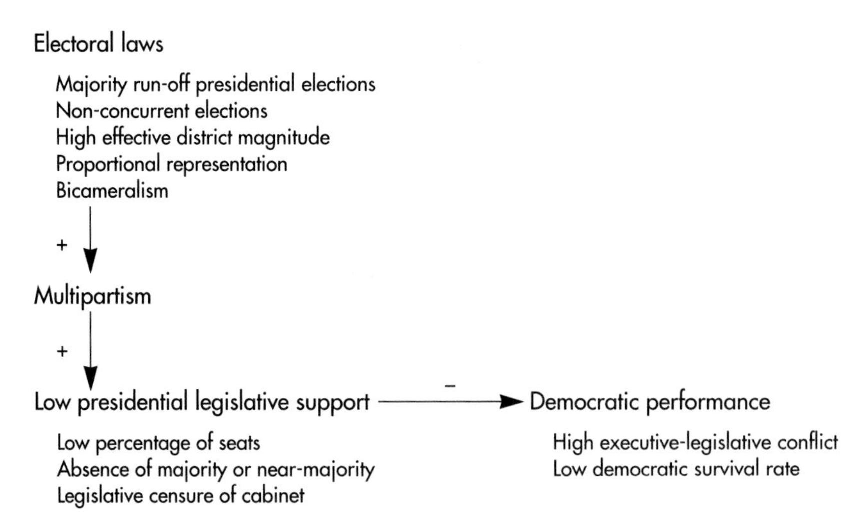

Figure 8.2 Electoral laws and democratic performance
Source: Summary of Jones (1995)

in terms of both executive–legislative conflict and democratic survival. The lesson for new democracies is to formulate electoral laws in order to reduce the number of political parties and make the legislature more compatible with successful presidential government (ibid.: 160).

The final study in this section concerns the relationship between party systems and democratic performance and also uses a sample of Latin American countries, the comparison of which adds two further dimensions to the conclusions reached by Jones (1995). Mainwaring and Scully (1995: 1–2) argue that beyond the problem of multipartism for presidential democracy, both the degree to which a party system is institutionalized and its level of ideological polarization are critical for its smooth functioning as well as the process of democratic consolidation. An institutionalized party system has four important characteristics: stable inter-party competition; parties with stable roots in society; the acceptance parties as institutions for determining who governs; and party organizations with stable rules and structures (ibid.: 1). Party polarization refers to the ideological 'distance' between political parties on the left–right spectrum (ibid.: 2). Their comparison of twelve Latin American countries over the period 1970–1993 examines the degree to which the party systems have become institutionalized and the level of ideological polarization – a two-dimensional scheme of classification that is linked to democratic performance.

Table 8.3 shows how the presence of each characteristic determines a rough classification of the party systems in the twelve countries (listed in the second column of the table), which is then linked to aspects of democratic performance, including legitimacy, accountability, corruption, and the quality of governance. By definition, institutionalized party systems have all the characteristics, while inchoate party systems are deficient across most of the characteristics, and hegemonic party systems fall somewhere in between. Both inchoate and hegemonic

Table 8.3 Party institutionalization and democratic performance

Party system type	*Countries*	*Democratic performance*
Institutionalized		
Stable competition	Venezuela	Compromise and coalitional governance
Deeply rooted	Costa Rica	Political process is structured
Accepted institutions for determining who governs	Chile	High levels of legitimacy
	Uruguay	Provides accountability
Strong organization	Colombia	Less corruption
	(Argentina)	Effective governance
Inchoate		
Unstable competition	Bolivia	Erratic politics
Less deeply rooted and personalistic	Brazil	Weak representation of interests
	Peru	Low level of legitimacy
Less accepted as institutions for determining who governs	Ecuador	Problems with accountability
		More corruption
Weak organization		Ineffective governance
Hegemonic		
Very little competition	Mexico	No full expression of interests
Deeply rooted	Paraguay	Weak representation
Little acceptance as institutions for determining who governs		Effective governance
Strong organization		

Source: Mainwaring and Scully (1995: 6–28)

party systems are problematic for democratic performance. Inchoate systems provide weak forms of representation, suffer problems of accountability, and make governance difficult since the political process is not well structured. Hegemonic systems provide effective governance since they control the political process, but they fail to represent interests.

In addition to the institutionalization of the party system, Mainwaring and Scully (1995) examine the number of effective parties (see above and Briefing Box 8.3) and the level of ideological polarization. Across the twelve countries, there is a positive association between the number of effective parties and the level of ideological polarization. Countries with a small number of effective political parties (e.g. Paraguay, Costa Rica, and Colombia) have low levels of ideological polarization, while those countries with a larger number of effective parties (e.g. Chile, Ecuador, Brazil, and Peru) have high levels of ideological polarization (ibid.: 31). The combination of multipartism and a high level of ideological polarization creates problems for democratic performance. Indeed, those countries from the region that have long-standing experiences with democracy have fewer parties and low levels of ideological polarization, while those that have had problems with democracy have the opposite combination (ibid.: 32).

Overall, these comparisons demonstrate that a low level of institutionalization in a multi-party system with high levels of ideological polarization produces problems of governance that threaten the stability and maintenance of democratic rule. Moreover, the authors claim that these inferences can be applied to countries beyond the confines of the Latin American region to the emerging party systems of Eastern and Central Europe, Africa, and elsewhere (ibid.: 6). Like the other studies in this chapter, this systematic comparison of key components of institutional design across a selection of countries yields important inferences for the architects of the new democracies about which arrangements are most likely to sustain democracy and promote effective governance (ibid.: 34).

Single-country studies

This final section examines the United States, whose institutions were intentionally designed to provide separate powers to three branches of government and electoral mandates to two branches of government. Its combination of pure presidential system with a plurality electoral system and two dominant political parties may produce a degree of conflict between the executive and the legislature. American history has experienced various periods in which a political party different from the party that controlled the executive has controlled the legislature, a phenomenon known as 'divided government'. During the post-war period in the United States, periods of divided government have been more prevalent than periods of unified government. Indeed, roughly 20 per cent of the period 1900–1968 experienced divided government, while the figure for the period 1968–1992 is over 80 per cent (McKay 1994: 517). Given this rise in the frequency of divided government, scholars have sought to examine both its origins and consequences. Since this chapter is concerned with the relationship between institutional design and democratic performance, it necessarily focuses on the consequences of divided government in the United States.

In contrast to the studies examined in this chapter that use other countries in their comparisons, democratic survival has never been a serious concern in the United States since the end of the Civil War in 1865. Thus, political scientists have concentrated on other key aspects of democratic performance to examine its relationship with institutional design. Three such studies include Mayhew's (1993) analysis of legislative output from 1946 to 1990, Peterson and Greene's (1993) analysis of executive–legislative conflict from 1947 to 1990, and Fiorina's (1996) assessment of additional indicators of democratic performance. Each study compares periods of divided government to periods of unified government in an effort to see if divided government has a negative effect on democratic performance. The inferences drawn from the United States have implications for the comparative study of divided government in other democracies (Fiorina 1996: 112). Thus, in keeping with the argument put forward in Chapter 2, this section demonstrates that the study of institutional design and democratic performance in a single country can have comparative merit that extends beyond its borders.[1]

In *Divided We Govern*, Mayhew assembles a time-series data set of 267 significant pieces of legislation that were passed during the period 1946–1990. Significant pieces of legislation were identified through a comprehensive reading of reports in the *New York Times* and the *Washington Post* as well as retrospective judgements in various policy studies (Mayhew 1993: 37–50). In addition, he examines thirty significant instances of congressional investigation and harassment of the executive (ibid.: 8–33). Both these sets of data are seen as key indicators of executive–legislative co-operation, where the latter measures congressional oversight of the president, and the former measures the political output (performance) of US government (McKay 1994: 526). The time period was chosen to provide a good and even contrast of divided and unified periods of governance, a long enough length of time to make strong generalizations, and a 'natural modern unit' (Mayhew 1993: 5). Somewhat surprising to those commentators who viewed divided government as a problem for democratic performance (e.g. Sundquist 1988), the comparisons over time demonstrate that periods of divided government make very little difference both in terms of congressional investigations (Mayhew 1993: 32) and the volume of legislative output (ibid.: 51–99). During periods of divided government, 12.8 legislative acts per Congress (two-year sessions) were passed while during periods of unified government, thirteen legislative acts per Congress were passed. With regard to congressional investigations, fifteen such investigations occurred under unified government while fourteen occurred under divided government. Thus, Mayhew's (ibid.: 4) study demonstrates that unified as opposed to divided government has not made an important difference in the incidence of high-publicity investigations or important legislation.

Like Jones (1995), Peterson and Greene examine the level of executive–legislative conflict over the period 1947–1990, which is measured as the conflict that arises when executive branch witnesses are questioned by congressional committees and subcommittees (Peterson and Greene 1993: 38). The potential quantity of such interactions is so large that the authors use a random sample of committees across five important policy areas (agriculture, armed services, finance, foreign policy, judiciary), and their total sample consists of 11,000 observations (ibid.: 41). In addition to their selection procedure, they ensured further variation across two dimensions: the degree to which the policy area was foreign or domestic, and the degree to which the issue area had local or national impact (ibid.). Apart from demonstrating different levels of executive–legislative conflict for the different committees and across the policy dimensions, their analysis shows more importantly that for the whole period 1947–1990, executive–legislative conflict actually *declined*. For the four decades, the level of conflict dropped from an average of 38.8 per cent to 26.7 percent, even after controlling for the increased volume of congressional committee activity during the period (ibid.: 46). Combined with the fact that the incidence of divided government has increased over the same period, their results suggest, in line with Mayhew's (1993) findings, that divided government does not adversely affect democratic performance in the United States.

Finally, Fiorina (1996) summarizes the main findings of Mayhew (1993) and Peterson and Greene (1993), while adding further indicators of democratic performance from the US case. Like the two previous studies, Fiorina (1996:

95–102) examines executive–legislative relations, but adds some new measures, including the Senate confirmation of presidential appointees (for executive offices and the judiciary), the signing of international treaties, and the use of presidential vetoes. His analysis demonstrates that divided government makes no difference for the confirmation of executive and judicial appointments, nor does it affect the president's ability to sign treaties. The only effect of divided government that is demonstrated by Fiorina (ibid.: 102) is that presidents who face a Congress controlled by the opposition are more inclined to veto unfavourable legislation.

Taken together, these studies provide a systematic analysis of the phenomenon of divided government in the United States. Each study raises the number of observations within the single country through an analysis of the time-series trends in key indicators of democratic performance while gauging the effects of divided government. With the exception of the use of the veto power, all three studies conclude that divided government in the United States does not have an effect on democratic performance. Methodologically, Mayhew (1993) has been criticized both for his definition and sources of 'significant' legislation, as well as his measure of legislation, which represents its supply rather than its demand (see Kelley 1993; McKay 1994: 527; Fiorina 1996: 88–89). Yet, Peterson and Greene's analysis, which uses a different measure of democratic performance, corroborates his results. For both studies using different measures of performance over the same period, divided government does not make a difference. Despite this corroboration, some scholars remain sceptical about the findings and still believe that divided government is at least a problem of perception as much as a problem of performance, which may ultimately erode the legitimacy of democratic institutions (McKay 1994: 532).

Beyond the basic conclusion that divided government does not affect performance, what comparative inferences can be drawn from these studies of the United States? Fiorina (1996: 111–124) argues that divided government in a presidential system is similar to coalition government in a parliamentary system, both of which are capable of sustained democratic performance. For him, what really needs to be addressed is the practice of split-ticket voting, which produces divided government in the first place. But by confining his comparative inferences to parliamentary and (mostly) European democracies, Fiorina fails to consider other presidential systems, for example those promulgated in the new democracies of Latin America, Africa, and Asia. While the two-party presidential system in the United States may produce conditions similar to coalition government in Europe, multiparty presidential systems in Latin America, as the comparisons outlined above have demonstrated, are fraught with problems of governance which may threaten democracy. Moreover, there may be 'exceptional' factors about the United States that have allowed its conflict-prone political system to continue to function.

Summary

Summarizing the results and conclusions of all the studies in this chapter shows a remarkable degree of consensus (see Table 8.4). The first conclusion is that parliamentary systems tend to perform better, both in terms of democratic survival

Table 8.4 Institutional design and democratic performance in comparative perspective

Method of comparison	*Number of countries*	*Exemplars*	*Result*
Many countries	Between 27 and 93 countries over time	Shugart and Carey 1992; Stepan and Skach 1994; Lijphart 1994	Overall, parliamentary systems appear to perform better than presidential systems; however, among presidential systems, the most problems occur in those with strong presidents facing weak party systems elected through non-concurrent elections For Lijphart, the effective threshold is the key aspect of the electoral system that can be manipulated to produce more proportional representation
Few countries	Between 12 and 18 countries	Lijphart 1994; Jones 1995; Mainwaring and Scully 1995	For Lijphart, proportional systems are better at providing the intrinsic goods of democracy and no worse at providing the extrinsic goods For Jones, certain features of the electoral system can produce multipartism, which translates into low legislative support for the president and problems with democratic performance For Mainwaring and Scully, low levels of party institutionalization and high levels of ideological polarization threaten the stability of Latin American presidential democracies
Single-country studies	United States	Mayhew 1993; Peterson and Greene 1993; Fiorina 1996	Across many measures of democratic performance, including executive–legislative conflict, the production of legislation, and the signing of treaties, divided government does not have a negative impact. Only the use of executive vetoes increases under conditions of divided government

and other aspects, than presidential systems. But this simple dichotomization between these two basic forms obscures the great variation among presidential systems and neglects the interaction among the electoral system, the party system, and the set of executive–legislative arrangements. Among presidential systems, it is those with strong presidents combined with weak and ideologically polarized parties that are the most problematic. They are more prone to conflict, have a greater tendency to use extra-constitutional means to achieve policy objectives (e.g. Iran-Contra in the US or the *autogolpes*[2] in Peru and Guatemala), and in certain cases, a greater propensity to encourage military intervention (Stepan and Skach 1994).

Thus, for the new democracies that seek survival and stability in the long run, certain lessons can be drawn from the comparison of comparisons presented in this chapter. If possible, new constitutions and institutional arrangements ought to establish parliamentary forms of rule. If, for reasons of culture and history, new democracies favour the establishment of presidential systems (see Foweraker 1998), then the electoral systems ought to be designed so as to minimize the worst qualities of multiparty systems. But these prescriptions must be viewed with a degree of caution. First, an examination of certain outliers has shown that manipulation of electoral and party systems can have unintended consequences. Second, more comparative research is needed on the coalitional behaviour within presidential multiparty systems, since many do exist and as yet have not experienced democratic breakdown during the third wave.

Notes

1 Although American politics constitutes a vibrant and comprehensive sub-field in political science, the United States is, after all, simply another country in the world and many of its research questions are applicable to other countries. It thus can be incorporated quite easily under the comparative umbrella.

2 In 1992 in Peru and 1993 in Guatemala, the presidents of both countries sought extra-constitutional means to pursue their political objectives. President Fujimori in Peru shut down the Congress with the support of the military, and President Serrano sought to do the same in Guatemala. The term '*autogolpe*' means 'self-coup'.

Further reading

Foweraker, J. (1998) 'Institutional Design, Party Systems, and Governability – Differentiating the Presidential Regimes of Latin America', *British Journal of Political Science*, 28: 651–676.

A comprehensive review of institutional design and democratic performance in Latin America.

McKay, David (1994) 'Review Article: Divided and Governed? Recent Research on Divided Government in the United States', *British Journal of Political Science*, 24: 517–534.

A comprehensive review of the origins and consequences of divided government in the United States.

Sartori, G. (1994) *Comparative Constitutional Engineering: An Inquiry into Structures, Incentives, and Outcomes, London*: Macmillan.

A theoretical and empirical exploration of institutional design and its effects.

Part III

COMPARATIVE METHODS AND NEW ISSUES

COMPARATIVE METHODS AND NEW ISSUES

This final section of the book summarizes the studies in Part II (Chapter 9) and discusses the new issues and challenges that will confront the field in the future (Chapter 10). Chapter 9 reviews the studies in Part II with respect to the ways in which they have highlighted the methodological trade-offs associated with different comparative methods and the contributions they have made to build theories in political science. In this way, the comparative architecture of Part I is brought to bear on the issues and methodological discussions in Part II. The key factors that are important for comparative research which emerge from this analysis include case selection (both number and type), the limitation of inferential aspirations, and the practice of good theorizing and adequate research design.

Chapter 10 explores the new issues and challenges that will confront comparative politics in the next century. The chapter summarizes briefly the developmental path that comparative politics has taken and where it is likely to lead in the years to come. It examines new developments in method and analytical software that will help the field to evolve as well as to break down traditional barriers in the discipline. Finally, it discusses the key challenges to comparative politics in the future, including transnational political activism, political diffusion, human rights, and globalization.

Chapter 9

Common themes and different comparisons

The chapters in Part II demonstrate clearly that comparative politics is an exciting, dynamic, and developing field in the social sciences both in terms of its substantive topics and methodological techniques (cf. Mair 1996: 309). Comparative politics as a field is not merely defined in terms of its primary activity – comparing countries – but as a broad research community that seeks to provide individual, structural, and cultural explanations for observed political phenomena (Lichbach 1997: 240–241). Each of the research topics in Part II has been examined using comparative methods, while the review of the specific studies illustrates that some have been more systematic in their comparisons than others. This 'comparison of comparisons' identifies similarities and differences among the studies with respect to the operationalization of key concepts, overall research design, choice of countries, and types of comparative inferences they are able to make.

With respect to the chapters in Part II, the research questions address common themes that are best examined using some form of comparison. The themes include the emergence of democracy (both in the past and more recently), violent and non-violent challenges to its institutions, and the institutional configurations that may facilitate its long-term survival (cf. Apter 1996: 373). The research questions were posed in such a way that comparison provided the best method for making substantive inferences. Whether searching for the objective preconditions of democracy, the individual and structural correlates of rebellion, the origins, trajectory and impact of social movements, the conditions for democratic transition, or the institutional arrangements for successful and effective democratic rule, systematic comparison of one or more countries helped to provide answers. This systematic comparison includes comparing many countries, few countries, and the intensive examination of single countries using both quantitative and qualitative techniques.

This chapter discusses these common themes and different comparisons to achieve several objectives. First, the issues and methodological concerns raised in Part I are brought to bear on the methods and substantive results in Part II in order to illustrate the methodological trade-offs associated with comparative politics. These trade-offs include those between the scope of countries and the types of inferences that can be drawn, generalizations based on the comparison of many countries and the presence of outliers, and different levels of analysis. In so doing, it identifies the methodological sources for the different substantive results obtained by the studies compared in Part II, including units of analysis, the selection of cases, and the inferential aspirations of the different studies. Second, the chapter summarizes the studies from Part II and examines how each has contributed to building individual, structural, and cultural theories of politics. Finally, the chapter outlines the key lessons scholars ought to draw from these observations.

Methodological trade-offs

Comparing many countries

The comparison of many countries provides statistical control and reduces the problem of selection bias; it gives extensive comparative scope and empirical support for general theories, and identifies deviant cases that warrant closer comparative examination. The many-country studies in Part II make important generalizations about the key issues identified in each chapter. Those in Chapter 4 identified important socio-economic correlates of democracy while the latter studies suggest that economic development causes democracy. For political violence, the studies identify a bundle of explanatory factors, while their different results are more due to their different theoretical conceptualizations and model specifications than to the method they have adopted (see below). The studies in Chapter 6 identify broad socio-economic changes and organizational factors as important explanations for social movement origins, while largely ignoring the trajectory, shape, and political impact of movements.

For democratic transition, Huntington's (1991) qualitative study argues that a crisis of legitimacy in the authoritarian regime, high levels of economic development, the national and international presence of the Catholic Church, other international influences, and the diffusion of democratic ideas all help account for the global spread of democracy since 1974. The quantitative studies either map descriptive attributes of the 'third wave' of democratic transition (Jaggers and Gurr 1995), or identify the importance of key socio-economic variables that lie behind it (Vanhanen 1997). Finally, the global evidence on institutional design and democratic performance demonstrates that parliamentary systems tend to perform better and break down less frequently than presidential systems.

What is clear from these studies is the identification of a parsimonious set of explanatory factors and sufficient degrees of freedom to allow for great variance in the variables, as well as the inclusion of control variables to rule out rival hypotheses. Of the issues in Part II, the most frequently verified empirical generalization is for the positive relationship between economic development and democracy. The second strongest generalization to emerge from these studies is the superior democratic performance (however measured) of parliamentary systems. There is less academic consensus, however, on the explanation for political violence, a dearth of many-country studies on social movements, and few quantitative global comparisons of democratic transition. These problems in the global comparative literature illustrate the key weaknesses of this method. For political violence, many of the theories posit relationships that exist at the individual level, yet the tests for them use the nation state as the unit of analysis. Indicators for social movement activity such as protest event data are difficult to collect for a large number of countries. Democratic transitions tend to be operationalized in dichotomous terms, while theoretically transition is often thought to be a longer *political process*, which makes its cross-national study more difficult (see Whitehead 1996a). Thus, for the many-country comparisons to provide more valid and reliable inferences, better specification and measurement of the key variables are needed. Given the advances in communication and information technologies, however, the collection and sharing of global data on a variety of social, economic, and political indicators will continue to be easier. Moreover, the establishment of an ethos of replication and data-sharing within the scholarly community will aid in this goal for improving global analysis (see Chapter 10).

Comparing few countries

The weaknesses associated with comparing many countries and the discomfort scholars may have in specifying parsimonious models of politics have led many to compare a smaller set of countries. As Part I made clear, this method of comparison also provides control through use of the most similar or most different systems design (or both). It uses concepts and variables that may be more sensitive to the nuances of the particular political contexts under investigation. It allows for historical and intensive examination of cases not possible in studies with a large sample of countries. Together, the strength of few-country studies lies in their lower level of abstraction and their inclusion of historical and cultural factors. While many of these studies do not seek universal aspirations for their inferences, they do seek to extend their generalizations beyond the immediate scope of the countries included in the analysis.

For economic development and democracy, few-country studies introduce a broader set of variables and, using a historical perspective, not only 'unpack' the simple bivariate relationship between development and democracy but also uncover the sequences through which countries have (or have not) become democratic. While the few-country studies do not dispute the generalizations of the global comparative literature, they are keen to point out that there are exceptions to every rule. Thus, the global comparative studies focus on the similarities across the sample, while the few-country comparisons focus on the differences. Both strategies of comparison are equally valid but will necessarily yield different results. Similarly, the studies on political violence introduce a broader set of explanatory variables and historical sequences, as well as the inclusion of full revolution as a dependent variable. These studies focus on the structure of the agricultural sector, capitalist transformation, the cultural and community features of key groups most likely to exhibit violent and revolutionary behaviour, group organization and support, the strength and legitimacy of state power, and the role of international actors. Rather than identifying a mono-causal explanation, all these studies seek to demonstrate the configuration of different explanatory factors and their likely association with political violence and revolution. Some of these studies select countries on the basis of having had a revolution (e.g. Wolf 1969), while others select a larger sample of countries to include positive, negative, and mixed cases of revolution (e.g. Paige 1975; Skocpol 1979; Wickham-Crowley 1993). Those that provide greater variance in the dependent variable through this type of selection necessarily can make stronger inferences from their comparisons.

Few-country studies of social movements move beyond explaining their origins to questions of their trajectory, shape, strategies, and political impact. They identify new sectors of the population that support movements, the changing political opportunities that allow for the emergence, shape and impact of movements, the differences between the so-called 'new' and 'old' social movements, as well as the different strategies they employ. The changing political opportunities include the level of repression in a political system, the variable provision of individual rights, and different sets of elite alignments. These studies use both quantitative and qualitative techniques to marshal the comparative evidence on movement activity. Overall, more comparative work on the nature and impact of social movement activity is needed, as this alternative form of politics will continue to be important.

Initially, democratization studies compared few countries and focused on uncertain outcomes of elite manoeuvring at critical moments of crisis during periods of authoritarian rule. More recently, studies have taken into account the nature of the prior regime, fundamental questions of 'stateness' (Linz and Stepan 1996), the political economy of the transition, and important international influences. Like the early studies of political violence and revolution, many of these studies suffer from selection bias as they focus on those countries that have made a democratic transition rather than comparing them to those that have not. While Linz and Stepan (1996) seek to redress this problem by looking at clusters of transitions and non-transitions, they introduce many other explanatory variables that create the problem of indeterminacy. In other words, their study does not quite overcome the problem of 'too many variables not enough countries' (see Chapter 3 above). Like the study of political violence and revolution, it is important to compare successful transitions to unsuccessful transitions across a sufficient number of cases to identify the key factors that help explain the process of democratic transition.

The few-country studies on institutional design and democratic performance do not conflict with the global comparisons, but complement their findings with a more intensive examination of the features of presidential systems that may or may not inhibit their overall performance. These comparisons provide a differentiation of presidential systems themselves to demonstrate that both strong presidential systems and those with multiple political party systems tend to have more problems than those with significant limits on presidential power and a small set of strong political parties. Thus, the generalizations made by the many-country comparisons warrant further investigation with a smaller set of countries. In this regard, Jones's (1995) study complements the global comparisons in examining the key differences among the presidential systems of Latin America. His study uses the most similar systems design since he compares countries with similar cultural and historical legacies and similar institutional arrangements. The many- and few-country comparisons of electoral systems complement one another since the general rule that proportional electoral systems tend to have multiparty systems identified by the global comparisons also holds in the comparisons of a smaller sample of countries. Moreover, it is precisely these types of electoral system that produce some of the major problems for the presidential systems examined in the few-country studies.

The biggest weakness in few-country comparisons is the problem of selection bias, particularly when the choice of countries relies on the outcome that is to be explained. For example, by including more countries from Europe in their study of capitalist development and democracy, Rueschemeyer *et al.* (1992) find that a violent break with the past is not an important factor for democracy, which contradicts Moore's (1966) findings. In addition, the extension of their study beyond Europe into Latin America and the Caribbean reveals that it is the working class, and not the bourgeoisie as Moore (1966) contends, that is the key agent for democracy. Whether the inclusion of Moore's (1966) cases of China and Japan would have altered the conclusions of Rueschemeyer *et al.* (1992) remains an empirical question; however, it appears that the inclusion of more countries in similar regions provides different substantive conclusions about the relationship between capitalist development and democracy.

Similar selection effects are apparent in the studies on violent political dissent and revolution. Wickham-Crowley's (1993) inclusion of positive, negative, and mixed instances of revolutionary activity at different periods of time provides a more robust understanding of revolution than that offered by Wolf's (1969) study. The most Wolf does is to identify a single explanatory factor across six countries that have experienced revolution, while Wickham-Crowley's (1993) analysis demonstrates the key factors for successful revolution as well as explaining the failure of many revolutionary attempts in Latin America. Thus in both research areas, Moore (1966) and Wolf (1968) select countries based on values of the dependent variable, while Rueschemeyer *et al.* (1992) and Wickham-Crowley (1993) select countries based on other criteria. Moore (1966) chooses particular examples of democratic, fascist, and communist outcomes, while Wolf (1968) chooses instances of revolutionary outcomes only. Rueschemeyer *et al.* (1992) and Wickham-Crowley (1993) choose countries on regional, cultural, and historical similarity while the outcome they are trying to explain – democracy or revolution – varies fully.

Single-country studies

By definition, there is great variation in results among the single-country studies. Part I argued that such studies are useful for comparative analysis if they make explicit use of comparative concepts or generate new concepts for application in countries beyond the original study. Such studies can generate hypotheses, infirm and confirm existing theories, and allow for the intensive examination of deviant cases identified by larger comparisons. Single-country studies, however well intentioned and well designed, have serious difficulty in making generalizations that are applicable at the global level. Two of the studies in Part II clearly establish a relationship between economic development and democracy (Argentina and South Korea), while three of them (Italy, Botswana, and India) find political culture to be an important intervening explanatory factor for the development of democracy. Thus for Italy, a certain 'civicness' explains good democratic performance. In Botswana, the presence of Tswana political culture inhibits the development of democracy beyond its formal components. The persistence of the caste system in India has meant that modern democracy is still embedded in traditional identities. Thus, closer attention to the historical and cultural specificities of individual countries enriches the understanding of the relationship between economic development and democracy which may be lost in larger comparisons.

The three case studies on rural rebellion in Mexico show a certain consensus that among other factors, the historical encroachment on land and lifestyle by outside agents has spurred on rebellious activity from the period of the Mexican Revolution to the latest peasant-based uprising from the Zapatistas in the southern state of Chiapas. Like the studies that compare many countries, the inference from these studies is that the encroachment and displacement of people whose livelihood is derived from land increase the likelihood that they will participate in rebellious and revolutionary activity. This inference is in line with Paige's (1975) comparison of agricultural sectors in seventy countries and it fits well with the types of explanation for rural rebellion offered by Wickham-Crowley (1993). Future single-country studies on rebellion and revolution can test whether the inferences from the Mexican case can be upheld in other contexts.

The single-country studies on social movements demonstrate how changing political opportunities interact with movement activity, as well as how the time-dependent dynamics of social movements can be described as a 'cycle of protest' (Tarrow 1989). The studies of social movements in the United States (Gamson 1975; Costain 1992) both show that protest activity can win concessions from the state. To compensate for some of the limits of the single-country study, both authors raise the number of observations to provide greater variance (see Chapter 3). Gamson (1975) compares the activities and outcomes of over fifty social movement organizations, while Costain (1992) uses time series indicators of social movement activity, government activity, and shifting patterns of public opinion. This greater variance allows both authors to make important inferences about social movement activity and political impact from a single country.

The quest to understand democratic transition has in large part been driven by studies of individual countries that have undergone such processes since 1974. Two of the studies compared in Part II demonstrate elite and popular struggle perspectives on transition. Colomer and Pascual (1994) develop a game theory model of transition, which is applied to the Polish case. The history of the transition is seen as a series of sequential games 'played' by the key political actors of the period. The strength of the analysis lies in the identification of all the outcomes possible from a combination of 'moves' by the players. Democratic transition is thus seen not as an inevitable outcome, but as one of many outcomes. In the Polish case, the authors demonstrate that democracy was indeed the outcome, yet their model is specified in such a way that it can be applied to other countries. Foweraker (1989) offers a more comprehensive analysis of the democratic transformation of Spanish civil society that preceded the moment of transition. Less attention is paid to elite political actors as the study focuses on the everyday activities of workers as they attempt to contest power through various representative organizations. Like Pascual and Colomer (1994), Foweraker's inferences concerning incremental struggle under conditions of authoritarian rule have application to countries other than Spain.

Finally, the exclusive focus on the problem of divided government in the United States shows that across a range of conflict and legislative measures, the simultaneous control of the presidency and Congress by different political parties does not appear to make a difference. Even though the post-war period in US political history has seen more years of divided government, the volume of legislation and level of conflict between the executive and legislature have remained unchanged. The global comparison of presidential and parliamentary democracies reveals a certain democratic weakness in presidential democracies and the few-country studies demonstrate that strong presidentialism combined with multiple political parties is particularly problematic. The case of the United States appears to be an outlier to the general rule established by the global comparisons and falls well within the expectations of the few-country comparisons. It is one case where a presidential system does not seem to inhibit democratic performance and it is one case where strong presidentialism combined with a weak two-party system functions.

Building theory

The book has throughout intentionally avoided a direct and full discussion of empirical political theory since it has sought to examine how different comparative methods contribute to theory-building. It also takes the view, contrary to some authors, that there is not a distinctive set of comparative theories (see Chilcote 1994). Rather, there is a collection of research problems that is best addressed through some form of comparison, which in turn helps build our theoretical understandings of the world. Cumulatively, the studies in Part II make contributions to theories that span a wide range of different perspectives. In a seminal piece on the contribution of comparative politics to social theory, Mark Lichbach (1997) delimits the following three broad theoretical perspectives and 'research communities' that have emerged in the field of comparative politics: (1) rationalist, (2) structuralist, and (3) culturalist. Each of these approaches has different assumptions about how the world 'works' and which aspects of the world deserve attention in order to understand and explain observed political phenomena. A short outline of each of these approaches is warranted before considering the ways in which the studies in Part II have contributed to them.

Rationalist perspectives concentrate on the actions and behaviour of individuals who make reasoned and intentional choices based upon sets of preferences, or interests. Those who adhere to the rationalist perspective are 'concerned with the collective processes and outcomes that follow from intentionality, or the social consequences of individually rational action' (Lichbach 1997: 246). Moreover, rationalists in political science believe 'that "bed rock" explanations of social phenomena should build upwards from the beliefs and goals of individuals' (Ward 1995: 79). The development of the rationalist perspective followed earlier individual theories that emphasize the non-rational aspects of human behaviour such as grievance and relative deprivation (see the discussion of Gurr 1968 in Chapter 5). In contrast to these earlier individual theories, rationalists claim that grievance alone is not enough to explain political action and that real choices at the individual level must be examined. While both perspectives concentrate on individual political behaviour, rationalists look for the intentional and 'means–ends' features of individual choice.

In contrast to the rationalist (and other individual) perspective(s), culturalist perspectives seek an understanding of political phenomena by focusing on the broader holistic and shared aspects of collectivities of individuals. Single individual interests and actions cannot be understood in isolation, but must be placed in the context of the shared understandings, inter-subjective relationships, and mutual orientations that make human communities possible (Lichbach 1997: 246–247). These shared meanings and understandings form broader cultures and communities that can be grouped together and analysed as whole units. Such cultures and communities are held together by certain social rules that are emblematic of the identities of both the individuals and the groups themselves (ibid.: 247). Identifying the boundaries of these cultural units and separate identities remains problematic for systematic comparative research; however, scholars have tried to examine the world views, rituals, and symbols that provide 'systems of meaning and the structure and intensity of political identity' across different geographical regions of the world (Ross 1997: 43–44).

Structuralists also focus on the holistic aspects of politics, but unlike the culturalists, they focus on the interdependent relationships among individuals, collectivities, institutions, or organizations. They are interested in the social, political, and economic networks that form between and among individuals. Adherents to this perspective insist that structures that have become reified over time constrain or facilitate political activity so that individual actors are not completely free agents capable of determining particular political outcomes (Lichbach 1997: 247–248). Rather, individuals are embedded in relational structures that shape human identities, interests, and interaction. These relational structures have evolved owing to large historical processes such as capitalist development, market rationality, nation state building, political and scientific revolutions, and technological progress (Katznelson 1997: 83). These large historical processes, it is argued, provide both possibilities and limits for human action.

Together, these three perspectives have variously sought to account for political phenomena in the world by emphasizing and examining key explanatory factors that adhere to the assumptions of their theories. Thus, rationalists focus on the *interests and actions* of individuals, culturalists focus on the *ideas and norms* of human communities, and structuralists focus on the *institutions and relationships* that constrain and facilitate political activity. These theoretical perspectives are not mutually exclusive, however, since scholars have examined the ways in which the interaction between and among the three perspectives helps explain certain outcomes. There are only very rare instances of work in comparative politics that rely exclusively on one of the three perspectives.[1] The comparative methods in this book have all been used to marshal evidence in support of these perspectives virtually across the range of research topics. With the exception of Chapter 8 on institutional design and democratic performance, which by definition focuses exclusively on the functions and effects of democratic institutions, the studies in all the other chapters contribute to individual, structural, and cultural theories of politics.

Table 9.1 summarizes the studies in Part II with reference to their location across individual, structural, and cultural theories of empirical political science. The first column in the table lists the research topics of each chapter while the remaining columns represent the three theoretical perspectives. Individual theories include the older theories that focus on grievances and deprivation as well as the

Table 9.1 Empirical theories of political science: topics and examples from Part II

Topics	*Individual (interests and actions)*	↔	*Structuralist (institutions and relationships)*	↔	*Culturalist (ideas and norms)*
Chapter 4 Economic development and democracy			Lipset (1959) Cutright (1963) Moore (1966) Neubauer (1967) Cutright & Wiley (1969) Dahl (1971) Jackman (1973) Bollen (1979) Waisman (1989) Helliwell (1994) Burkhart & Lewis-Beck (1994) Rueschemeyer et al. (1992) Landman (1999)	Lerner (1958) De Schweinitz (1964) Putnam (1993) Holm (1996) Moon & Kim (1996) Kaviraj (1996)	
Chapter 5 Violent political dissent and social revolution		Womack (1969) Gurr (1968) Hibbs (1973) Sigelman & Simpson (1977) Muller & Seligson (1987) Nugent (1993) Harvey (1998)	Wolf (1968) Hibbs (1973) Paige (1975) Skocpol (1979)	Hibbs (1973) Scott (1976) Wickham-Crowley (1993) Nugent (1993) Harvey (1998)	

Table 9.1 continued

Topics	*Individual (interests and actions)*	↔	*Structuralist (institutions and relationships)*	↔	*Culturalist (ideas and norms)*
Chapter 6					
Non-violent political dissent and social movements	Gamson (1975)	Dalton (1988) Tarrow (1989) Costain (1992) Gurr (1993) Foweraker & Landman (1997) Bashevkin (1998)	Powell (1982) Haas & Stack (1983) Kitschelt (1986) Kriesi *et al.* (1995)	Gurr (1993) Inglehart (1997)	
Chapter 7					
Transitions to democracy	Colomer & Pascual (1994)	O'Donnell *et al.* (1986a–c) Foweraker (1989) Peeler (1992) Maxwell (1995) Linz & Stepan (1996)	Jaggers & Gurr (1995) Linz & Stepan (1996) Vanhanen (1997)	Huntington (1991) Linz & Stepan (1996)	
Chapter 8					
Institutional design and democratic performance			Shugart and Carey (1992) Mayhew (1993) Peterson & Greene (1993) Stepan & Skach (1993) Lijphart (1994a) Lijphart (1994b) Jones (1995) Mainwaring and Scully (1995) Fiorina (1996)		

newer rational choice theories that focus on preferences and interests. The structuralist column refers to the presence of broad socio-economic changes, the development of key institutions, and the relational structures in which individuals are embedded. The culturalist column concerns the importance of ideas, shared understandings, and accepted norms and rules for behaviour. The arrows between the main columns capture the notion that many studies seek to examine the interplay between these theories.

The studies on the relationship between economic development and democracy are located in the cells extending from the structuralist to the culturalist approaches. The studies focus on the broad socio-economic changes and processes of modernization that were accompanied by changes in class structure, class alliances, the nature and power of the state, as well as the impact of transnational structures of power. In addition these studies imply, or in some cases state explicitly, that the development of democracy also depends on the formation of a sustainable political culture that emphasizes tolerance and promotes democratic norms. While earlier studies suggested that this political culture would be fomented by an emerging middle class, later studies recognize the importance of the working class in its role as an agent for democratic inclusion. In either case, these studies examine the interaction between broad structural changes and the development of political culture.

The studies on violent political dissent and revolution are located around the middle columns of the table since they seek to explain these political phenomena with a combination of individual and structural theories on the one hand and structural and cultural theories on the other. For example, Wolf's (1968) study shows that capitalist transformation of agriculture is a structural change that produces grievance among a particular set of rural cultivators who then become involved in revolutionary activity. Scott (1976) argues that similar structural changes transformed the moral economy and the culture of reciprocity that had become a key feature of the peasant communities in Burma and Vietnam. Hibbs's (1973) comprehensive set of explanatory variables captures a whole range of individual, structural, and cultural concepts.

The comparative studies from Chapter 6 are equally located in the middle columns as they seek to explain the origins, trajectory, and impact of social movements. All three theoretical perspectives have been used to explain the origin of social movement activity. Rationalists examine the key incentives that may or may not lead individuals to join a social movement. Structuralists look at long-term socio-economic fluctuations and the changing set of opportunities for social protest and political transformation. Culturalists are concerned with the changing nature of collective identities and how these identities provide the shared understanding and common will necessary for sustained political mobilization. The studies that combine these rational and structural theories (column three) look at how individual and collective behaviour in social movements is facilitated or constrained by broader structural changes, while those that combine structural and cultural theories (column five) examine how new values and identities form from broader structural changes.

The initial quest to understand democratic transition centred on the strategic interaction of elites and thus primarily adopted a rationalist perspective. Colomer and Pascual's (1994) application of game theory is a classic example of a strong rationalist effort to explain the democratic transition in Poland. Other elite-centred accounts such as those found in O'Donnell *et al.* (1986a, 1986b) examine the ways in which changing structural conditions lead to opportunities for 'hard-liners' and 'soft-liners' within the authoritarian regime to manoeuvre for political advantage. Popular struggle perspectives, on the other hand, are concerned with the opportunities for social mobilization and democratic transformation that are provided by changing structural conditions. Finally, studies that adopt culturalist explanations examine patterns of democratic 'habituation' and the acceptance of rules and democratic norms, as well as the cross-national diffusion of democratic ideas.

As mentioned above, the studies on institutional design and democratic performance necessary ground themselves in structural explanations since they examine the ways in which formal institutions of democracy (e.g. parties, electoral systems, presidential versus parliamentary systems) structure the activities of key political actors. This structuring of action has immediate implications for democratic performance. The studies in Chapter 8 suggest that the nexus between structure and agency can have direct effects on governance. For example, strong presidents facing multiple parties in the legislature may find it difficult to bring about new legislation or may face recurring governmental gridlock, which can have adverse effects on democratic performance, particularly in new democracies. Indeed, Stepan and Skach (1993) argue that presidents facing such constraints may flout the constitution, seek extra-constitutional means to achieve their objectives, and even encourage military intervention, particularly in countries with a past history of such intervention.

Conclusion: drawing the lessons

This review of over sixty comparative studies across a range of different methods and techniques shows both the trade-offs associated with conducting comparative research as well as the valuable contribution to theory that such studies can make. From this review and analysis, the following three key factors are important for scholars to bear in mind when embarking on comparative research: case selection, inferential aspirations, and theorizing. First, case selection significantly affects the answers that are obtained to the research questions that are posed (cf. Geddes 1990). Both the actual countries in the sample and the number of countries that comprise it can lead to different results. In order to make stronger inferences, the rule of thumb for political science method is to raise the number of observations (King *et al.* 1994), which for comparative politics means either a larger sample of countries or more observations within a smaller sample of countries.

Second, the substantive conclusions and inferential aspirations of a particular comparative study should not go too far beyond the scope of its sample. A single-country study of democratic transition may provide some important inferences that can be examined in countries with a similar set of circumstances but it does not provide a universal set of inferences for democratic transition in general. A study of social mobilization under authoritarian rule can make inferences relevant to social mobilization in other countries under similar conditions of authoritarian rule. On the other hand, a study of social movement activity under democratic rule cannot make inferences about such activity under authoritarian rule (see Chapter 7). Many-country studies may have universal aspirations yet must remain sensitive to the fact that there are exceptions to every rule. In short, comparative scholars must recognize the limits of their own enterprise in making generalizations about the political world they observe.

Finally, comparativists ought to spend more time on careful theorizing and research design. Once the assumptions of a theory are established and the observable implications of that theory are identified, then the research can be designed in such a way to provide the best set of comparisons given the available resources. Careful theorizing about political events and political outcomes will lead scholars to compare similar outcomes in different cases, or different outcomes in similar cases. The differences and similarities that are identified through comparison help provide an explanation for the outcomes themselves. Together, case selection, self-limiting inferential aspirations, and careful theorizing provide the foundation for comparative politics. What remains to be examined are the new issues, new methods, and new challenges that confront the field in the next century. It is to these issues that the final chapter turns.

Note

1 There are exceptions to this rule for each perspective. For the rationalist perspective, see for example Bates's (1989) study of the political economy of Kenya, Tsebelis's (1990) study of European political behaviour, and Geddes's (1991, 1994) work on state reform in Latin America. For the structural perspective, see Leubbert's (1991) study of regime origins in inter-war Europe and Poulantzas's (1976) study of dictatorships in Greece, Spain, and Portugal. For the cultural perspective, see Scott's (1985) study of peasant resistance in Malaysia and his comparison of Burma and Vietnam (Scott 1976) as examined in Chapter 5.

Further reading

Hay, C. (1995) 'Structure and Agency', in D. Marsh and G. Stoker (eds) *Theory and Methods in Political Science*, London: Macmillan, 189–208.

An excellent overview of the dialogue between rationalist and structuralist theories of political science.

Lichbach, M. (1997) 'Social Theory and Comparative Politics', in M. Lichbach and A. Zuckerman (eds), *Comparative Politics: Rationality, Culture, and Structure*, Cambridge: Cambridge University Press, 239–276.

A concise model of rational, structural, and cultural theories and how comparative politics has contributed to their development.

Chapter 10

New challenges for comparative politics

This book has consistently argued that the systematic comparison of countries is an effective method for making inferences about the political world we observe. The basic methods of comparative politics (many-, few-, and single-country studies) and its basic unit of analysis (the independent nation state) will not change for the foreseeable future. Comparative politics as a field and a method fits squarely in the 'evidence–inference methodological core' of political science (see Chapter 1 of present volume; cf. Almond 1996: 52), and the application of comparative methods to real-world problems will continue to play a valuable role in the incremental accumulation of knowledge. Indeed, for many, comparative politics should be the central concern of political science, as well as a central feature in helping us to understand current affairs in the world (see Peters 1998: 212; Pennings *et al.* 1999: 2–3).

This chapter addresses these claims and examines the way in which the field has evolved and is likely to evolve, the challenges it will face in the near future, as well as the ways in which it can adapt to our rapidly changing and increasingly global political environment. In so doing, it answers several important questions for the field. How has comparative politics as a field evolved since the early 'public law' days of institutional comparison? What new issues will confront comparativists in the future? What new methods and techniques of comparison will be developed? How can area studies contribute to comparative politics? Is comparative politics possible in a globalized world? In answering these questions, this final chapter seeks to provide scholars with the inspiration and tools to confront the challenges that lie ahead.

Full circle

In many respects, comparative politics has come full circle since its early days as a new field in the social sciences (Mair 1996: 315–316). Rather than simply returning to earlier research questions and methods, however, the field has evolved, effectively retaining key developments and rediscovering problems not addressed thoroughly in the past. In this way, the field has mirrored the history of political science more generally. Described as an 'eclectic progressive' development, the discipline started with formal legal and institutional comparisons, moved to an almost exclusive focus on individuals (the 'behavioural revolution'), rediscovered the importance of institutions (the advent of the 'new institutionalism'), while continuously struggling with the question of culture (see Almond 1996; Mair 1996). Today, both the substantive foci and theoretical perspectives with which to examine them are more eclectic and open to change than ever before. What has not changed, however, is the importance of systematic comparison and the need for inferential rigour (Almond 1996: 89).

The evolution in method, detailed throughout this book, also mirrors the substantive evolution in the field. Earlier 'legalistic' and formal institutional comparisons were carried out on a small sample of countries usually isolated to the United States and Western Europe, or to areas such as Latin America (see Valenzuela 1988). The relegation of formal institutional comparisons for more general comparisons was accompanied by the increase in the number of countries

Table 10.1 Evolution of comparative politics: substantive foci and dominant methods

Period	*Substantive focus*	*Comparative method*
Public law phase Inter-war period	Institutional design and political order Objects of inquiry: presidential vs. parliamentary regimes, federal vs. unitary systems, political party organizations, legal and legislative instruments, democratic, fascist, and socialist regimes	Few- and single-country studies Descriptive history Formal and configurative analysis Basic unit of analysis: individual countries (mostly in Europe and North America)
Behavioural revolution 1940s–1960s	Political behaviour Explaining patterns of political development, including democracy, political instability, and political violence Objects of inquiry: interest groups, parties, elections, decision making, rules of the game, the military, peasants, students, and workers	Many-country comparisons Cross-national indicators Quantitative analysis Search for covering laws and universal generalizations Basic unit of analysis: individuals and individual countries (global and regional samples)
Institutional revival 1970s and 1980s	Relationship between institutions and political actors Objects of inquiry: democracy and democratic transition, revolution, economic and political dependency, political protest, public policy mechanisms and outcomes, and the welfare state	Few-country comparisons Qualitative and quantitative techniques Inferences limited to similar countries outside scope of comparison Basic unit of analysis: individuals and individual countries (global and regional samples)
New eclecticism 1990s	Individual, institutional, and cultural foundations of politics Objects of inquiry: democratic transition, institutional design, social movements, globalization, transnational networks, political and cultural diffusion	Many-, few-, and single-country studies Qualitative and quantitative techniques Universal generalizations, as well as regional and country-specific inferences Basic unit of analysis: individuals and individual countries (global and regional samples)

Sources: Valenzuela (1988); Erickson and Rustow (1991); Rustow and Erickson (1991); Mair (1996); Apter (1996); Lichbach (1997)

in the sample, aided by the advent of computer technology and a commitment to providing comparable indicators of politics. A certain disillusionment with large-scale comparisons and the 'rediscovery' of institutions (particularly the state) led to an increase in few-country studies, and in some corners of the discipline, a definitive call for a conscious return to few-country studies (ibid.: 86). Thus, the contemporary era of comparative politics includes many-country studies, few-country studies, and single-country studies, all of which comprise the methodological universe of the field and all of which are devoted to providing explanation and understanding of observed political phenomena in the world.

Table 10.1 summarizes the evolution of comparative politics in terms of its substantive foci and dominant comparative methods. This evolution has in part been reflected in the chapters that comprise Parts I and II. On the one hand, large questions in Part II concerning the establishment and maintenance of political institutions, patterns of violent and non-violent political behaviour, and the relationship between institutions and political performance map on to the history of the field detailed in column two of the table, while on the other hand, the chapters in both parts have demonstrated the evolution towards a more inclusive set of comparative methods. Contrary to the observations of some comparative scholars (e.g. Mair 1996; Peters 1998), all three methods of comparison are valid and continue to be employed by scholars in the field. The period of 'new eclecticism' recognizes and even celebrates the plurality of topics, theories, and methods in comparative politics. As Part I has made clear, the method adopted and the research design that is formulated are a function of both the type of research question that is being addressed and the theoretical perspective that has been adopted.

New methods

In addition to the many strengths and weaknesses of the different comparative methods outlined in this book, there are several new developments in the field that will continue to improve its ability to make strong inferences about the political world. These include important issues of data collection and analysis, the transcendence of traditional boundaries in the field, and the development of new analytic software and comparative techniques. Each of these developments relates directly to the concerns raised throughout the book, but in particular, to those in Part I.

At the height of the behavioural revolution, there was a sanguine view about the ability to collect meaningful indicators on global samples of countries in an effort to make universal generalizations about politics and political events. Many criticized this optimistic view of the 'new' comparative politics (Apter 1996), yet now more than ever, the global collection of meaningful data is possible. The tremendous advance in information and communication technologies (ICTs), such as the Internet and the World Wide Web, have made the production, collection, and analysis of global data much easier than in the past. For example, the entire UNDP *Human Development Report 1999* is available on the World Wide Web and can be downloaded on to personal computer systems in a matter of minutes. The format of the files is particularly stable for importation to any number of computer platforms. In addition, the major international development agencies such as the World Bank, the International Monetary Fund, as well as the European Union, the United Nations, and other international governmental and non-governmental organizations have made increasingly large amounts of data available for scholars. In addition to official statistics offered by these various organizations, political scientists of all persuasions and research traditions are making their data available either directly from their own websites or through intermediary organizations such as the Inter-University Consortium for Political and Social Research at the University of Michigan (ICPSR), the Roper Center at the University of Connecticut, and the UK Data Archive at the University of Essex.

But beyond the increase in the availability of data for comparative research, the field needs to develop better systematic ways of collecting, documenting, and diffusing data. Scholars need to explain the sources, coding, problems, and potential areas for error in their data collection efforts. These need to be fully documented in the accompanying codebooks. Moreover, the field, and political science more generally, needs to develop an ethos of replication and data-sharing. Once data have been collected, documented, and analysed, scholars should make them available through the direct or indirect means mentioned above. Replicating and performing secondary analysis on published articles and books provides corroboration, incremental advancement in knowledge, and an excellent way to teach future generations of comparativists. Overall, technology now allows to a greater extent than ever before, the development of a networked comparative research community.

The benefits of better data collection and diffusion are not isolated to many-country comparisons using quantitative analysis. They apply equally to other comparative methods. Global indicators put regional comparisons, other few-country studies, and single-country studies in a broader comparative perspective. Likewise, comparative studies with a smaller sample size can demonstrate the limits of the global data and increase our understanding of political processes and events at the local level. In addition, as Part I made clear, the term 'data' is a broad one that includes all empirical information marshalled for systematic comparative analysis. Thus, in echoing the call articulated by King *et al.* (1994), the improvement in data collection and diffusion practices ought to extend to non-quantitative evidence. Comparative histories and single-country studies using qualitative methods should provide details and documentation of their collection of evidence.

The advent of new analytic techniques and computer software supports this general call for data improvement. New advances in qualitative data software allow new types of analysis that seek to provide structures and clusters of meaning from texts collected through traditionally qualitative means, such as in-depth interviewing, participant observation, or published official statements by political elites and policy-makers. In this sense, texts themselves provide the data from which inferences can be drawn. The new computer software can draw connections, perform word counts, develop typologies and classification schemes, and calculate word, phrase, or sentence frequencies for more advanced analysis. In the past, this type of work has often been completed by hand. For example, Ian Budge and his collaborators (Budge *et al.* 1987; Klingemann *et al.* 1994) have coded political party manifestos published since the Second World War into thematic categories in an effort to compare policy and ideological positions of political parties in Europe and North America. Using the new software, these texts can now be scanned and analysed more easily. In addition, these new advances in text and qualitative analysis software packages allow for more systematic comparative studies that adopt discursive approaches to politics more generally (see Howarth 1995; Beer and Balleck 1994; Howarth 1998a; Howarth *et al.* forthcoming).

For quantitative analysis, new software and techniques are being developed to handle new types of data. Typically, cross-sectional data analysis of the kind performed on a large sample of countries at one point in time (see, for example, the earlier many-country studies outlined in Chapters 4 and 5), was a relatively straightforward exercise. Time series data, 'event count' data such as protest events, and dichotomous data collected on such events as wars, coups, and revolutions require more advanced kinds of analysis to overcome some of their inherent biases. Skewed distributions (i.e. some countries with particularly high or low values), 'ceiling' problems (i.e. no events in one year followed by 4,000 events in the next), and 'either–or' outcomes require different kinds of analytical techniques to avoid drawing erroneous inferences. Developments in this area of quantitative comparative analysis continue to be made to deal with these new indicators and forms of data.

Finally, new techniques for combining quantitative and qualitative methods have been developed to offer more holistic explanations for political outcomes. Wickham-Crowley's (1993) comparison identified necessary and sufficient conditions for successful revolution in Latin America. He used what is called Boolean algebra to eliminate those conditions that did not appear to be important for revolution while retaining those that did (see Chapter 5 and Table 5.5 above). The values of these supportive conditions were derived in qualitative fashion through a deep reading of the events surrounding these (non) revolutionary moments in Latin American history. In this way, he combines the strengths of a 'variable-oriented' study with the strengths of a 'case-oriented' study to reach substantive conclusions about social revolution (see Ragin 1987; Peters 1998: 162–171). Other comparative studies have used the 'either–or' categories of Boolean analysis (see De Meur and Berg-Schlosser 1994; Foweraker and Landman 1997: Chapter 7) to reduce the complexity of qualitative information while harnessing the strengths of logical analysis. As in other areas of political methodology, this type of analysis has been aided by the development of computer software (Qualitative Comparative Analysis, or QCA), which reduces the burden of calculating the key conditions by hand (see Drass and Ragin 1991). Future comparative studies may want to adopt this strategy, which strikes a balance between quantitative and qualitative approaches.

Taken together, these advances in methods, techniques, and software strengthen our ability to conduct systematic comparative research and help to break down traditional barriers that exist within the discipline. No longer should qualitative practitioners be pitted against their quantitative colleagues. Rather, the insights of both communities can inform each other. Regionally based comparative studies that traditionally inhabit the faculties of area studies programmes (e.g.

Latin America, Africa, and Asia) can contribute to more general theories and research communities in political science. Many of the regionally based studies reviewed in this book either developed new concepts and theories applicable to contexts outside the scope of the original comparison, or used particular parts of the world as natural 'laboratories' to test theories and ideas developed elsewhere. There thus must be an ongoing intellectual conversation among the practitioners of different comparative methods, across different levels of analysis, and across different theoretical perspectives, as well as across different parts of the world.

New issues

The history of political science suggests that the field has been preoccupied with the formation and maintenance of different political institutions and with developing ways in which to evaluate their performance on both empirical and normative grounds (Almond 1996). The chapters in Part II of this book reflect in part this preoccupation. The criteria for the selection of topics included their wide attention in the literature, their popularity with students, and their ability to demonstrate the different ways in which comparative methods have been employed in the field. Yet the chapters variously demonstrated the field's preoccupation with the ways in which political order is made possible. In addition to these concerns, key issues of political science such as representation, political parties, interest groups, political culture, political participation, legislative behaviour, public policy, and political economy will continue to animate the minds of comparative researchers in years to come. There have been a number of developments in the world, however, that are particularly suited to systematic comparative analysis of the type advocated in this book. Although not an exhaustive list, these issues include transnational political influences, the diffusion of political ideas and political culture, universal human rights, and the broad category of globalization. Each of these new issues implies political activity and political processes that extend beyond the confines of the nation state, but their brief discussion below will demonstrate the value that can be added to their explanation and understanding using systematic comparative analysis.

Transnational political influence

Chapter 5 in Part II focused on the comparative study of the origins, shape, and impact of social movements. One key factor that has emerged in the study of social movements during the contemporary period is the increasing prevalence of social movement organizations (SMOs) whose capacity for political activism transcends national boundaries. Sometimes called 'transnational advocacy networks' (Keck and Sikkink 1998a, 1998b), these organizations are able to build memberships and articulate the many demands of their different constituencies in a multitude of political contexts. These global networks of activists, whether of the right or the left, seek to make claims against authorities and organize global campaigns for change.[1] Yet, they most often represent an alternative to mass action, using

information and communication technologies to make claims for those unable to do so in political contexts where access to authorities is blocked or dramatically limited (Keck and Sikkink 1998a: 217–221). As an extension of domestic social movement activity, this type of political activism is a research area ripe for comparative analysis that seeks to identify the multiple 'nodes' of such advocacy networks, the type of information and tactics that are shared, the ways in which particular struggles can be framed in a global context, and the types of political impact that they are capable of achieving.

The analysis of transnational influences brings comparative politics closer to the field of international relations, since activities between states become important features of the comparison. Insights from both disciplines appear particularly fruitful for future research and have already featured in some areas of research. For example, comparativists and international relations scholars have become interested in the relationship between democratizing countries and warfare. Ward and Gleditsch (1998) compare a global sample of countries with measures of democratization and inter-state war and find that unstable and rocky democratic transitions increase the likelihood of inter-state warfare, while the process of democratization itself does not. In this example, key concepts from comparative politics (democratization) and comparative methods (many-country quantitative comparison) are combined with key concepts of international relations (state weakness and warfare).

Political diffusion

In addition to agents embedded in global networks fighting for political change, comparative politics must remain sensitive to larger processes of political diffusion. For example, Huntington's (1991) comparative study of democratization (see Chapter 7 of present volume) is concerned with the cross-national and cross-cultural diffusion of democratic ideas. In this account and others, political diffusion of democracy is seen as almost a 'contagion' (Whitehead 1996b) that moves from one political system to another. For Huntington, this diffusion of democratic ideas helps explain the third wave of democratization. Indeed, regional proximity alone accounts for a large number of countries that have become democratic this century (N > 40; see Whitehead 1996b: 6). But the recent spread of global communications technologies means diffusion effects are becoming more like 'demonstration' effects, where democratic activists in one corner of the globe can now learn of the grievances, strategies, and outcomes of democratic struggles in other parts of the globe. For example, Castells (1997: 72–83) shows how the Zapatista rebellion in the southern Mexican state of Chiapas employed the Internet and global media to communicate their struggle for rights, social justice, and democracy to audiences and potential sympathizers outside the confines of Mexico. Future comparative studies of democracy and democratization must include these international diffusion effects.

Human rights

Related to the struggle for democracy is the issue of the promotion and protection of universal human rights. Since the Universal Declaration of Human Rights in 1948, the academic study of human rights has flowered into an interdisciplinary research and activist community comprising lawyers, political scientists, philosophers, anthropologists, psychologists, and sociologists. This research area is particularly suited for comparative analysis since it sets an ideal and legal standard of rights that ought to be protected (civil, political, economic, social, and cultural) in all countries of the world. This ideal standard is laid out in a series of international legal instruments to which countries can become signatories, such as the Covenant on Civil and Political Rights; the Covenant on Economic, Social, and Cultural Rights; the Convention on the Prevention and Punishment of the Crime of Genocide; etc. Between 125 and 191 countries are signatories to these various instruments (UNDP 1999), yet global evidence suggests that 'there are more countries in the world today where fundamental rights and civil liberties are regularly violated than countries where they are effectively protected' (Robertson and Merrills 1996: 2). Indeed, in its 1999 tabulation of freedom in the world, Freedom House (1999) reports that 46 per cent of the world is considered 'free', 28 per cent is considered 'partly free', while the remaining part is considered 'not free'. In addition, the Human Development report for 1999 shows the persistence of great disparities in wealth, trade, and investment, as well as use of and access to the Internet, all of which constitute violations of economic, social, and cultural rights.

This disparity between official proclamations and actual implementation of human rights protection is a fruitful area for comparative research. What economic, social, and political factors explain the continued violation of human rights? How can rationalist, structuralist, and culturalist perspectives help us explain these violations? In other words, the gap between so-called 'rights in principle' and 'rights in practice' can be compared across any number of countries to uncover the key explanatory factors that may account for this difference (see Foweraker and Landman 1997). While the academic study of human rights tends to be dominated by single-country studies, the availability of global and regional reports allows for few- and many-country comparisons to be carried out that seek to explain the degree to which human rights are protected. For example, Poe and Tate (1994) code both the Amnesty International and US State Department human rights reports and analyse the violation of civil and political rights world-wide. Poe *et al.* (1994) use similar methods to examine the relationship between US foreign aid and the protection of human rights in Latin America. Martin and Sikkink (1993) compare the effects of US foreign policy on human rights practices in Argentina and Guatemala. Finally, de Brito (1997) compares the efforts of post-transition Uruguay and Chile in dealing with their long periods of authoritarian rule. In each of these examples, human rights as an ideal provide the benchmark against which countries in the particular sample can be compared. Moreover, like the studies on democratization and warfare, those studies that examine the promotion of human rights by outside agents introduce key insights from the field of international relations.

Globalization

Together these new issues demonstrate the presence of a new global level of political activity, the origins, patterns, and impact of which may be subsumed under the broader category of *globalization*. The term has been variously used to describe a state of affairs, to account for a historical process, to represent an 'end-state' to which all countries are moving, and as both the cause and effect of the changing nature of our political, economic, and social environment (see Gray 1999; Held *et al.* 1999). As a description, globalization refers to the increasing interconnectedness of the world across all aspects of life. As a historical process, it is a pattern of relationships and trends in the evolution of nation states from the first empires to the present day. As an end-state, it is a world where all countries enjoy freedom, democracy, and wealth. As a cause, it accounts for disparities in wealth, dominance of capital, the erosion of local communities, the effective disenfranchisement of individuals, subordination, exploitation, and increasing levels of global inequality. As an effect, it is the world-wide spread of a homogeneous culture that celebrates the consumption of goods and products produced in the West.

These various definitions of globalization suggest that without proper care, the term will mean everything and nothing at the same time. To redress this conceptual and analytical confusion, clear definitions of globalization and proper theorizing about its causes and effects are needed (see Held *et al.* 1999). The ability to theorize about the different dimensions of globalization will provide the means to operationalize them for comparative analysis, and draw substantive conclusions about the implications of globalization for politics, economics, and culture. Whether globalization poses a threat to the traditional nation state is an *empirical question*, which requires *systematic comparative analysis* of the type this book has advocated. Moreover, whether studying transnational political networks, political diffusion, universal human rights, or the many different aspects of globalization, data and evidence will continue to be collected, organized, and compared across nation state units.

Conclusion

The future for comparative politics is bright. The proliferation of new issues and the examination of old ones continue to provide an ample supply of research topics for systematic comparative analysis. The accretion of comparative methods that has developed over the years provides scholars with a rich 'toolchest' to examine and explain observed political phenomena in the world. Continued developments in information and communications technology will make the world a smaller place and ought to encourage an ethos of replication, develop a network of shared knowledge, build a stronger comparative research community, and for certain research areas, promote links with the field of international relations. It is hoped that this book will make scholars more careful in their choice of countries, their collection of evidence, and their substantive conclusions about the particular research questions that have motivated them.

Note

1 While Keck and Sikkink (1998a, 1998b) focus on a collection of advocacy groups that comprise a broad leftist agenda for right and social justice, the radical right has shown itself to be equally adept at global mobilization of its main constituencies.

Further reading

Erickson, K. P. and Rustow, D. A. (1991) 'Global Research Perspectives: Paradigms, Concepts and Data in a Changing World', in D. A. Rustow and K. P. Erickson (eds) *Comparative Political Dynamics: Global Research Perspectives*, New York: Harper Collins, 441–459.

An excellent summary of new directions for the field of comparative politics.

Gray, J. (1999) *False Dawn: The Delusions of Global Capitalism*, London: Granta Books.

A critical review of globalization and the 'easy' association between political freedom and economic freedom. Chapter 3, entitled 'What Globalization Is Not', is highly recommended.

Held, D., McGrew, A., Goldblatt, D., and Perraton, J. (1999) *Global Transformations: Politics, Economics, and Culture*, Cambridge: Polity Press.

A comprehensive study of globalization in the past and in the present, including a survey of arguments relating to globalization, new conceptualizations, and global comparative evidence.

Glossary

aggregate statistics Any quantitative indicators collected at the country level. Examples include per capita gross domestic product (GDP), inflation, income inequality, population size, number of riots, and the number of televisions per capita. Also referred to as official statistics.

behaviouralism A period (1950s and 1960s)/methodology of political science that concentrates on the analysis of observed political phenomena in the search for universal laws of politics. Post-behaviouralism concedes that the collection of indicators and subsequent analysis may not be free of value biases of the researcher, nor are the resultant inferences necessarily universal.

binary comparison The comparison of two countries, which can either be 'most similar' or 'most different'. Greater analytical leverage is achieved through the comparison of two 'most different' countries that have a similar outcome that is to be explained. This is sometimes called the 'contrast of contexts'. See also **most similar systems design** and **most different systems design**.

bivariate relationship A significant relationship between two variables, such as economic development and democracy. Theory specifies which variable is dependent and which is independent. See also **dependent variable**, **independent variable**, and **multivariate relationship**.

case (s) The individual country or countries that feature in a comparison.

case-oriented Type of comparison that emphasizes the holistic qualities of the individual cases (or countries) that are being compared. This method of analysis is opposed to **variable-oriented** analysis.

coding The process by which either numerical or categorical values are assigned to observed political phenomena, such as 'violent' or 'non-violent' political protest, 'left' vs. 'right' ideological position, or the 'degree of democracy' in a political system. See also **measurement**.

configurative Holistic aspects of observed political phenomena, such as the necessary and sufficient conditions for revolution. Emphasis is not the additive independent effects, but the combination of favourable conditions. See also **case-oriented**.

control The practice of isolating the effects of some variables while examining the effects of others. Control can be introduced through statistical methods in many-country studies, or through the intentional selection of countries in few-country studies.

correlation Any significant association between two or more variables, such as age and income, or education and income. Mathematically, a correlation of 0 means no relationship, while a correlation of 1 means a perfect correlation. Correlation does not mean causation. See also **bivariate relationship** and **multivariate relationship**.

counterfactual Hypothetical situations that examine what may have happened given a different set of conditions. For example, what would have happened in the 1997 General Election in the United Kingdom if the electoral system were based on proportional representation? Since history cannot be repeated, comparativists compare similar countries with different electoral systems to examine their effects on party systems. In this way, comparison is a substitute for the counterfactual.

culturalist approaches Theoretical perspectives that concentrate on the shared meanings, understandings, identities, and overall 'worldview' within identifiable communities of people. For example, the 'moral economy' is a concept that captures the ethos of reciprocity and the shared sense of economic vulnerability among individuals in peasant communities (Scott 1976). See also **rationalist approaches** and **structuralist approaches**.

data Any information collected and organized systematically by a comparative scholar. The word 'data' is plural (as opposed to 'datum'), and may be quantitative or qualitative in nature.

data set The organized collection of data. In quantitative comparative studies, data are organized into a matrix of columns and rows, while in qualitative analysis, data may be organized into files, transcripts, recordings, archives, scanned text, etc.

deduction The logical process where conclusions are derived from starting assumptions. For example, one version of game theory assumes the presence of two players with two options from which four possible outcomes can be deduced. Such logical deduction identifies all possible outcomes which are then reflected in real-world events. See also **induction**.

degrees of freedom The number of pieces of information that can vary independently from one another. In comparative politics, it is important for a research design to have a sufficient number of countries to allow the variables in the analysis to have full variation. Few-country comparativists argue that careful selection of countries alleviates this problem.

dependent variable The political outcome, event, or situation that is to be explained by the comparative analysis. This variable is identified by the research question and specified in the theory and research design of the comparison. For example, in the study of institutional design and democratic performance, democratic performance is presumed to be dependent on institutional design. The dependent variable is alternatively referred to as an outcome variable, an endogenous variable, or the explanandum. See also **independent variable**.

deviant cases (or countries) Those countries that appear to be the exception, or 'outlier' to an empirical generalization. Such countries are normally identified through the quantitative analysis of many countries. For example, in the many-country quantitative study of economic development and democracy, both Saudi Arabia and Costa Rica appear as deviant countries since the former is a rich non-democratic country while the latter is a poor democratic country.

diachronic Comparison over time. See also **synchronic**.

dialectic relationship Two-way relationship between two antagonistic forces or agents that ultimately becomes resolved by a new set of conditions. For example, under capitalism Karl Marx posited a dialectic relationship between the bourgeoisie and the proletariat, which through social revolution would bring about the establishment of communism.

dichotomous Any concept, idea, or category that has two values. For example, countries may be democratic or non-democratic, experience social revolution or not experience social revolution, have a democratic breakdown or not have a democratic breakdown.

dummy variable Any variable with two values or two categories that helps introduce control into systematic analysis. For example, in a comparison of all Latin American countries, the analysis may include a dummy variable for Central America and the Southern Cone to control for presumed sub-regional variation. Thus, in the sample of countries, each dummy variable is coded '1' for the countries that fit the criteria (Central America or Southern Cone) and '0' for those that do not.

ecological fallacy Drawing false conclusions about individuals through the analysis of aggregates. For example, Gurr (1968) compares 114 countries across a range of indicators to make inferences about individual violent political behaviour. See also **individualist fallacy**.

empirical generalization Making inferences about empirical relationships and event regularities without specifying a direct cause for the outcomes that are observed. For example, the following statements are empirical generalizations: 'Countries with proportional representation tend to have multiple political parties'; 'Rich countries tend to be democratic'; 'Democracies tend not to fight one another.'

equivalence The same underlying meaning associated with different actions, terms, structures, or categories. Survey instruments develop different questions that have the same meaning across different countries, and comparativists identify different structures that perform similar functions in different contexts. For example, the World Values Survey uses a battery of questions to construct measures of post-materialism across forty-three societies, and some comparativists look for the key structures in society that perform the functions of interest articulation and interest aggregation. In both examples, the underlying equivalence of measures or functions allows for comparison.

external validity The extent to which the inferences of a study can be extended beyond the scope of countries in the original analysis. See also **internal validity**.

functional form The actual shape of a relationship between two or more variables. For example, the relationship between the level of income inequality and political violence can be in the shape of a U, an inverted U, a straight line, or some other form. Each form suggests a different type of relationship. The linear form is still the most common form of relationship that is posited in comparative politics. See also **monotonic relationship** and **regression**.

hypothesis A statement about a possible relationship between two or more variables derived from a more general theory and tested using systematic comparative analysis. Hypotheses generally take the form: if *A*, then *B*. For example, a typical hypothesis would be stated as follows: 'A reduction in government repression will lead to an increase in social movement activity.'

independent variable The variable or variables included in the comparative analysis that are presumed to account for some or all of the variation in the dependent variable. The independent variable is alternatively labelled a causal variable, an explanatory variable, an exogenous variable, or the explicandum.

indeterminate research design A comparative analysis that is designed in such a way that the research answer cannot truly be answered. For example, a comparative study may identify four independent variables for an outcome that is to be explained, but have only two countries in the comparison. There are not enough countries for the variables to assume their different values and logical combinations. This is a problem of insufficient **degrees of freedom** or 'too many variables, not enough countries'.

individualist fallacy Drawing false conclusions about aggregates through the analysis of individuals. For example, Inglehart (1997) compares surveys with approximately 2,000 respondents from forty-three countries to identify cultural clusterings, but it is not clear that a country can be considered 'traditional' even if all of the respondents in the survey express such attitudes. See also **ecological fallacy**.

induction The process by which conclusions are drawn from direct observation of empirical evidence. See also **deduction**.

inference The process by which comparative researchers use facts they do know about the world to make statements about things they do not know.

internal validity The extent to which the inferences drawn from a study are due precisely to the factors that have been analysed and not to some other factors. See also **external validity**.

intervening variable An explanatory variable presumed to provide the causal link between two other variables. For example, the positive association between income and health is explained by the presence of expenditure on healthcare, the intervening variable.

level of analysis The degree to which political units are aggregated for comparative analysis. For example, a single-country study can examine individuals, cities, regions (counties), and sub-regions (states, federal districts). Few- and many-country comparisons use the nation state as the basic unit of analysis. The higher the level of analysis, the less specificity a study can have and vice versa.

macro-causal A specification of causal relationships among macro-level variables, such as class, class alliances, the state, and processes of socio-economic modernization.

majoritarian Refers to an electoral system that produces and gives power to majority political parties in the legislative assembly.

measurement Assigning values to objects of comparative inquiry for further quantitative analysis. See also **coding**.

method of agreement Part of J. S. Mill's logic that identifies similar features across different units. Forms the basis of the **most different systems design**.

method of difference Part of J. S. Mill's logic that identifies different features across similar units. Forms the basis of the **most similar systems design**.

methodology The study of different methods of research, including the identification of research questions, the formulation of theories to explain certain events and political outcomes, and the development of research design.

model A simplified representation of relationships between variables usually depicted graphically. The different relationships that form the structure of the model can then be tested empirically.

monotonic relationship Any **bivariate** relationship where an increase in one variable necessarily is associated with an increase in the other variable.

most different systems design A research design that compares instances of similar variation across different countries.

most similar systems design A research design that compares instances of different variation across similar countries.

multivariate relationship A significant relationship with at least two **independent variables** that account for the **dependent variable**.

observable implications All possible instances in which expected political outcomes ought to occur, or where significant relationships ought to be upheld.

observations The values that variables take on specific units. For example, a code of 1 for 'democracy' at time t in country A is an observation.

operationalize The process by which theoretical concepts become transformed into variables for quantitative or qualitative comparative analysis. See also **coding** and **measurement**.

parsimonious explanation The type of explanation that uses the least amount of evidence to explain the most amount of variation. This is also referred to as maximizing the analytical leverage of a comparative study.

post-behaviouralism A period (after 1970)/methodology of political science that accepts that observation and analysis of the political world are not free from certain theoretical and value biases, yet strives to make strong inferences through empirical analysis.

qualitative analysis Any method that examines the inherent traits, characteristics, and qualities of the political objects of inquiry. Examples of qualitative analysis include comparative history, participant observation, in-depth interviews, and ethnographic field research. Studies in this vein tend to be more holistic and interpretative, as well as conducted for a small selection of countries.

quantitative analysis Any method that uses numerical indicators of political phenomena and seeks to establish the existence of relationships between them across a selection of countries, time periods or both.

rationalist approaches Theoretical perspectives that place the actions and choices of individuals at the centre of the analysis. These individuals are assumed to have sets of preferences, the utility of which is maximized through rational 'cost-benefit' analysis.

regression An analytical technique that estimates relationships between two or more variables by fitting a line to data points that minimizes the distance between actual observations and those predicted by the analytical model. Standard regression fits a straight line to these data points (called linear regression), while more advanced versions of the technique fit curves of various shapes to the data points. See also **functional form**.

research design The framework of analysis that is derived both from the research question and the theoretical attempt to provide a plausible answer to the research question. Research design includes the choice of countries, the ways in which the dependent and independent variables are operationalized, and the collection and analysis of the evidence. A good research design should answer the three questions: (1) What does the analysis seek to find out? (2) How does it propose to find it out? (3) How will the researcher know if the answer is wrong?

sample A group of countries selected from a larger group of countries, which when analysed will reveal something about the larger group (known as the population). Even comparisons of many countries represent a sample, since their analysis is limited to a particular time-frame, and their inferences are meant to extend to all time. The general rule in comparative politics is that the larger the sample, the stronger the **inferences** that can be drawn about the population.

selection bias The problem of choosing countries based on criteria that are somehow related to the dependent variable. For example, selection bias is present in studies that analyze exclusively countries in which only the outcome to be explained is present, such as military coups, revolutions, or democratic transitions.

spuriousness The false establishment of an empirical relationship between two or more variables that is actually due to a third variable not included in the analysis. For example, the seemingly positive relationship between authoritarian governments and superior economic performance is spurious, since authoritarian governments tend to collapse in periods of poor economic performance, while democracies extend over periods of good and bad economic performance.

structuralist approaches Theoretical perspectives that concentrate on the sets of relations, networks, and interconnectedness between and among individuals, and how these 'structures' constrain or facilitate human agency.

synchronic A comparison of countries at one point in time. See also **diachronic**.

theory A definitive and logical statement (or groups of statements) about how the world (or some key aspect of the world) 'works'. Known collectively as empirical theory (as opposed to normative theory), these statements make claims about relationships between variables that can be tested using systematic comparative analysis.

theory confirming Crucial single-country studies, which are either 'least likely' or 'most likely' can confirm the expectations of a theory. For example, the presence of social revolution in Mexico and continued mobilization from subordinate rural groups confirms a number of theories about peasant rebellion.

theory infirming Crucial single-country studies, which are either 'least likely' or 'most likely' can infirm the expectations of a theory. For example, the absence of social revolution in Brazil despite the presence of key socio-economic conditions infirms certain theories of revolution.

time-series Data that are collected over time and arranged in chronological order. These data have special attributes that need to be addressed when using advanced quantitative methods.

unit of analysis The objects of comparative political inquiry upon which data are collected, such as individuals, elections, or countries.

value bias The introduction of contamination in measurement due to the cultural or theoretical predispositions of the researcher.

variable Any object in comparative analysis whose values vary across units, such as income across individuals, or the degree of democracy across countries.

variable-oriented Type of comparative analysis that emphasizes the empirical relationships between variables across a selection of countries. See also **case-oriented**.

References

Achen, C. H. and Snidal, D. (1989) 'Rational Deterrence Theory and Comparative Case Studies', *World Politics*, 41 (2): 143–169.

Almond, G. (1990) *A Discipline Divided: Schools and Sects in Political Science*, Newbury Park, CA: Sage.

—— (1996) 'Political Science: The History of the Discipline', in R. E. Goodin and H. Klingemann (eds) *The New Handbook of Political Science*, Oxford: Oxford University Press.

Almond, G. and Bingham Powell, G. (1966) *Comparative Politics: A Developmental Approach*, Boston: Little Brown.

Almond, G. and Genco, S. J. (1977) 'Clouds, Clocks, and the Study of Politics', *World Politics*, 29 (4): 489–522.

Almond, G. and Verba, S. (1963) *The Civic Culture: Political Attitudes and Democracy in Five Nations*, Princeton, NJ: Princeton University Press.

Andrain, C. F. (1994) *Comparative Political Systems*, Armonk, NY: M. E. Sharpe.

Apter, D. E. (1958) 'A Comparative Method for the Study of Politics', *American Journal of Sociology*, 64 (November): 221–237.

—— (1996) 'Comparative Politics, Old and New', in R. E. Goodin and H. Klingemann (eds) *The New Handbook of Political Science*, Oxford: Oxford University Press, 372.

Aristotle (1958) *The Politics*, trans. E. Barker, Oxford: Clarendon Press.

Axelrod, R. (1984) *The Evolution of Cooperation*, New York: Basic Books.

Banks, A. S. (1994) *Cross-Polity Time-Series Data Archive*, Binghamton, NY: State University of New York at Binghamton.

Bashevkin, S. (1998) *Women on the Defensive: Living through Conservative Times*, Chicago: University of Chicago Press.

Bates, G. (1989) *Beyond the Market: The Political Economy of Agrarian Development in Kenya*, Cambridge: Cambridge University Press.

Beck, N. and Katz, J. N. (1995) 'What to Do (and Not to Do) with Time-Series Cross-Section Data', *American Political Science Review*, 89 (3): 634–647.

Beer, F. and Balleck, B. (1994) 'Realist/Idealist Texts: Psychometry and Semantics', *Peace Psychology Review*, 1: 38–44.

Bill, J. and Hardgrave, R. L., Jr. (1973) *Comparative Politics: The Quest for Theory*, Columbus, OH: Charles Merrill Co.
Blalock, H. M., Jr. (1961) *Causal Inferences in Nonexperimental Research*, Chapel Hill: University of North Carolina Press.
Bollen, K. (1979) 'Political Democracy and the Timing of Development', *American Sociological Review*, 44 (August): 572–587.
Boyle, K. and Sheen, J. (1997) *The Freedom of Religion and Thought: A World Report*, London: Routledge.
Brito, A. B. de (1997) *Human Rights and Democratization in Latin America: Uruguay and Chile*, Oxford: Oxford University Press.
Budge, I., Robertson, D., and Hearl, D. (1987) *Ideology, Strategy, and Party Change: Spatial Analysis of Post-War Election Programmes in 19 Democracies*, Cambridge: Cambridge University Press.
Burkhart, R. E. and Lewis-Beck, M. (1994) 'Comparative Democracy, the Economic Development Thesis', *American Political Science Review*, 88 (4): 903–910.
Burton, M., Gunther, R., and Higley, J. (1992) 'Introduction: Elite Transformation and Democratic Regimes', in John Higley and Richard Gunther (eds), *Elites and Democratic Consolidation in Latin America and Southen Europe*, Cambridge: Cambridge University Press, 1–37.
Cammack, P. (1997) *Capitalism and Democracy in the Third World: The Doctrine for Political Development*, London and Washington: Leicester University Press.
Campbell, D. T. (1975) '"Degrees of Freedom" and the Case Study,' *Comparative Political Studies*, 8 (2): 178–193.
Campbell, D. T. and Stanley, J. C. (1963) *Experimental and Quasi-Experimental Designs for Research*, Chicago: Rand McNally.
Caporaso, J. A. (1995) 'Research, Falsification, and the Qualitative–Quantitative Divide', *American Political Science Review*, 89 (June): 457–460.
Carr, R. and Fusi, J. P. (1979) *Spain: Dictatorship to Democracy*, 2nd edn, London: Allen & Unwin.
Castells, M. (1997) *The Information Age: Economy, Society, and Culture, Volume II: The Power of Identity*, Oxford: Blackwell.
Chilcote, R. H. (1994) *Theories of Comparative Politics: The Search for a Paradigm Reconsidered*, 2nd edn, Boulder, CO: Westview Press.
Cioffi-Revilla, C. (1998) *Politics and Uncertainty: Theory, Models and Applications*, Cambridge: Cambridge University Press.
Cioffi-Revilla, C. and Landman, T. (1999) 'The Rise and Fall of Maya City States in the Ancient Meso-American System', *International Studies Quarterly*, December.
Clarke, S. E. and Gaile, G. (1998) *The Work of Cities*, Minneapolis and London: University of Minnesota Press.
Cohen, J. and Arato, A. (1992) *Civil Society and Political Theory*, Cambridge, MA: MIT Press.
Cohen, Y. (1987) 'Democracy from Above: The Origins of Military Dictatorship in Brazil', *World Politics*, 30–54.
—— (1994) *Radicals, Reformers, and Reactionaries: The Prisoner's Dilemma and the Collapse of Democracy in Latin America*, Chicago: University of Chicago Press.
Collier, D. (ed.) (1979) *The New Authoritarianism in Latin America*, Princeton, NJ: Princeton University Press.
—— (1991) 'New Perspectives on the Comparative Method', in D. A. Rustow and K. P. Erickson (eds) *Comparative Political Dynamics: Global Research Perspectives*, New York: Harper Collins, 7–31.
—— (1993) 'The Comparative Method', in A. Finifter (ed.) *Political Science: The State of the Discipline*, Washington, DC: The American Political Science Association.

—— (1995) 'Translating Quantitative Methods for Qualitative Researchers: The Case of Selection Bias', *American Political Science Review*, 89 (June): 461–466.
Collier, D. and Collier, R. B. (1991) *Shaping the Political Arena: Critical Junctures, the Labor Movement, and Regime Dynamics*, Princeton, NJ: Princeton University Press.
Collier, D. and Mahoney, J. (1996) 'Insights and Pitfalls: Selection Bias and Qualitative Research', *World Politics*, 49: 56–91.
Colomer, J. (1991) 'Transitions by Agreement: Modelling the Spanish Way', *American Political Science Review*, 85 (4): 1283–1302.
Colomer, J. M. and Pascual, M. (1994) 'The Polish Games of Transition', *Communist and Post-Communist Studies*, 27 (3): 275–294.
Costain, A. N. (1992) *Inviting Women's Rebellion: A Political Process Interpretation of the Women's Movement*, Baltimore, MD: Johns Hopkins University Press.
Costain, A. N. and Majstorovic, S. (1994) 'Congress, Social Movements and Public Opinion: Multiple Origins of Women's Rights Legislation', *Political Research Quarterly*, 47 (1):111–135.
Couvalis, G. (1997) *The Philosophy of Science: Science and Objectivity*, London: Sage.
Cutright, P. (1963) 'National Political Development: Its Measurement and Social Correlates', in N. Polsby, R. A. Denther, and P. A. Smith (eds) *Political and Social Life*, Boston: Houghton Mifflin, 569–582.
Cutright, P. and Wiley, J. A. (1969) 'Modernization and Political Representation: 1927–1966', *Studies in Comparative International Development*, 23–41.
Dahl, R. A. (1971) *Polyarchy: Participation and Opposition*, New Haven, CT: Yale University Press.
—— (1998) *On Democracy*, New Haven, CT: Yale University Press.
Dalton, R. (1988) *Citizen Politics in Western Democracies*, Chatham, NJ: Chatham House Publishers.
—— (1994) *Green Rainbow: Environmental Groups in Western Europe*, New Haven, CT: Yale University Press.
De Mesquita, B., Morrow, J. D., and Zorick, E. R. (1997) 'Capabilities, Perception, and Escalation', *American Political Science Review*, 91 (March): 15–27.
De Meur, G. and Berg-Schlosser, D. (1994) 'Comparing Political Systems: Establishing Similarities and Dissimilarities', *European Journal of Political Research*, 26: 193–219.
De Schweinitz, K. (1964) *Industrialization and Democracy: Economic Necessities and Political Possibilities*, New York: Free Press.
De Vaus, D. A. (1991) *Surveys in Social Research*, 2nd edn, London: Unwin Hyman.
Della Porta, D. (1996) 'Social Movements and the State: Thoughts on the Policing of Protest,' in D. McAdam, J. McCarthy, and M. N. Zald (eds) *Comparative Perspectives on Social Movements*, Cambridge: Cambridge University Press, 62–92.
Della Porta, D. and Reiter, H. (1998) *Policing Protest : The Control of Mass Demonstrations in Western Democracies*, Minnesota: University of Minnesota Press.
Devine, F. (1995) 'Qualitative Analysis', in D. Marsh and G. Stoker (eds) *Theories and Methods in Political Science*, London: Macmillan, 137–153.
Diamond, L. (1999) *Developing Democracy: Toward Consolidation*, Baltimore, MD: Johns Hopkins University Press.
Dogan, M. and Kazancigil, A. (1994) *Comparing Nations: Concepts, Strategies, Substance*, Oxford: Blackwell.
Dogan, M. and Pelassy, D. (1990) *How to Compare Nations: Strategies in Comparative Politics*, 2nd edn, Chatham, NJ: Chatham House.
Drass, K. A. and Ragin, C. C. (1991) *Qualitative Comparative Analysis 3.0*, Evanston, IL: Center for Urban Affairs and Policy Research, Northwestern University.
Duverger, M. (1954) *Political Parties*, trans. B. and R. North, London: Methuen.

Eckstein, H. (1964) *Internal War*, New York: Free Press.

—— (1975) 'Case-study and Theory in Political Science', in F. I. Greenstein and N. S. Polsby (eds) *Handbook of Political Science, Vol. 7: Strategies of Inquiry*, Reading, MA: Addison-Wesley, 79–137.

Erickson, K. P. and Rustow, D. A. (1991) 'Global Research Perspectives: Paradigms, Concepts and Data in a Changing World', in D. A. Rustow and K. P. Erickson (eds) *Comparative Political Dynamics: Global Research Perspectives*, New York: Harper Collins, 441–459.

Ersson, S. and Lane, J. E. (1996) 'Democracy and Development: A Statistical Exploration', in A. Leftwich (ed.) *Democracy and Development*, Cambridge: Polity, 45–73.

Escobar, A. and Alvarez, S. E. (eds) (1992) *The Making of Social Movements in Latin America: Identity, Strategy, and Democracy*, Boulder, CO: Westview.

Eulau, H. (1996) *Micro–Macro Dilemmas in Political Science: Personal Pathways through Complexity*, Norman, OK: University of Oklahoma Press.

Faure, A. M. (1994) 'Some Methodological Problems in Comparative Politics', *Journal of Theoretical Politics*, 6 (3): 307–322.

Fay, B. (1975) *Social Theory and Political Practice*, London: Allen & Unwin.

Ferguson, N. (ed.) (1997a) *Virtual History: Alternatives and Counterfactuals*, London: Picador.

—— (1997b) 'Virtual History: Towards a Chaotic Theory of the Past', in N. Ferguson (ed.) *Virtual History: Alternatives and Counterfactuals*, London: Picador, 1–90.

Feyerabend, P. (1993) *Against Method*, London: Verso Press.

Finer, S. E. (1997) *The History of Government, Vol. I: Ancient Monarchies and Empires*, Oxford: Oxford University Press.

Fiorina, M. P. (1996) *Divided Goverment*, 2nd edn, Needham Heights, MA: Simon & Schuster.

Firebaugh, G. (1980) 'Cross-National Versus Historical Regression Models: Conditions of Equivalence in Comparative Analysis', *Comparative Social Research*, 3: 333–344.

Fischer, M. E. (ed.) (1996) *Establishing Democracies*, Boulder, CO: Westview Press.

Fitzgibbon, R. H. (1967) 'Measuring Democratic Change in Latin America', *Journal of Politics*, 29: 129–166.

Foweraker, J. (1989) *Making Democracy in Spain: Grassroots Struggle in the South, 1955–1975*, Cambridge: Cambridge University Press.

—— (1995) *Theorizing Social Movements*, London: Pluto.

—— (1998) 'Institutional Design, Party Systems and Governability: Differentiating the Presidential Regimes of Latin America', *British Journal of Political Science*, 28: 651–676.

Foweraker, J. and Landman, T. (1997) *Citizenship Rights and Social Movements: A Comparative and Statistical Analysis*, Oxford: Oxford University Press.

—— (1999) 'Individual Rights and Social Movements: A Comparative and Statistical Inquiry', *British Journal of Political Science*, 29 (April): 291–322.

Fox, J. (1997) *Applied Regression Analysis, Linear Models, and Related Methods*, Thousand Oaks and London: Sage Publications.

Freedom House (1995) *Freedom in the World: Political and Civil Liberties, 1994–1995*, New York: Freedom House.

—— (1999) *Freedom in the World: Political and Civil Liberties 1998–1999*, New York: Freedom House [http://www.freedomhouse.org]

Fuentes, M. and Frank, G. A. (1989) 'Ten Theses on Social Movements', *World Development*, 17 (2): 179–191.

Gamson, W. A. (1975) *The Strategy of Social Protest*, Homewood, IL: Dorsey Press.

Gautier, D. (1986) *Morals by Agreement*, Oxford: Clarendon Press.

Geddes, B. (1990) 'How the Cases You Choose Affect the Answers You Get: Selection Bias in Comparative Politics', *Political Analysis*, 2: 131–150.

—— (1991) 'A Game Theoretic Model of Reform in Latin American Democracies', *American Political Science Review*, 85 (June): 371–392.
—— (1994) *Politician's Dilemma: Building State Capacity in Latin America*, Berkeley and Los Angeles: University of California Press.
Geertz, C. (1973) 'Thick Description: Toward an Interpretative Theory of Culture', in *The Interpretation of Cultures*, New York: Basic Books, 3–30.
Gerschenkron, A. (1962) *Economic Backwardness in Historical Perspective*, Cambridge: Belknap Press of Harvard University Press.
Gleditsch, K. and Ward, M. (1997) 'Double Take: A Reexamination of Democracy and Autocracy in Modern Polities', *Journal of Conflict Resolution*, 41 (3): 361–383.
Golembewski, R. T., Welsh, W. A., and Crotty, W. J. (eds) (1969) *A Methodological Primer for Political Scientists*, Chicago: Rand McNally.
Goodin, R. E. and Klingemann, H. (eds) (1996a) 'Political Science: The Discipline', in R. E. Goodin and H. Klingemann (eds) *The New Handbook of Political Science*, Oxford: Oxford University Press, 3–49.
—— (eds) (1996b) *The New Handbook of Political Science*, Oxford: Oxford University Press.
Goodwin, J. and Skocpol, T. (1989) 'Explaining Revolutions in the Contemporary Third World', *Politics and Society*, 17 (4): 489–509.
Gray, J. (1999) *False Dawn: The Delusions of Global Capitalism*, London: Granta Books.
Gross, P. R. and Levitt, N. (1994) *Higher Superstition: The Academic Left and Its Quarrels with Science*, Baltimore, MD: Johns Hopkins University Press.
Gujarati, D. N. (1988) *Basic Econometrics*, 2nd edn, London: McGraw-Hill.
Gurr, T. R. (1968) 'A Causal Model of Civil Strife', *American Political Science Review*, 62: 1104–1124.
—— (1970) *Why Men Rebel*, Princeton, NJ: Princeton University Press.
—— (1993) 'Why Minorities Rebel: A Global Analysis of Communal Mobilization and Conflict since 1945', *International Political Science Review*, 14 (2): 161–201.
Haas, M. (1962) 'Comparative Analysis', *The Western Political Quarterly*, 15 (June): 292–304.
Haas, M. and Stack, S. (1983) 'Economic Development and Strikes: A Comparative Analysis', *The Sociological Quarterly*, 24 (Winter): 43–58.
Hagopian, F. (1996) *Traditional Politics and Regime Change in Brazil*, Cambridge: Cambridge University Press.
Hague, R., Harrop, M., and Breslin, S. (1992) *Political Science: A Comparative Introduction*, New York: St Martin's Press.
Hartlyn, J. and Valenzuela, A. (1994) 'Democracy in Latin America since 1930', in L. Bethell (ed.) *Cambridge History of Latin America*, Volume VI: Part 2, Cambridge, Cambridge University Press.
Harvey, N. (1998) *The Chiapas Rebellion: The Struggle for Land and Democracy*, Raleigh, NC: Duke University Press.
Hay, C. (1995) 'Structure and Agency', in D. Marsh and G. Stoker (eds) *Theories and Methods in Political Science*, London: Macmillan, 189–206.
Held, D., McGrew, A., Goldblatt, D., and Perraton, J. (1999) *Global Transformations: Politics, Economics, and Culture*, Cambridge: Polity Press.
Helliwell, J. F. (1994) 'Empirical Linkages between Democracy and Economic Growth', *British Journal of Political Science*, 24: 225–248.
Hibbs, D. (1973) *Mass Political Violence: A Cross-National Causal Analysis*, New York: Wiley.
Hirschman, A. O. (1971) 'The Search for Paradigms as a Hindrance to Understanding', *World Politics*, 22: 329–343.
Holm, J. D. (1996) 'Development, Democracy, and Civil Society in Botswana', in A. Leftwich (ed.) *Democracy and Development*, Cambridge: Polity Press, 97–113.

Holt, R. T. and Turner, J. E. (eds) (1970) *The Methodology of Comparative Research*, New York: The Free Press.

Howarth, D. (1995) 'Discourse Theory', in D. Marsh and G. Stoker (eds) *Theories and Methods in Political Science*, London: Macmillan, 115–136.

—— (1998a) 'Discourse Theory and Political Analysis', in E. Scarbrough and E. Tanenbaum (eds) *Research Strategies in the Social Sciences: A Guide to New Approaches*, Oxford: Oxford University Press, 268–293.

—— (1998b) 'Paradigms Gained? A Critique of Theories and Explanations of Democratic Transition in South Africa', in D. Howarth and A. Norval (eds) *South Africa in Transition: New Theoretical Perspectives*, London: Macmillan, 182–214.

Howarth, D., Norval, A., and Stavrakakis, Y. (forthcoming) *Discourse Theory and Political Analysis*, Manchester: University of Manchester Press.

Hume, D. [1748] (1962) *On Human Nature and the Understanding*, ed. Antony Flew, New York: Collier Books.

Huntington, S. P. (1968) *Political Order in Changing Societies*, New Haven, CT: Yale University Press.

—— (1991) *The Third Wave: Democratization in the Late Twentieth Century*, Norman, OK: University of Oklahoma Press.

—— (1996) *The Clash of Civilizations and the Remaking of the New World Order*, New York: Simon & Schuster.

Inglehart, R. (1977) *The Silent Revolution: Changing Values and Political Styles among Western Publics*, Princeton, NJ: Princeton University Press.

—— (1990) *Culture Shift in Advanced Industrial Societies*, Princeton, NJ: Princeton University Press.

—— (1997) *Modernization and Postmodernization*, Princeton, NJ: Princeton University Press.

—— (1998) 'Political Values' in Jan W. van Deth (ed.), *Comparative Politics: The Problem of Equivalence*, London: Routledge.

Jackman, R. W. (1973) 'On the Relation of Economic Development to Democratic Performance', *American Journal of Political Science*, 17 (3): 611–621.

—— (1975) *Politics and Social Equality*, New York: Wiley.

—— (1985) 'Cross-National Statistical Research and the Study of Comparative Politics', *American Journal of Political Science*, 29 (1): 161–182.

Jackson, J. E. (1996) 'Political Methodology: An Overview', in R. E. Goodin and H. Klingemann (eds) *The New Handbook of Political Science*, Oxford: Oxford University Press, 717–748.

Jaggers, K. and Gurr, T. R. (1995) 'Tracking Democracy's Third Wave with the Polity III Data', *Journal of Peace Research*, 32 (4): 469–482.

Janos, A. C. (1997) 'Paradigms Revisited: Productionism, Globality, and Postmodernity in Comparative Politics', *World Politics*, 50: 118–149.

Jones, M. P. (1995) *Electoral Laws and the Survival of Presidential Democracies*, Notre Dame, IN: University of Notre Dame Press.

Kalleberg, A. (1966) 'The Logic of Comparison: A Methodological Note for the Comparative Study of Political Systems', *World Politics*, 19 (January): 69–82.

Kant, I. (1977) *Prolegomena to any Future Metaphysics*, trans. J. W. Ellington, Indianapolis: Hackett Publishing.

—— (1990) *Foundations of the Metaphysics of Morals*, 2nd edn, trans. L. White Beck, London: Macmillan.

Karl, T. L. (1990) 'Dilemmas of Democratization in Latin America', *Comparative Politics*, 23: 1–21.

Katznelson, I. (1997) 'Structure and Configuration in Comparative Politics', in M. Lichbach and A. Zuckerman (eds.) *Comparative Politics: Rationality, Culture, and Structure*, Cambridge: Cambridge University Press, 81–112.

Kaviraj, S. (1996) 'Dilemmas of Democratic Development in India', in A. Leftwich (ed.) *Democracy and Development*, Cambridge: Polity Press, 114–138.

Keck, M. and Sikkink, K. (1998a) 'Transnational Advocacy Networks in the Movement Society' in D. S. Meyer and S. Tarrow (eds) *The Social Movement Society: Contentious Politics for a New Century*, Lanham: Rowman & Littlefield Publishers, 217–238.

—— (1998b) *Activists beyond Borders: Advocacy Networks in International Politics*, Ithaca, NY: Cornell University Press.

Kelley, S. Q. (1993) 'Divided We Govern: A Reassessment', *Polity* 25: 475–484.

Keman, H. (1993) *Comparative Politics*, Amsterdam: Free University Press.

King, G. (1989) *Unifying Political Methodology: The Likelihood Theory of Statistical Inference*, Cambridge: Cambridge University Press.

—— (1997) *A Solution to the Ecological Inference Problem: Reconstructing Individual Behaviour from Aggregate Data*, Princeton, NJ: Princeton University Press.

King, G., Keohane, R. O., and Verba, S. (1994) *Designing Social Inquiry: Scientific Inference in Qualitative Research*, Princeton, NJ: Princeton University Press.

Kirkpatrick, J. (1979) 'Dictatorships and Double Standards', *Commentary*, November: 34–45.

Kitschelt, H. (1986) 'Political Opportunity Structures and Political Protest: Anti-nuclear Movements in Four Democracies', *British Journal of Political Science*, 16 (January): 57–85.

Klingemann, H. D., Hofferbert, R. I., and Budge, I. (1994) *Parties, Policies, and Democracy*, Boulder, CO: Westview Press.

Knapp, T. R. (1996) *Learning Statistics through Playing Cards*, Thousand Oaks, CA: Sage.

Kohli, A., Evans, P., Katzenstein, P. J., Przeworski, A., Rudolph, S. H., Scott, J. C., and Skocpol, T. (1995) 'The Role of Theory in Comparative Politics: A Symposium', *World Politics*, 48: 1–49.

Kriesi, H. (1996) 'The Organizational Structure of New Social Movements in a Political Context', in D. McAdam, J. D. McCarthy, and M. N. Zald (eds) *Comparative Perspectives on Social Movements*, Cambridge: Cambridge University Press, 152–184.

Kriesi, H., Koopmans, R., Duyvendak, J. W., and Giugni, M. G. (1995) *New Social Movements in Western Europe*, London: UCL Press.

Kuhn, T. (1970) *The Structure of Scientific Revolutions*, Chicago: University of Chicago Press.

La Polombara, J. (1968) 'Macro-theories and Micro-applications in Comparative Politics: A Widening Chasm', *Comparative Politics*, 1 (October): 52–78.

—— (1974) *Politics within Nations*, Englewood Cliffs, NJ: Prentice Hall.

Laakso, M. and Taagepera, R. (1979) '"Effective" Number of Parties: A Measure with Application to Western Europe', *Comparative Political Studies*, 12 (1): 3–27.

Laitin, D. (1995) 'Disciplining Political Science', *American Political Science Review*, 89 (June): 454–456.

Laitin, D. and Warner, C. M. (1992) 'Structure and Irony in Social Revolutions', *Political Theory*, 20 (1): 147–151.

Lakatos, I. (1970) 'Falsification and the Methodology of Scientific Research Programs,' in I. Lakatos and A. Musgrave (eds) *Criticism and Growth of Knowledge*, Cambridge: Cambridge University Press, 91–196.

Landman, T. (1995) '"El Chipiro" wins: The Venezuelan Elections of 1993', *Electoral Studies*, 14 (1): 100–109.

—— (1999) 'Economic Development and Democracy: The View from Latin America', *Political Studies*, 47 (4).

Lane, R. (1996) 'Positivism, Scientific Realism, and Political Science: Recent Developments in the Philosophy of Science', *Journal of Theoretical Politics*, 8 (3): 361–382.

Lawson, T. (1997) *Economics and Reality*, London: Routledge.
Leftwich, A. (ed.) (1996) *Democracy and Development*, Cambridge: Polity Press.
Lerner, D. (1958) *The Passing of Traditional Society: Modernizing the Middle East*, Glencoe, IL: The Free Press of Glencoe.
Levi, M. (1997) 'A Model, a Method, and a Map: Rational Choice in Comparative and Historical Analysis', in M. Lichbach and A. Zuckerman (eds), *Comparative Politics: Rationality, Culture, and Structure*, Cambridge: Cambridge University Press, 19–41.
Levine, D. (1989) 'Paradigm Lost: Dependency to Democracy', *World Politics*, 40 (3): 377–394.
Lewis, D. (1973) *Counterfactuals*, Cambridge, MA: Harvard University Press.
Lichbach, M. (1989) 'An Evaluation of "Does Economic Inequality Breed Political Conflict" Studies', *World Politics*, 41: 431–470.
—— (1994) 'What Makes Rational Peasants Revolutionary? Dilemma, Paradox, and Irony in Peasant Collective Action', *World Politics*, 46 (April): 383.
—— (1995) *The Rebel's Dilemma*, Ann Arbor: University of Michigan Press.
—— (1997) 'Social Theory and Comparative Politics', in M. Lichbach and A. Zuckerman (eds), *Comparative Politics: Rationality, Culture, and Structure*, Cambridge: Cambridge University Press, 239–276.
Lichbach, M. and Zuckerman, A. (eds) (1997) *Comparative Politics: Rationality, Culture, and Structure*, Cambridge: Cambridge University Press.
Lieberson, S. (1987) *Making It Count: The Improvement of Social Research and Theory*, Berkeley: University of California Press.
—— (1991) 'Small *N*'s and Big Conclusions: An Examination of the Reasoning in Comparative Studies Based on a Small Number of Cases', *Social Forces*, (December): 307–320.
—— (1994) 'More on the Uneasy Case for Using Mill-Type Methods in Small-*N* Comparative Studies', *Social Forces*, 72 (June): 1225–1237.
Lieberson, S. and Hansen, L. K. (1974) 'National Development, Mother Tongue Diversity, and the Comparative Study of Nations', *American Sociological Review*, 39: 523–541.
Lijphart, A. (1971) 'Comparative Politics and Comparative Method', *The American Political Science Review*, 65 (3): 682–693.
—— (1975) 'The Comparable Cases Strategy in Comparative Research', *Comparative Political Studies*, 8 (2): 158–177.
—— (1994a) *Electoral Systems and Party Systems: A Study of Twenty Seven Democracies, 1945–1990*, Oxford: Oxford University Press.
—— (1994b) 'Democracies: Forms, Performance, and Constitutional Engineering', *European Journal of Political Research*, 25: 1–17.
Linz, J. J. (1964) 'An Authoritarian Regime: Spain', in E. Allardt and S. Rokkan (eds) *Mass Politics*, New York: Free Press.
—— (1990) 'The Perils of Presidentialism', *Journal of Democracy*, 1: 51–69.
Linz, J. J. and Stepan, A. (1978) *The Breakdown of Democratic Regimes*, Baltimore, MD: Johns Hopkins University Press.
—— (1996) *Problems of Democratic Transition and Consolidation: South America, Southern Europe, and Post-Communist Europe*, Baltimore, MD: Johns Hopkins University Press.
Lipset, S. M. (1959) 'Some Social Requisites for Democracy: Economic Development and Political Legitimacy', *The American Political Science Review*, 53: 69–105.
Lipset, S. M. and Rokkan, S. (1967) *Party Systems and Voter Alignments: Cross-National Perspectives*, New York: Free Press.
—— (1960) *Political Man*, London: Mercury Books.
—— (1994) 'The Social Requisites of Democracy Revisited', *American Sociological Review*, 59 (February): 1–22.

Luebbert, G. (1991) *Liberalism, Fascism, or Social Democracy: Social Classes and the Political Origins of Regimes in Inter-war Europe*, New York: Oxford University Press.
Lustick, I. (1996) 'History, Historiography, and Political Science: Multiple Historical Records and the Problem of Selection Bias', *American Political Science Review*, 90 (3): 605–618.
McAdam, D., McCarthy, J. D., and Zald, M. N. (1996) *Comparative Perspectives on Social Movements*, Cambridge: Cambridge University Press.
McCarthy, J. D. and Zald, M. N. (1977) 'Resource Mobilization and Social Movements: A Partial Theory,' *American Journal of Sociolgy*, 82: 1212–1241.
Macauley, N. (1967) *The Sandino Affair*, Chicago: Quadrangle Books.
McClelland, J. S. (1997) *A History of Western Political Thought*, London: Routledge.
Macintyre, A. (1971) 'Is a Science of Comparative Politics Possible?', *Against the Self-Images of the Age*, London: Duckworth, 260–279.
McKay, D. (1994) 'Review Article: Divided and Governed? Recent Research on Divided Government in the United States', *British Journal of Political Science*, 24: 517–534.
Mackie, T. and Marsh, D. (1995) 'The Comparative Method', in D. Marsh and G. Stoker (eds) *Theory and Methods in Political Science*, London: Macmillan, 173–188.
Macridis, R. C. and Brown, B. E. (eds) (1986) *Comparative Politics*, 6th edn, Chicago: Dorsey Press.
Mainwaring, S. (1993) 'Presidentialism, Multipartism, and Democracy: The Difficult Combination', *Comparative Political Studies*, 26 (2): 198–228.
Mainwaring, S. and Scully, T. R. (1995) 'Introduction: Party Systems in Latin America', in S. Mainwaring and T. R. Scully (eds) *Building Democratic Institutions: Party Systems in Latin America*, Stanford: Stanford University Press, 1–34.
Mair, P. (1996) 'Comparative Politics: An Overview', in R. E. Goodin and H. Klingemann (eds) (1996) *The New Handbook of Political Science*, Oxford: Oxford University Press, 309–335.
March, J. G. and Olsen, J. P. (1984) 'New Institutionalism: Organizational Factors in Political Life', *American Political Science Review*, 78: 734–749.
Marsh, D. and Stoker, G. (eds) *Theories and Methods in Political Science*, London: Macmillan.
Martin, L. L. and Sikkink, K. (1993) 'US Policy and Human Rights in Argentina and Guatemala, 1973–1980', in P. B. Evans, H. K. Jacobson, and R. D. Putnam (eds) *Double-Edged Diplomacy: International Bargaining and Domestic Politics*, Los Angeles: University of California Press, 330–362.
Maxwell, K. (1995) *The Making of Portuguese Democracy*, Cambridge: Cambridge University Press.
Mayer, L. C. (1983) 'Practicing What We Preach: Comparative Politics in the 1980s', *Comparative Political Studies*, 16 (2): 173–194.
—— (1989) *Redefining Comparative Politics: Promise versus Performance*, Newbury Park, CA: Sage.
Mayhew, D. (1993) *Divided We Govern: Party Control, Lawmaking, and Investigations, 1946–1990*, New Haven, CT: Yale University Press.
Merkl, P. H. (1970) *Modern Comparative Politics*, New York: Holt, Rinehart, & Winston.
Merritt, R. L. (1970) *Systematic Approaches to Comparative Politics*, Chicago: Rand McNally.
Midlarsky, M. and Roberts, K. (1985) 'Class, State, and Revolution in Central America: Nicaragua and El Salvador Compared', *Journal of Conflict Resolution*, 29 (2): 163–193.
Mill, J. S. (1872) *A System of Logic*, London: Longman.
Miller, W. L. (1995) 'Quantitative Analysis', *Theories and Methods in Political Science*, London: Macmillan, 154–172.
Moon, C. and Kim, Y. (1996) 'A Circle of Paradox: Development, Politics and Democracy in South Korea', in A. Leftwich (ed.) *Democracy and Development*, Cambridge: Polity Press, 139–167.

Moore, B. (1966) *The Social Origins of Dictatorship and Democracy: Lord and Peasant in the Making of the Modern World*, Boston, MA: Beacon Press.
—— (1978) *Injustice: The Social Bases of Obedience and Revolt*, London: Macmillan.
Muller, E. N. and Seligson, M. A. (1987) 'Inequality and Insurgency', *American Political Science Review*, 81 (2): 425–451.
Neubauer, D. E. (1967) 'Some Conditions of Democracy', *American Political Science Review* 61: 1002–1009.
Nichols, E. (1986) 'Skocpol and Revolution: Comparative Analysis vs. Historical Conjuncture', *Comparative Social Research*, 9: 163–186.
Nugent, D. (1993) *Spent Cartridges of Revolution: An Anthropological History of Namiquipa, Chihuahua*, Chicago: University of Chicago Press.
O'Donnell, G. (1973) *Economic Modernization and Bureaucratic Authoritarianism*, Berkeley, CA: Institute of International Studies.
O'Donnell, G., and Schmitter, P. C. (1986) *Transitions from Authoritarian Rule: Tentative Conclusions about Uncertain Democracies*, Baltimore and London: Johns Hopkins University Press.
O'Donnell, G., Schmitter, P. C., and Whitehead, L. (eds) (1986a) *Transitions from Authoritarian Rule: Southern Europe*, Baltimore and London: Johns Hopkins University Press.
—— (1986b) *Transitions from Authoritarian Rule: Latin America*, Baltimore and London: Johns Hopkins University Press.
—— (1986c) *Transitions from Authoritarian Rule: Comparative Perspectives*, Baltimore and London: Johns Hopkins University Press.
Olson, M. (1965) *The Logic of Collective Action*, Cambridge, MA: Harvard University Press.
Opp, K. D., Finkel, S. E., Muller, E. N., Wolsfield, G., Dietz, H. A., and Green, J. D. (1995) 'Left–Right Ideology and Collective Political Action: A Comparative Analysis of Germany, Israel, and Peru', in J. C. Jenkins and B. Klandermans (eds), *The Politics of Social Protest: Comparative Perspectives on States and Social Movements*, London: UCL Press, 63–95.
Page, E. (1990) 'British Comparative Politics and Political Science', *Political Studies*, 38: 275–305.
Paige, J. (1975) *Agrarian Revolution: Social Movements and Export Agriculture in the Underdeveloped World*, New York: Free Press.
Peeler, J. A. (1992) 'Elite Settlements and Democratic Consolidation: Colombia, Costa Rica, and Venezuela', in J. Higley and R. Gunther (eds.) *Elites and Democratic Consolidation in Latin America and Southern Europe*, Cambridge: Cambridge University Press, 81–112.
Pennings, P., Keman, H., and Kleinnijenhuis, J. (1999) *Doing Research in Political Science: An Introduction to Comparative Methods and Statistics*, London: Sage.
Peters, Guy (1998) *Comparative Politics: Theory and Methods*, New York: New York University Press.
Peterson, P. and Greene, J. P. (1993) 'Why Executive-Legislative Conflict in the United States Is Dwindling', *British Journal of Political Science*, 24: 33–55.
Poe, S. C. and Tate, C. N. (1994) 'Repression of Human Rights to Personal Integrity in the 1980s: A Global Analysis', *American Political Science Review*, 88 (4): 853–872.
Poe, S., Pilatovcky, S., Miller, B., and Ogundele, A. (1994) 'Human Rights and US Foreign Aid Revisited: The Latin American Region', *Human Rights Quarterly*, 16: 539–558.
Popkin, S. (1979) *The Rational Peasant: the Political Economy of Rural Society in Vietnam*, Berkeley: University of California Press.
Popper, K. (1959) *The Logic of Scientific Discovery*, London: Hutchinson.

—— (1997) *The Lesson of This Century*, London: Routledge.

Poulantzas, N. (1976) *The Crisis of the Dictatorships: Portugal, Spain, Greece*, New York: Schocken Books.

Powell, G. Bingham (1982) *Contemporary Democracies: Participation, Stability, and Violence*, Cambridge, MA: Harvard University Press.

Przeworski, A. (1991) *Democracy and the Market*, Cambridge: Cambridge University Press.

Przeworski, A. and Limongi, F. (1993) 'Political Regimes and Economic Growth', *Journal of Economic Perspectives*, 7 (3): 51–69.

—— (1997) 'Modernization: Theories and Facts', *World Politics*, 49 (January): 155–183.

Przeworski, A. and Teune, H. (1970) *The Logic of Comparative Social Inquiry*, New York: Wiley.

Putnam, R. D. (1993) *Making Democracy Work: Civic Traditions in Modern Italy*, Princeton, NJ: Princeton University Press.

Rae, D. (1967) *The Political Consequences of Electoral Laws*, New Haven, CT: Yale University Press.

—— (1971) *Political Consequences of Electoral Laws*, New Haven, CT: Yale University Press.

Ragin, C. (1987) *The Comparative Method: Moving beyond Qualitative and Quantitative Strategies*, Berkeley: University of California Press.

—— (1994) 'Introduction to Qualitative Comparative Analysis,' in T. Janoski and A. Hicks (eds) *The Comparative Political Economy of the Welfare State*, Cambridge: Cambridge University Press, 299–320.

Ragin, C., Berg-Schlosser, D., and de Meur, G. (1996) 'Political Methodology: Qualitative Methods' in R. E. Goodin and H. Klingemann (eds) *The New Handbook of Political Science*, Oxford: Oxford University Press, 749–768.

Robertson, A. H. and Merrills, J. G. (1996) *Human Rights in the World: An Introduction to the Study of the International Protection of Human Rights*, 4th edn, Manchester: University of Manchester Press.

Robinson, W. S. (1950) 'Ecological Correlations and the Behaviour of Individuals', *American Sociological Review*, 15: 351–357.

Rosenau, P. M. (1992) *Post-Modernism and the Social Sciences: Insights, Inroads, and Intrusions*, Princeton, NJ: Princeton University Press.

Ross, M. H. (1997) 'Culture and Identity in Comparative Political Analysis', in M. Lichbach and A. Zuckerman (eds.) *Comparative Politics: Rationality, Culture, and Structure*, Cambridge: Cambridge University Press, 42–80.

Rostow, W. W. (1961) *The Stages of Economic Growth: A Non-Communist Manifesto*, Cambridge: Cambridge University Press.

Rueschemeyer, D., Stephens, E. H., and Stephens, J. (1992) *Capitalist Development and Democracy*, Cambridge: Polity Press.

Rustow, D. A. (1970) 'Transitions to Democracy: Toward a Dynamic Model', *Comparative Politics*, 2: 337–363.

Rustow, D. A. and Erickson, K. P. (1991) 'Introduction', in D. A. Rustow and K. P. Erickson (eds) *Comparative Political Dynamics: Global Research Perspectives*, New York: Harper Collins, 1–4.

Sanders, D. (1981) *Patterns of Political Instability*, London: Macmillan.

—— (1994) 'Methodological Considerations in Comparative Cross-national Research', *International Social Science Journal*, 46: 43–49.

—— (1995) 'Behavioural Analysis', in D. Marsh and G. Stoker (eds) *Theories and Methods in Political Science*, London: Macmillan, 58–75.

Sartori, G. (1970) 'Concept Misinformation in Comparative Politics', *American Political Science Review*, 64: 1033–1053.

—— (ed.) (1984) *Social Science Concepts: A Systematic Analysis*, Beverly Hills, CA: Sage.

—— (1994) 'Compare Why and How: Comparing, Miscomparing and the Comparative Method', in M. Dogan and A. Kazancigil (eds) *Comparing Nations: Concepts, Strategies, Substance*, London: Basil Blackwell, 14–34.

Savolainen, J. (1994) 'The Rationality of Drawing Conclusions Based on Small Samples: In Defense of Mill's Methods', *Social Forces*, 72 (June): 1217–1224.

Scarrow, H. A. (1969) *Comparative Political Analysis: An Introduction*, New York: Harper & Row.

Scheuch, E. K. (1966) 'Cross-national Comparisons Using Aggregate Data: Some Substantive and Methodological Problems', in R. L. Merritt and S. Rokkan (eds) *Comparing Nations: The Use of Quantitative Data in Cross-National Research*, New Haven, CT: Yale University Press, 131–167.

—— (1969) 'Social Context and Individual Behaviour', in M. Dogan and S. Rokkan (eds) *Quantitative Ecological Analysis in the Social Sciences*, Cambridge, MA: MIT Press, 133–155.

Scott, J. (1976) *The Moral Economy of the Peasant: Rebellion and Subsistence in Southeast Asia*, New Haven and London: Yale University Press.

—— (1985) *Weapons of the Weak: Everyday Forms of Peasant Resistance*, New Haven, CT: Yale University Press.

Seligson, M. (1987) 'Development, Democratization, and Decay: Central America at the Crossroads' in J. Malloy and M. Seligson (eds) *Authoritarians and Democrats: Regime Transition in Latin America*, Pittsburgh: University of Pittsburgh Press.

Serra, J. (1979) 'Three Mistaken Theses Regarding the Connections between Industrialization and Authoritarian Regimes', in D. Collier (ed.) *The New Authoritarianism in Latin America*, Princeton, NJ: Princeton University Press, 99–164.

Shugart, M. and Carey, J. M. (1992) *Presidents and Assemblies: Constitutional Design and Electoral Dynamics*, Cambridge: Cambridge University Press.

Sigelman, L. and Gadbois, G. (1983) 'Contemporary Comparative Politics: An Inventory and Assessment', *Comparative Political Studies*, 16 (3): 275–307.

Sigelman, L. and Simpson, M. (1977) 'A Cross-National Test of the Linkage between Economic Inequality and Political Violence', *Journal of Conflict Resolution*, 21 (1): 105–128.

Skocpol, T. (1979) *States and Social Revolutions: A Comparative Analysis of France, Russia, and China*, Cambridge: Cambridge University Press.

—— (1994) *Social Revolutions in the Modern World*, Cambridge: Cambridge University Press.

Skocpol, T. and Somers, M. (1980) 'The Uses of Comparative History in Macrosocial Inquiry', *Comparative Studies in Society and History*, 22: 174–197.

Smelser, N. (1976) *Comparative Methods in the Social Sciences*, Englewood Cliffs, NJ: Prentice-Hall.

Steinmo, S., Thelen, K., and Longstreth, F. (eds) (1992) *Structuring Politics: Historical Institutionalism in Comparative Analysis*, Cambridge: Cambridge University Press.

Stepan, A. (1978) 'Political Leadership and Regime Breakdown: Brazil', in J. J. Linz and A. Stepan (eds) *The Breakdown of Democratic Regimes: Latin America*, Baltimore, MD: Johns Hopkins University Press, 110–137.

Stepan, A. and Skach, C. (1993) 'Constitutional Frameworks and Democratic Consolidation: Parliamentarism and Presidentialism', *World Politics* 46 (Oct.): 1–22.

—— (1994) 'Presidentialism and Parliamentarism in Comparative Perspective', in J. Linz and A. Valenzuela (eds) *The Failure of Presidential Democracy*, Baltimore, MD: Johns Hopkins University Press, 119–136.

Stimson, J. (1985) 'Regression in Space and Time: A Statistical Essay', *American Political Science Review*, 29: 914–947.

Stoker, G. (1995) 'Introduction', in D. Marsh and G. Stoker (eds) *Theory and Methods in Political Science*, London: Macmillan.

Suleiman, E. (1994) 'Presidentialism and Political Stability in France', in J. Linz and A. Valenzuela (eds) *The Failure of Presidential Democracy*, Baltimore: Johns Hopkins University Press, 137–162.

Sundquist, J. L. (1988) 'Needed: A Political Theory for the New Era of Coalition Government in the United States', *Political Science Quarterly*, 103: 613–635.

Tarrow, S. (1989) *Democracy and Disorder: Protest and Politics in Italy, 1965–1975*, Oxford: Clarendon Press.

—— (1994) *Power in Movement: Social Movements, Collective Action, and Politics*, Cambridge: Cambridge University Press.

—— (1995) 'Bridging the Quantitative – Qualitative Divide in Political Science', *American Political Science Review*, 89 (2): 471–474.

Taylor, C. and Hudson, M. (1972) *World Handbook of Political and Social Indicators*, 2nd edn, New Haven, CT: Yale University Press.

Taylor, C. and Jodice, D. A. (1983) *World Handbook of Political and Social Indicators*, 3rd edn, New Haven, CT: Yale University Press.

Teune, H. (1975) 'Comparative Research, Experimental Design, and Comparative Method', *Comparative Political Studies*, 8 (2): 195–199.

Therborn, G. (1977) 'The Rule of Capital and the Rise of Democracy', *New Left Review*, 103: 3–42.

Tilly, C. (1978) *From Mobilization to Revolution*, Englewood Cliffs, NJ: Prentice Hall.

—— (1984) *Big Structures, Large Processes, Huge Comparisons*, New York: Russell Sage.

Tilly, C., Tilly, L., and Tilly, R. (1975) *The Rebellious Century 1830–1930*, Cambridge, MA: Harvard University Press.

Todaro, M. P. (1994) *Economic Development*, 5th edn, London: Longman.

—— (1997) Economic Development, 6th edn, London: Longman.

Tsebelis, G. (1990) *Nested Games: Rational Choice in Comparative Politics*, Berkeley: University of California Press.

UNDP (1999) *Human Development Report*, New York: Oxford University Press.

Valenzuela, A. (1988) 'Political Science and the Study of Latin America', in C. Mitchell (ed.) *Changing Perspectives in Latin American Studies: Insights from Six Disciplines*, Stanford, CA: Stanford University Press, 63–86.

Valenzuela, J. S. and Valenzuela, A. (1978) 'Modernization and Dependency: Alternative Perspectives in the Study of Latin American Underdevelopment', *Comparative Politics*, 10, 535–557.

Vanhanen, T. (1984) *The Emergence of Democracy: A Comparative Study of 119 States, 1850–1979*, Helsinki: The Finnish Society of Science and Letters.

—— (1990) *The Process of Democratization: A Comparative Study of 147 States, 1980–1988*, New York: Crane Russak.

—— (1997) *The Prospects of Democracy*, London: Routledge.

Verba, S. (1967) 'Some Dilemmas in Comparative Research', *World Politics*, 20 (October): 111–127.

Vogt, W. P. (1999) *Dictionary of Statistics and Methodology: A Non-Technical Guide for the Social Sciences*, 2nd edn, London: Sage.

Von Wright, G. H. (1971) *Explanation and Understanding*, London: Routledge & Kegan Paul.

Waisman, C. H. (1989) 'Argentina: Autarkic Industrialization and Illegitimacy', in L. Diamond, J. J. Linz, and S. M. Lipset (eds) *Democracy in Developing Countries, Vol. 4: Latin America*, London: Adamantine Press, 59–109.

Wang, T. Y. (1993) 'Inequality and Political Violence Revisited', *American Political Science Review*, 87 (4): 979–993.

Ward, H. (1995) 'Rational Choice Theory', in D. Marsh and G. Stoker (eds) *Theories and Methods in Political Science*, London: Macmillan, 76–93.

Ward, M. and Gleditsch, K. (1998) 'Democratizing for Peace', *American Political Science Review*, 92 (1): 51–61.

Weber, M. (1949) *On Methodology of the Social Sciences*, ed. E. Shils, New York: Free Press.

Whitehead, L. (1996a) 'Comparative Politics: Democratization Studies', in R. E. Goodin and H. Klingemann (eds) *The New Handbook of Political Science*, Oxford: Oxford University Press.

—— (1996b) *The International Dimensions of Democratization*, Oxford: Oxford University Press.

Wickham-Crowley, T. (1993) *Guerrillas and Revolution in Latin America*, Princeton, NJ: Princeton University Press.

Wolf, E. (1969) *Peasant Wars of the Twentieth Century*, New York: Harper Torchbooks.

Womack, J. (1969) *Zapata and the Mexican Revolution*, New York: Knopf.

Zald, M. N. and Ash, R. (1966) 'Social Movement Organizations: Growth, Decay and Change', *Social Forces*, 44: 327–341.

Index